# Transforming the Word

***Frontispiece for Samuel Butler's "Hudibras"* by William Hogarth, 1725/6. The University of Chicago Library.**

# Transforming the Word

## Prophecy, Poetry, and Politics in England, 1650–1742

Margery A. Kingsley

DELAWARE

Newark: University of Delaware Press
London: Associated University Presses

Associated University Presses
440 Forsgate Drive
Cranbury, NJ 08512

Associated University Presses
16 Barter Street
London WC1A 2AH, England

Associated University Presses
P.O. Box 338, Port Credit
Mississauga, Ontario
Canada L5G 4L8

The paper used in this publication meets the requirements of the American National Standard for Permanence of Paper for Printed Library Materials Z39.48-1984.

**Library of Congress Cataloging-in-Publication Data**

Kingsley, Margery A., 1965–
Transforming the word : prophecy, poetry, and politics in England, 1650–1742/ Margery A. Kingsley.
p. cm.
Includes bibliographical references (p. ) and index.
ISBN 0-87413-749-7 (alk. paper)
1. English poetry—Early modern, 1500–1700—History and criticism. 2. Politics and literature—Great Britain—History—17th century. 3. Politics and literature—Great Britain—History—18th century. 4. English poetry—18th century—History and criticism. 5. Political poetry, English—History and criticism. 6. Prophecies in literature. 7. Prophecy in literature.

PR545.H5 K56 2001
821'.409358—dc 21

2001027382

PRINTED IN THE UNITED STATES OF AMERICA

*For My Parents*

# Contents

# Acknowledgments

Any projects as long in the making as this one accumulates numerous debts of gratitude. Above all, I owe the completion of this volume to Max Novak. He is without question the most learned and generous man I know, and he has served over the years as a tireless source of information, advice, and encouragement. Many others have offered insights along the way. Jonathan Post read and commented voluminously on numerous early drafts, and if the final product is readable, it is due in large part to his efforts. His seminar on Andrew Marvell contributed significantly to my thinking about problems of representation in the 1650s. Jayne Lewis likewise slogged through an earlier version of the argument presented here, and her theoretical acumen and her sensitivity as a reader saved me from many obfuscations that might otherwise have made it into print unchallenged. Richard Kroll, who first introduced me to many of the literary pleasures of the Restoration and eighteenth century, contributed helpful feedback on individual chapters, as did Debra MacComb, Leigh Holmes, Carolyn Kinslow, and Larry Shanahan. John Brewer's observations helped to define and shape the project at a preliminary stage, and the faculty and participants in a 1996 NEH Institute—among them David Cressy, Lori Anne Ferrell, Peter Lake, Kevin Sharpe, and Phyllis Mack—lent me a far greater appreciation of both religion and society in the mid-seventeenth century. James Holstun and Laura Lunger Knoppers each generously made forthcoming material available for my use. My thanks, too, to David Mell and my readers at the University of Delaware Press and to my editors at Associated University Presses, Christine Retz and Wyatt Benner, who have saved me from countless embarrassing miscues. All of these people have made this book far stronger than it would otherwise have been; remaining gaffes and blunders I can only acknowledge—with regret—to be my own.

Dissertation fellowships from the William Andrews Clark Memorial Library, the UCLA Graduate Division, and the UCLA Department of English provided time and resources, as have subsequent grants from the Clark

Library, the Oklahoma Foundation for the Humanities, and the Cameron University Research Fund. The invaluable assistance of the NEH Institute, "Religion and Society in Early Modern England," I have already mentioned, and a summer sabbatical from Cameron University provided additional time and funding for travel. The staffs of the Clark, the Huntington, the Houghton, and the British Library have kept me on the right path time after time; in particular, Carol Sommer, John Bidwell, Suzanne Tatian, and Steve Tabor deserve special thanks. I am also grateful for the permission to reprint material from my own previously published essays. A version of chapter 4 originally appeared in *Modern Philology* 93 (1996) and is here reprinted by permission of the University of Chicago Press, and an earlier rendition of chapter 3 was included in *Wonders, Marvels, and Monsters in Early Modern Culture,* ed. Peter Platt (University of Delaware Press, 2000).

Above all my thanks to Eric, who has patiently endured all of the neglects and tribulations that spousal flesh is heir to. Without his loving support and his occasional reminders that there is life beyond the computer, both this book and its author would undoubtedly have suffered for the worse.

# Introduction

When William Hogarth delivered his twelve illustrations for Samuel Butler's *Hudibras* to two hundred or so subscribers in February 1726, he literally laid the enduring images of the English civil wars before his clients, their friends, and all the frequenters of the two London print shops that carried his designs. The fat and unwieldy Presbyterian knight, his austere sectarian squire, the antiheroic battle over traditional revelry and bearbaiting, even the conjoined figures of hypocrisy, ignorance, and rebellion that adorn the frontispiece—all publicly demonstrated the grotesquerie of civil conflict, while simultaneously helping to define the historically important terms of that seventeenth-century struggle for an eighteenth century wrestling with its own versions of intestine conflict.

The appeal of Hogarth's prints, and indeed the continued popularity of the highly topical *Hudibras* subject itself, typify an eighteenth-century obsession with the images of civil war. For the late seventeenth and early eighteenth centuries, political reminders of the divisions that had so disturbed the 1640s and 1650s (reminders of just how fragile British society could seem well after 1660) were all too unpleasantly frequent, as the Popish Plot and Exclusion Crisis of 1679–81, the Glorious Revolution in 1688–89, the parliamentary conflicts that followed the death of Queen Mary in 1694, and the Jacobite rising of 1715 threatened renewed internal violence. In such an environment, authors, as well as artists like Hogarth, understandably turned to images of civil conflict in order to represent the world around them—both as they knew it and as they sought to understand it. During the Restoration, amidst the instability and uncertainty of the Restoration settlement, Samuel Butler, with his several parts of *Hudibras*, and John Dryden, in poems like *Annus Mirabilis* and *Mac Flecknoe*, used images of the civil wars to historicize and to interpret ongoing conflict, and to define the boundaries of Restoration society. Histories of the civil wars, both public and private, from Clarendon's *History of the Great Rebellion* to Lucy Hutchinson's

*Memoirs*, reasserted continuities between past and present well into the eighteenth century. Later writers—Swift, Defoe, and Pope—represented the conflicts of the mid-seventeenth century in order to contextualize and authorize their own eighteenth-century political, religious, and cultural battles. And from the anonymous authors collected in the *Poems on Affairs of State* to ministers of the Anglican Church, lesser writers equally sought to locate the origins of their own political, religious, and even economic identities in the turmoil of the mid-seventeenth century. Arguments over latitudinarianism, attacks upon British Catholics, and the rantings of French enthusiasts were assigned false origins in the so-called Great Rebellion; civil war even became a defining metaphor for the theatrical competitions of the 1720s. For several generations after 1660, it seemed that there was no escaping the political, philological, and hermeneutic legacy of the 1640s and 1650s.

To trace all of the many varied and infinitely complex reverberations of civil war through the cultural and discursive landscape of late-seventeenth and early-eighteenth-century England would be a task both monumental and superfluous, given the significant efforts of other students of the field.[1] Instead, this study concentrates upon one particular manifestation of the post-Restoration preoccupation with the images and discourse of civil war: namely, the recurrence of the figure and rhetoric of civil war radical prophecy. My general contentions are essentially twofold: first, that prophetic discourse itself was far more prevalent, more pervasive, and more influential in the decades following 1660 than has traditionally been acknowledged, and second, that the post-Restoration association of prophecy with civil war made it a compelling discourse for writers—particularly, but not exclusively, royalist—who sought to redefine the terms of political, religious, social, and cultural division after 1660. Examining the figuration (and reconfiguration) of prophecy both in traditionally canonical texts—Butler's *Hudibras*, Dryden's *Annus Mirabilis* and *Mac Flecknoe*, Bernard Mandeville's *Fable of the Bees*, and Pope's *Dunciad*—and in the popular literature of the period, this book explores the ways in which prophetic discourse was deliberately reshaped by a postwar culture eager to master the conflicts poignantly etched in its collective memory. Above all, it describes how prophecy was rewritten, transformed, and disarmed, but never completely disavowed, in the post-1660 attempt to generate new and viable relationships between society and its representations.

In insisting that radical prophecy was important to the Restoration as a genre, a rhetoric, and a social phenomenon, I am building on the work of earlier historians and literary critics who undertook the more fundamental (and in many ways more difficult) task of asserting that the radical prophecy of the civil wars was significant at all. Christopher Hill's picture of an "Island of Great Bedlam" seething with religious fanatics in *The World Turned Upside Down*, while perhaps overstated and hardly undisputed, did much to raise a scholarly awareness that the tribulations of mid-seventeenth-century England encouraged self-proclaimed latter-day prophets who railed against the social iniquities of their day, envisioned the coming of the New Jerusalem, and graphically threatened the demise of their unholy enemies. The historical research of Hill and others has slowly revealed a complex variety of prophetic agendas and rationales among groups and sects ranging from the Levellers, to the Quakers, to the more elusive Ranters, linked in many ways by the reformist impulses that characterized the 1640s and 1650s but also subject to the fracturing and factionalization that political and religious ferment produced. Yet these studies also suggest that taken as a whole the prophets of the mid-seventeenth century had a significant cultural and political influence. From the naked radical quoting Jeremiah in the streets to the scribbling astrologer penning his predictions in a dark garret, they not only captured and focused the attention of the society around them but also contributed to the political and intellectual ferment of the period.

In part under the influence of the new historicism, literary scholars have likewise broadened their understanding of prophecy to acknowledge that the radical prophetic texts of the mid-seventeenth century warrant significant literary study. Narrow definitions of the prophetic as a "public mode, concerned to mediate through testimony, archetypal symbol, and story the prophet's inspired visions of transcendent reality or of apocalyptic transformations, present or future," traditionally banished the harsher prophetic voices of the English civil wars that seldom attempted to subordinate their clear (even hysterical) political, social, and religious polemic to a prominent or self-conscious artistry, and literary scholars were long content to seek in the writings of Spenser, Milton, and even the early George Wither the traces of a transcendent vatic voice that could serve to link divine inspiration with the essential "truth" of poetry.[2] More recent work, however, has done much to suggest that the writing and thought of the radical prophets can and should be taken seriously. James Grantham Turner's work on the Ranters, Quakers, and Adamites locates the controversial sexuality of those groups in the context of mainstream seventeenth-century theological debate and insists upon the logical and intellectual integrity of the individuals who advocated free love and sex without sin.[3] James Holstun, in a series of articles published in and after 1989, argues in the face of critics like MacGregor and Davis that the Ranters—one of the more nebulous groups of the period—not only existed but exhibited a serious sense of collective purpose, though not perhaps an institutional identity; for him the sustained opposition to official authority that the Ranters represented in their writing and actions suggests their very real significance to the political dialogue of the period.[4] For both of these scholars, in fact, the radical prophets of the period were not only significant and worthy of study but also crucial to the atmosphere of opposition and debate fostered by the rebellion of the 1640s.

And it has become increasingly clear that the radical prophets not only played a significant role in the political dialogue of the period but also self-consciously located themselves in the context of the movements for social, cultural, and economic reform that characterized the 1640s and 1650s. Phyllis Mack's study of seventeenth-century female Quakers in *Visionary Women* argues convincingly that the prophetic word was an utterance inextricably linked to both public action and public performance and was always politically engaged. Her description of female prophets who were not merely ranting lunatics beset by emotional instability and a severe case of the vapors, but rather social activists who "organized a system of charity, a communications network, care of prisoners, safe houses, and negotiations with magistrates" provides us with a picture of prophetic writers who "translated their sense of personal guilt into a vision of external evil, of a society corrupted by sin, and embraced the challenge of expelling that sin from the world," always believing that the textual representation of sin carried with it the necessity of action.[5] Clement Hawes's more recent examination of male and female radical prophecy expands and qualifies Mack's work to illuminate the attempts of radical prophets of both sexes to achieve not only reform but also real institutional change. [6] Treating radical prophecy not as incidental fanatical ravings but as serious, self-conscious, and generically sophisticated utterance, Hawes makes a convincing argument that the prophecy of the 1640s and 1650s should be treated as a significant form of social protest; he contends that the self-proclaimed prophets of the period deliberately adopted what he defines as a "manic" rhetoric—characterized by enthusiasm, grandiosity, omnipotence, and a belief in divine election—and asserts that that rhetoric provided a means of rebelling against "traditional hierarchies of socio-economic privilege and their related hierarchies of discourse."[7] Likewise James Holstun's examination of the career of Fifth Monarchist Anna Trapnel illuminates what he calls her "complex oppositional praxis," demonstrating in part that her ecstatic prophecy helped to provide a unifying focus to Fifth Monarchist resistance to Cromwellian power.[8] Thus identifying both a unifying style and a controlling intent in the seemingly anarchic and often marginally literate barrage of hysterical utterance that characterized these civil war texts, these studies enable the discussion of prophecy as a coherent and socially engaged literary form, and remind us of the original social potency of seventeenth-century prophetic writing.

Yet despite the recent reevaluation of civil war prophecy, we have continued to underestimate its role in Restoration society and its long-term impact on the political and representational strategies of the period following 1660. Most scholars have chosen to follow Christopher Hill's *Experience of Defeat* in its assumptions about the rapid decline and disappearance of English religious radicalism after 1660. Those who do address prophecy and its representations after the Restoration have tended to assume that where it does appear, it does so only to be excluded, derided, and contained as Restoration and early-eighteenth-century governments sought to put the divisiveness of the wars behind them.[9] Hawes does a convincing job of suggesting the importance of civil war prophecy to the mid-eighteenth-century writings of Christopher Smart; Shaun Irlam has likewise argued for the importance of seventeenth-century enthusiasm in the writings of Thomson and Young.[10] But for both of these scholars, the period from 1660 to 1710 represents the temporary failure of the prophetic genre; Hawes's discussion of *Tale of a Tub* insists that Swift's representation of manic enthusiasm renders prophecy "a grotesque foil for both sanity and proper authorship."[11] Even Hillel Schwartz, concerned in *The French Prophets* with the phenomenon of early-eighteenth-century enthusiasm, explains the English enthusiasts of the 1710s more as a result of the teachings of imported French radicals than as the outgrowth of a native prophetic tradition that prepared English malcontents to receive the French exiles.[12] And thus we have been surprisingly reluctant to trace the continuous influence of English prophecy through the Restoration and into the early eighteenth century.

Admittedly, many of our assumptions about the relative insignificance of radical prophecy after 1660 undoubtedly stem from our sense of the violence with which it was persecuted by Restoration government. By 1660 prophecy had become for royalists not only a reminder but a symbol of insurrection, civil turmoil, and violence, best pursued and degraded wherever it could be found. It did not seem to matter much that the radical prophets of the 1640s and 1650s were not the men responsible for either the outbreak of war in 1642 or the execution of Charles I, nor did it seem to make a difference that the prophets themselves had frequently been persecuted by the Commonwealth. Their rhetorical insistence upon the power of the prophetic word to transform existing social structures, together with their relative vulnerability, was itself sufficient to render them the sign of internal discord, and numerous writers complained of the "indigested Rhapsody of fanatical Nonsense" that seemingly threatened a stability still perceived as fragile and insecure in the early eighteenth century.[13] Throughout the Restoration, civil war prophets who continued to write—men like William Bayly, Christopher Taylor, and Ambrose Rigge—were actively pursued and imprisoned, particularly under the leadership of censor Roger L'Estrange; when George Wither was imprisoned and denied pen and paper in 1662, the king was publicly thanked for his arrest.[14] In the early eighteenth century, English prophets were deliberately but often erroneously linked with French Enthusiasm, Jacobitism, and Catholicism—associations born out of fears of French invasion and cultural tyranny—and punished accordingly.

And yet, as such examples should also suggest, the very intensity with which prophets and their writings were persecuted and satirized well into the eighteenth century makes a strong argument for their continued political, religious, and cultural significance. In fact, despite assumptions about the rapid decline of prophecy after 1660, it remained a common genre in which to couch popular protest, particularly complaints about religious, social, and economic inequities. Many of the Quaker prophets who began their careers during the 1650s continued to write well after 1660; and the plague of 1664–65 provided a particularly potent opportunity to point out the failures of Restoration government and predict its imminent demise. The Quaker Ambrose Rigge was still active—if somewhat less outspoken—during the 1690s, while other less restrained figures like the Quakeress Joan Whitrowe continued to hurl vitriol through the last decades of the century. If many of the more radical groups of the 1650s seemed tamed by the Restoration, moreover—either persecuted out of existence or depressed by their failure to achieve the social change they had envisioned—their works were frequently reprinted well into the 1670s and 1680s, sometimes outliving the radicalism of their authors. Even later, their rhetoric was appropriated by others who had not even been born during the civil wars, as those discontented with society continued to predict its divinely ordained destruction throughout the early eighteenth century. Welcome or not, radical prophecy did not simply go away after the restoration of Charles II.

At the same time, a number of scholars working in the period have quite sensibly warned us of the dangers of equating political and cultural failure, as we are too often wont to do in the case of the radical prophets. In *The Literary Culture of Nonconformity*, N. H. Keeble suggests that "we have been misled into identifying the political defeat of Puritanism [as a more general movement] with its cultural demise," when in fact "the contrary seems rather to be the case: political defeat was the condition of cultural achievement." In *The Daring Muse*, Margaret Doody has likewise reminded us how deeply the roots of Augustan poetics run in the popular poetry of the Commonwealth.[15] The failure of the radical prophets to drive social and political practice after 1660 (or after 1653, for that matter) did not mean that their influence was negligible. In fact, as Lawrence Klein and Anthony La Vopa have suggested in their introduction to *Enthusiasm and Enlightenment in Europe, 1650–1850*, attacks upon prophecy and enthusiasm in the Restoration and eighteenth century did not mean an abandonment of the forms and strategies of prophetic writing, nor a simple containment of the opposition—or "counter-public"—that it often represented.[16] Rather, despite its associations with radicalism and revolution, prophetic discourse was frequently adopted by royalists like Butler and Dryden who sought not change but the reconsolidation of monarchical authority. And as prophecy was so employed, it helped to construct the terms in which authority was represented after 1660.

There were a number of reasons why radical prophecy was an important influence upon conservative rhetoric in the wake of the Restoration. Most simply, perhaps, in the wake of the civil wars prophetic language—which often encoded, as John Stachniewski has suggested, a "quest for stability" that could be in itself quite conservative—answered to a political and rhetorical situation that could not simply return to the politics and iconography of the early Stuarts, but demanded new polemical strategies—strategies that did not merely ignore the divisions that the civil wars had created but rather sought to acknowledge and account for them.[17] The civil wars had created crises that were not merely political in the strictest sense, but also institutional and cultural. In particular, they created glaring disruptions in two crucial arenas intrinsically linked in the late Renaissance English political mind: the theorization and justification of political authority and the understanding of the authority and nature of representation itself. The changes they wrought on the cultural landscape, once accomplished, could not be easily erased, and those changes demanded new theories of power, both political and textual, as well as new strategies for its representation.

In 1649, the execution of Charles I realized a political vacuum that was at once practical and theoretical, leaving the country with neither a visible head nor a common theory of the basis of political authority.[18] For many traditionalist historians, the civil wars marked the end of an age of political absolutism, the trial and execution of the king a space in which competing theories of government could arise and flourish. And while revisionist historians have often successfully challenged the assumption that Englishmen after 1642 were desperately seeking a political alternative to a monarchical system of government, their portrait of a British monarchy that continued to grow in power throughout the eighteenth century despite the setbacks of the civil wars if anything highlights the need for monarchy itself to reconceptualize the terms of its power after 1660. If the civil wars were not a sign that the English were tired of kings, they were certainly an indication that the monarchy as the early Stuarts had conceived of it had ceased to be conducive to its own prosperity as an institution.[19] Despite their many differences, both traditional and revisionist narratives share a belief that the monarchy after 1660 was forced to respond to the fact of the civil wars and to the residual effects of twenty years of civil conflict—political, social, and economic realities that unquestionably affected the rhetoric of English postwar politics. And not the least of these was simply the unavoidable presence (or perhaps awareness) of difference itself—the only reality for an entire generation raised between 1640 and 1660. The work of Peter Lake and others on earlier religious polemic reminds us, of course, that representations of political and religious differences did not simply appear out of nowhere in 1642, but those earlier divisions remained to some extent unrealized, threatening neither massive numbers of human lives nor the gold that, by 1660, Samuel Pepys had experience enough to hide from Monk's army even at the risk of his life.[20] After 1660, the recognition that ideological differences could have real systemic and institutional consequences beyond the occasional execution of the poor or out of favor demanded new strategies for the consolidation and representation of authority.

At the same time, the civil wars had precipitated changes—both perceived and real—in the political and economic structure of English print culture, changes that themselves contributed to an overwhelming public awareness of the simple facts of division and difference. Recent studies of the textual explosion that in many ways defined the mid-seventeenth century have made us more aware than ever of the impact of the civil wars on perceptions of the relationship between text and the political sphere. In particular, a growing body of scholarship addressing the textual construction of the "public sphere" during the mid-seventeenth century has emphasized the extent to which shifts—both perceived and real—in the political and economic structure of English print culture contributed to a need for the reconsideration and reconstruction of the very idea of authority—both political and textual. Sharon Achinstein, Paula McDowell, and David Norbrook, all writing about the effects of the explosion of the popular press after 1641 upon the concept of an English public, have individually shown compelling arguments for locating the development of an English public sphere not, as Habermas would have it, in the periodical culture of the early eighteenth century, but rather in the unprecedented polemical wars of the Great Rebellion.[21] As each has suggested, a recognition of the utility of wide-scale polemic in political struggle, along with the demand for information, however biased, in uncertain times, created tremendous pressure upon the popular press during the civil wars, even as the occasional failure of censorship provided that press with intermittent freedom, and as perceptibly rising political and religious stakes encouraged unlicensed printing at a greater rate than ever before. The emergence of overtly polemical news books and periodicals, along with a rapidly expanding pamphlet market, thus registered a significant change in the demographics of print culture, while literacy rates among the lower classes were on the rise: Achinstein has estimated that over twenty-two thousand pamphlets were published between 1640 and 1661, while the adult male literacy rate in London, at least, approached 60 percent.[22] To the average Londoner, literate or not, suddenly barraged by a cacophony of disparate polemics, sold perhaps in shops but also cried in the streets so that even those who could not read must certainly have been aware of much of the content, it must indeed have seemed as though Babel had come again.

That such changes in the world of print in turn precipitated new theories and strategies of representation in traditionally "literary" texts has been made clear through the works of those who, like Michael Wilding and Nigel Smith, have attempted to assess the impact of the civil war period on the general landscape of English rhetoric and aesthetics.[23] As David Norbrook and Laura Knoppers have both suggested, moreover, this print explosion of the 1640s and 1650s also posed a special challenge to traditional Stuart strategies of representing monarchical authority, founded predominately in the overlapping imagery of Augustan imperialism and divine right. As Norbrook's work suggests, the political debates conducted in print throughout the 1640s gave rise to a sense of citizenship, of popular participation in political dialogue, and of the ability of the common people to effect political change—a sense that, whether accurate or not, unquestionably challenged both the Augustan and the divine-right imagery of personal rule.[24] And while Norbrook has suggested that the Restoration responded to this challenge by endorsing an essentially reactionary aesthetics, Knoppers and others have noted in both Restoration poetry and prose a significant attempt to rework the representation of authority. Michael McKeon's early study of *Annus Mirabilis* describes John Dryden's attempt to create both a new textual model for political authority and a new relationship between the act of reading and the formulation of obedience. Arguing that the polemical crises of the civil wars rendered traditional methods of representing authority ineffective, McKeon points to the postwar emergence of an affective rhetoric marked by models of political hegemony that relied primarily on familial metaphors.[25] Elizabeth Skerpan, likewise interested in the effects of the civil wars upon a reading audience, has identified similar changes in the nature of post-Restoration political polemic, suggesting that the rejection of absolutism that resulted from the experience of the civil wars necessitated new and often essentially affective strategies for representing and consolidating political authority.[26] Knoppers's recent study examines the mechanisms by which "Cromwellian print" "transformed the courtly forms of Caroline ceremony, portraiture, and panegyric" and suggests that the print culture of Cromwell's reign did not merely set up an opposition to be reacted against, but rather "complicated and altered the cultural forms available to Charles II" in his efforts to represent monarchical power.[27]

As it sought to develop its own explanation of textual and political authority, the radical prophecy of the civil wars was both a participant in and a product of the opening of discourse in the mid-seventeenth century. Yet ironically, in the process of redefining the relationship between text and social order, the prophetic voice also offered a compelling rhetorical opportunity for royalists seeking to reconstruct authority and its representations after 1660, for the rhetoric of radical prophecy encoded important assertions about the relationship between text and social order. As the work of Clement Hawes suggests, much of the power of prophecy resided for that period in the particular relationship that prophecy traces between social order—however it is conceived—and the process of representation. The Old Testament prophets—upon whom the self-proclaimed prophets of the seventeenth century frequently modeled themselves—were understood to be prophets because their speech was not human and individual utterance, but divine and national action. Often neither their word nor their selves were thought of as their own at the moment of representation, but rather as the enactment of divine presence and thus as the visible and audible conflation of the word that is symbol and the Word that is deed. For the Jeremiah, Isaiah, or Daniel who predicted in 1662 that "the *day* of the *Lord* is coming upon you [England], *his* day is drawing *near* you, yea it is *Even* come, *he* will Visit your *Iniquity* upon you, and your *Transgressions*, and ye shall *know* that *he* is the *Lord,*" retribution was neither distant nor hypothetical, but real, present, and institutional, effected in part by the writings of the prophets themselves.[28] Published "that you may be left without excuse in the day when the Lord will come to reckon with you," the prophetic text ultimately claimed not simply to predict but to ensure the destruction of those it identified as persecuting, dissipated, and ungodly.[29] For both prophets and readers in the seventeenth century the translation of the divine will into human speech was understood to be an inherently and unavoidably public act, meaningless except in interaction with the society whose fate the prophetic writings decreed: the power of the Word to pass national judgment was thought to be manifest only as it verbally enacted that judgment upon a human nation and thus precipitated radical change in institutions that were inevitably social and political in nature. Radical prophecy, that is, defined the nature of representation as essentially instrumental and essentially generative rather than mimetic, and thus as capable of effecting both social change and social order.

As the example of the prophet inveighing against transgression and declaring impending judgment might suggest, moreover, the instrumentality of prophecy meant that as it claimed to effect social change, it also asserted its own abilities to set the limits, boundaries, and regulations of a workable and functioning society, an attractive characteristic for royalists in search of an authoritative genre after 1660. Patrick Collinson, in his study of religious voluntarism in Elizabethan and Jacobean England, has suggested that the purposeful isolation of radical sectarians in general "from conventional society and its mores and recreations" allowed those groups to define their own sense of what both he and John Bossy have called "community"—a society whose boundaries were fenced, he argues, not by "a separation of the godly but a forcible separation of the ungodly: the driving of the bondswoman Hagar and her son Ishmael out of the tent and into the wilderness."[30] Substituting, as their authors frequently asserted, the divine Word for socially negotiated human power, the radical prophecies of the mid-seventeenth century likewise asserted their own ability both to set the boundaries between acceptable and unacceptable social behavior and to create a society whose boundaries were established solely according to those definitions. As Collinson's allusion suggests, moreover, one of the most common forms that they employed in this effort was the prophetic complaint or jeremiad, which identified the sins of the ungodly and predicted the manifestations of divine wrath that would result from those transgressions. The prophets of the civil wars generated long lists of possible transgressions—labeling their opponents anything from "raylers, swearers, cursed speakers, lyars and slanderers, . . . Drunkards, Whoremongers, and Adulterers, [to] blasphemers [and] . . . filthy unclean persons"—and those transgressions in turn frequently served as the basis not merely for censure, but for extermination, becoming themselves self-regulating betrayals that ensured their own exclusion from a godly society.[31] Such texts did not merely demand the redistribution of power or the redefinition of existing institutions; rather, as Collinson suggests, they claimed the ability to create a community with its own rules and principles—defining cohesion and hegemony in the face of sin, transgression, and chaos.

As a form that dealt specifically with the depicted human transgression of divine ordinance and with the prospect of textually anticipated punishment, moreover, prophetic complaint already encoded the terms of conflict and obedience within its very structure, inscribing relationships among represented order (social, political, religious, economic, and cultural), represented disobedience, disaffection, incoherence, or rebellion, and authorial intervention—the self-conscious authorial negotiation between order and civil conflict necessary for rebuilding society and recasting its representations. In 1656 the Quaker Martha Simmonds warned "the Lost Sheep of the House of Israel" that "If thou wilt not improve thy measure of light, but wilt run on in thy head-strong Rebellion, . . . and if thou slight this day of small things, then will this precious Pearl, the measure of Light, be taken from thee, and given to him that is more worthy, and the gnawing worm will enter into thee, which will never die, but will torment thee to all eternity, and then wilt thou be shut up in darkeness and unbelief."[32] For her, disobedience of divine law (the refusal to recognize the "day of small things" that warns of impending condemnation) leads logically and inexorably to divine punishment (the entry of the "gnawing worm" that will remove all hope), thus ensuring the division between transgressors and the godly few who will remain after the desolation, and so identifying the boundaries of a desired community.

As the prophetic text defines these distinctions, moreover, it asserts its own role in the creation of communal boundaries, for in these texts the process of social formation ultimately depends upon the author's ability to establish contact (to negotiate) between divine Word and human reader. The very kinds of authorial claims—both epistemological and ontological—particular to the prophetic complaint described an active dynamic among divine law (providential order), the act of human disobedience (the open defiance of hegemonic order or unifying law), and the human prophetic voice—a dynamic that was crucial to the conceptualization of the relation between written text and the construction of social stability in the years after 1660. In merely suggesting that the "day of small things" has come, Simmonds demands that the reader choose between a belief in divine law and a divinely ordained punishment, providing a place for both author and human text in the process of negotiating the new social order that will result from the collective choices of a now-informed readership. And thus she implicitly defines the role of human textual authority in the creation of a stable community—a process very much a concern for those trying to establish order after 1660.

Thus, ironically, even while the belated prophets of the Restoration and early eighteenth century were financially persecuted, whipped, and imprisoned in the attempt to expunge past sins and avoid present conflict, the perceived ability of the prophetic text to define a causal relationship between representation and social order was itself attractive to those who sought to generate order out of seeming chaos. Even as royalists in particular attacked and derided both prophet and prophetic text, they also used the rewriting and representation of both the prophetic text and the prophet to reconfigure the special relationship between text and world that civil war prophecy not only represented but also came to symbolize. From Butler's Hudibras, to Dryden's Mac Flecknoe, to the Settle of Pope's first *Dunciad*, prophets roam the pages of Restoration and early-eighteenth-century literature, helping to redefine the societies to which they belong.

I do not want merely to suggest, however, that conservative writers simply used their prophetic rewritings as a means of appropriating or containing the radical voices that they echoed. Rather, I want to emphasize the extent to which the generative potential of prophetic discourse enabled a new postwar conservative aesthetics—an understanding of text and power based in a language of production, material, trade, and above all negotiation. At the same time, I want to suggest that the aestheticization of prophecy—its transformation into what was in some sense a cultural rather than a political language, though the distinction between the two is hardly firm in this period—did not mean that it was simply contained or disempowered. Rather, in a world increasingly dependent on and determined by text, its generative rhetoric was itself a source of power, only partially harnessed, for the poetics of political reconstruction. Postwar writers sought almost fetishistically to transform, not eliminate, their prophets, and they never abandoned the political and social potential promised by a prophetic tradition even while continually, obsessively, reworking its implications. Thus even as they call into question the prophet's ability to uphold and execute either earthly or divine law, Butler's Hudibras and his divinely inspired squire also reenact and reembody the physical and ideological battles of the 1640s, which are left unresolved and without closure. Dryden's public depiction of the equally Presbyterian Shadwell—the "last great prophet of tautology"—links prophecy and bathos at the very moment at which the terms of earlier civil conflict threatened to replay themselves in the Exclusion Crisis, ultimately transforming the prophetic voice into something neither subversive, nor fully contained, but rather (reluctantly) exposing the weakness of social constructs and social institutions based upon those alternatives.

In so doing, these texts challenge recent studies in the field that have attempted to construct (or reconstruct) the social function of early modern writing along a strict axis of opposition between the desire for social order and the fear of division, chaos, and anarchy.[33] To a great extent, I am indebted to the writing of those students of the eighteenth century—Terry Castle, Carol Houlihan Flynn, Ronald Paulson, and Paula Backsheider among them—who have defined, as it were, an aesthetics of difference for the period. Acutely conscious of the self-proclaimed ability of early modern representational strategies to negotiate social cohesion by alternately illuminating and effacing difference, disorder, and disobedience, their examinations structure Restoration and eighteenth-century discourse according to its own depicted recognition of the distinction between loyalty and disobedience, containment and subversion—concepts hardly new to the postwar period, but certainly focused in the public consciousness by the represented memory of civil division and the world turned upside down. Yet at the same time, a study of the specific nature of prophetic complaint during this period also uncovers certain contemporary Restoration and eighteenth-century reservations about the assumptions typical of those studies that suggest that power (political, religious, social, and economic) was essentially defined by the capacity to exclude difference and the ability to effect public punishment upon those who transgressed preordained social boundaries. There is no question, I think, that these were important discourses throughout the early modern period, as texts from Foxe's *Book of Martyrs* to Pope's *Dunciad* self-consciously depict the spectacle of punishment. In the wake of the civil wars, however, an English consciousness of the relations between transgression and punishment, order and disorder, was markedly different from that of either prewar England or the eighteenth-century France that Michel Foucault describes in *Discipline and Punish.*[34] Ultimately, those were differences that themselves seriously affected eighteenth-century English thinking about representational strategies, the social implications of text, and the representation of alterity in Restoration and eighteenth-century writing.

For one thing, the mere fact that England had experienced civil war, and the crisis of representation that accompanied it, made it difficult after 1660 to put implicit faith in the absolute power of any form of spectacle, or any depicted definition of alterity. For many who had seen (or memorialized) the wars as a product of political and religious differences constructed and focused, made real and palpable, by the proliferation of printed polemic as well as the force of arms, the very legacy of civil war print culture revealed the extent to which the terms of obedience and transgression, order and disorder, were self-interested representations that had enabled not only the expression but also the iteration of civil conflict. The cynicism of an audience barraged by print and the efforts of a factionalized press that sought to reach an ever more sophisticated, more wary, and more jaded reading public gave rise to a culture poignantly aware of the all too real power of the press, yet equally afraid of the meaninglessness of the truth it purported to represent, and thus powerfully skeptical about the usefulness of polemic of any kind. For the writer who had proclaimed early in the civil wars that the state of polemic was such that "the world is growne into a new confused Chaos, or a Babell of balling, and foolish disputing," order and obedience were hardly political absolutes, but rather rhetorical weapons, abstract concepts useful only as they were deliberately cut loose from any fixed point of reference.[35] For those writing after the Restoration, such recognitions were a matter of political survival, as the return of Charles II had hardly begun to answer important questions both about the way in which order and authority were constructed and about the reconceptualization of obedience itself. The resulting shift from a Renaissance ideal of rhetoric as the most genteel form of authority to a Restoration vision of the writer as one always already stained by the taint of self-interest and driven by the pressing needs of both belly and purse underscores a fundamental distrust of both writers and the definitions of difference endemic to the "paper bullets" they produced.

At the same time, in part as a direct result of the radical prophetic text, postwar England often doubted representations of absolute distinctions that were based upon providential arguments. Intellectual historians have extensively documented the period's shift away from a belief in direct providential intervention, citing the emergence of a doctrine of second causes and the increasing philosophical popularity of deism. In this shift prophetic polemic itself played a significant part, as the skepticism bred of competing providential claims led inexorably to the voicing of public doubts about the human ability to successfully read the visible signs of providence. And thus while the France that Foucault describes, for instance, still seemingly believed in the absolute authority of both God and king, assuming that the efficacy of the spectacle of punishment in the maintenance of order stemmed from the popular belief that human representation imaged the absolute authority of a divine will, for a country like England whose recent experience had called both the basis upon which monarchy was built and the reliability of the visible evidence of divine providence radically into question, such assumptions could not and did not go unchallenged. Men like Simon Ford and Nicholas Brady, both ordained clergymen with low-church leanings, publicly agonized in their writings over precisely that relationship between human punishment and divine retribution, desperately trying to develop a logic that would ensure that public trial and execution could in fact approximate the will of God and thus ensure an orderly society.[36] Ultimately unable to satisfy themselves that there was in fact a direct correlation between the two, both were forced into arguments by analogy; Ford even relied upon the laws of probability to suggest that there was in fact a chance that any execution reflected divine will. Unable to guarantee the truth of any representation of transgression, these texts thus called radically into question the human ability to define absolute distinctions between transgression and obedience, disorder and hegemony.

Thus even as, at one level, the persistent rewriting of civil war prophecy ensured that English society continued to be conceived according to a polar logic of transgression and obedience, on another it served equally well to continually expose those poles as themselves artificial constructions and the product of representation. Frequently poking fun at those who claimed to be able to make such absolute distinctions (namely, the prophets themselves), those rewritings often consciously avoided the definition of arbitrary boundaries, and sought new ways to describe social order. Prophecy was rewritten most often in ways that suggest discomfort with an absolutist structuring of civic, religious, and cultural boundaries. As it was reshaped by a period eager to avoid the conflicts so poignantly etched in its collective memory, as well as in its print shops, the writers of the Restoration and the early eighteenth century instead used the prophetic voice to develop models of social order based on compromise, irresolution, and exchange, rather than upon the terms of polar opposition—reworking even the notions of textual authority that prophecy had encoded in order to generate more viable understandings of both rhetoric and representation.

Exploiting increasingly available discourses of commercialism, bipartisanship, and individual subjectivity that were based upon the assumed continuity and interdependence of transgression and obedience rather than upon their difference, these writings sought to make sense of the nature of social, political, religious, and cultural difference amid the changing contexts of Restoration society, helping in turn to shape the way that period defined authority, obedience, and difference according to new deliberately nonpolar formulations. From the language of trade that defined new relations between satire and satirized in the antiprophetic writings of the early Restoration to the psychology of the aesthetics of punishment that informs the renunciation of prophecy in Pope's *Dunciad*, we can trace the development of postwar theories of social hegemony in the discursive models adopted and adapted by the rewriting of prophecy. The rest of this book will be concerned with precisely that process of rewriting, with all of its political, economic, religious, and cultural implications, and with the results of that process as they appear to achieve some focus or occasional resolution within individual texts. Centered around literary adaptations of prophecy and the prophetic voice—adaptations specifically in the service of larger cultural issues of division, hegemony, and arbitration—each chapter will explore the ways in which key texts in a late-seventeenth- and early-eighteenth-century literary tradition sought to express their own understanding of the mechanisms of post–civil war English culture.

Chapter 1 places the Restoration and eighteenth-century rewriting of the prophetic text in a historical context, examining the radical prophecy of the civil wars and some of the early reactions to it in order to assess the ways in which prophetic rewritings saw themselves responding to prophetic texts. Arguing that the rhetoric of radical prophetic texts—disdaining as it explicitly did both the human author and human motivations—served to focus anxiety about emerging models of authority in the period that were often explicitly economic in nature and emphatically self-interested, the first chapter is particularly interested in the dynamic exchange between the prophetic text and its Commonwealth and royalist opponents, both as a register of the impact of the perceived commercialization of political power during and after the civil wars, and as those exchanges served to provide both a context and a rationale for later rewritings of the prophetic voice.

The next two chapters then explore the fate of prophetic and providential rhetoric in the early Restoration, as restored monarchists and the court itself sought to rethink and to restructure notions of national hegemony in the face of fears of renewed civil unrest. Chapter 2 focuses upon *Hudibras,* Samuel Butler's early attempt to reevaluate the role of political opposition in an orderly society in the wake of civil war. Examining the poem's adaptation of a prophetic rhetoric, primarily figured in the person of its pseudoprophetic antihero, the unwieldy knight himself, that chapter locates Butler's parody of mid-century prophecy in the context of a concerted royalist effort to use the increasingly commercial sphere of print culture to refigure cultural difference, which reluctantly emerges from Butler's text not as the potentially destructive absolute opposition represented by prophecy but rather as a process of economic negotiation. Chapter 3, concentrating upon Dryden's *Annus Mirabilis*, examines the still fragile nature of post-Restoration political society in 1666. Placing Dryden's text in the context of the remarkable resurgence of prophetic writing in and around the year of wonders, the chapter explores the terms in which Dryden presses a besieged court to understand the changing nature of social hegemony, as he too rewrites providential rhetoric. Suggesting that Dryden uses popular adaptations of prophecy common in the wake of the fire of London to offer a workable alternative to both absolutist and affective rhetoric, it evaluates the extent to which the prophetic voice in that period was transformed into a royalist instrument of social negotiation and economic power.

Chapter 4 turns once again to Dryden, this time in the context of royalist political rhetoric during the Popish Plot and Exclusion Crisis of 1678–81.

That chapter reads Dryden's satire *Mac Flecknoe* as a parody of the prophetic voice that attempts to renegotiate the relationship that civil war polemic had established between political and cultural opposition. Arguing that the 1670s, fraught by the political strains of an emerging party politics, witnessed a transference of the debate over the nature of social hegemony from a political to a cultural sphere, it treats Dryden's attack on Thomas Shadwell as a manifestation of his desperate, but ultimately futile, desire to further rework the terms of hegemony and rescue a failing Restoration settlement. Examining, in particular, the Restoration theater as an arena that deliberately conflated the terms of religious, political, and cultural transgression, it suggests a turning in Dryden's own mind from the rhetoric of negotiation so common to royalist representations in the early Restoration to an attempt to find new ways of once again defining strict social, political, cultural, and religious boundaries.

*Mac Flecknoe* thus becomes an important pivotal point for this study, as it identifies the point at which the emergence of party politics, and the inevitable changes in the very structure of social hegemony that that emergence dictated, altered the nature of prophetic reappropriation itself. In many ways, English prophecy after 1680 has been almost invisible in scholarly discourse, neglected in favor of the seemingly more exciting French enthusiasts, a fascination with continental discourse in the period, and even assumptions about the pervasiveness of the ascendance of science, the decline in providential logic and religious radicalism, and the emergence of a more "rational" belief in second causes.[37] In fact, however, prophecy did not go away, and changes in the nature of providential thinking, acting in conjunction with political changes that forced a reevaluation of both polemic and the nature of hegemony, made both the prophetic text and its adaptations once again the register of cultural anxiety, albeit in a rather different form. The rigidification of party politics, affecting the experience of both reading and writing polemic, the further commercialization of text, and the greater commitment of society as a whole to capitalist economies—radically affecting, as Colin Nicholson has recently argued in *Writing and the Rise of Finance*, the relationship between the state and the individual reader—all led to the perpetual renegotiation and the overt politicization of rhetorical models between 1680 and 1740.[38] Jonathan Swift, Bernard Mandeville, and even Alexander Pope all turned to the re-presentation of prophecy as a means of exploring alternative models of social structure and ultimately restructuring polemical discourse itself in the age of trade and party.

Thus chapters 5 and 6, in turn, explore the way in which the early eighteenth century used the prophetic tradition to respond to what was, in essence, the failure of the tradition of negotiated opposition represented by

Butler and Dryden, and the ineradicable presence of a new form of organized party politics. Chapter 5, which examines Bernard Mandeville's *Fable of the Bees* in the context of the postrevolutionary politics of the 1790s and early eighteenth century, attempts to define developing Whig strategies for coping with their own radical prophetic legacy as they sought to rework and reconsolidate both political and economic power after 1689. A final chapter on Pope's *Dunciad* looks at his use of the expired monarch/prophet Settle as an expression of his own ambivalence about the very usefulness of concepts such as cultural and political hegemony in a postprophetic and increasingly imperialist political and cultural environment. Both chapters, ultimately, are concerned with the emerging skepticism of English society regarding the organizing potential of economic explanations of power, while they recover an anti-imperial rhetoric that grew not out of the careful examination of Britain's foreign dealings but rather out of anxieties about the status of cultural economy at home.

Each of these chapters thus seeks, in its own way, to explain the continued presence of the prophetic text as a means of understanding the mechanisms of social order in an age that was forced to accept, among other things, the new inevitability of political, religious, economic, and social alterity. In each I have chosen to depict canonical texts in dialogue with those obscure and often anonymous pieces that have traditionally been excluded from discussions of "literature" as such, in part to suggest the extent to which the relationship between "high" and "low" forms in the period was very much a two-way street—a vital interdependence that defined the very nature of public writing in the late seventeenth century. For much the same reason, I have sought to set conservative voices not against, but in interchange with, their more radical contemporaries, again to emphasize the process of negotiation and dialogue that was as central to the construction of the most self-consciously literary production as it was to the most blatant of political polemics in the period. Such confessions are perhaps de rigeur these days, given the influence of the new historicism, but here they are also part and parcel of the attempt to recover the essentially dialogic nature of prophecy after 1660, as the form itself was recreated and redefined by the polemical battle over its structure, rhetoric, and meaning, and as the transformation of prophetic discourse itself generated new strategies for representation and debate. Thus the following chapter attempts first and foremost to describe this dialogue as it developed during the 1650s and 1660s, as the radical prophets of the seventeenth century, their immediate heirs, and their early opponents sought to define the nature and purpose of prophetic discourse for a society often convinced that the judgment of God lay heavily upon them.

# Transforming the Word

# 1

# Polemic, Culture, and Conflict

Fed up with Cromwell's repeated attempts to silence the Quakers during the 1650s, and angered by rumors of Quaker plots to overthrow the Commonwealth government, Edward Burrough issued a warning in 1657 to all those who refused to hear the message of the brethren. "This we give all to know," he declared,

> That the Lord will be avenged on all them who hates the way of righteousness, and all that opposeth the Lord and his way, and despiseth his truth which he hath revealed, they shall be confounded and broken to pieces, and shall confess to the Lord, and his way, and his truth in the day of their destruction.
>
> Again, let all the earth know, that against all unrighteousness, injustice, oppression, whoredom, murder and drunkenness; and all sin what soever, we do declare and acknowledge our selves to be enemies against all sin, and they that commit it . . . and this is that Government onely which is the Government of sin and death, which we declare our selves enemies to . . . and this is that Government which we testifie against, and warres against by the sword of the Spirit of God, and by his power and not by the carnall weapons or subtil conspiracies, or violent insurrections.[1]

Defending the Quakers against charges of wrongdoing and accusations that they represented a physical threat to the safety and stability of the Commonwealth, Burrough insists that the aims of the brethren are spiritual, not political, and that they eschew all "carnall weapons" in their attempt to gain the more desirable kingdom of heaven. At the same time, his protestations that the Quakers will not be responsible for the destruction of the Commonwealth government hardly prevent him from assuring his listeners that that government will be destroyed; the Lord has declared that vengeance will be his, and the Quakers can rest comfortably knowing that those powerful perpetrators of "unrighteousness, injustice, oppression, whoredom, murder and drunkenness" will be "broken to pieces" without their involvement in civil insurrection.

In many ways, Burrough's text epitomizes both the reformist impulse and the resistance to entrenched and oppressive power that Hawes and Holstun have cited as central to the mission of the radical prophets. In asserting that the Quakers would stand against "all unrighteousness, injustice, oppression, whoredom, murder and drunkenness; and all sin what soever" Burrough envisions a society freed of both antisocial behavior and the abuse of power, equating moral and political reformation. Doubtless his own experience as part of a group whose members were pursued, harassed, and imprisoned by a government that feared their resistance made the promise of such reforms particularly meaningful, and Burrough in fact used this pamphlet to assert the independence of the Brethren from an unsympathetic Commonwealth, declaring that "[wicked] Rulers and Government we cannot be subject to for conscience sake, but doth rather fulfill the law and will of God, though we transgress their wills and unrighteous laws."[2] In the context of such oppression, his assertion that God will deal with Cromwell and his agents seems a defiant proclamation that there is a power great enough to accomplish the resistance and ultimate rebellion that the Quakers themselves were powerless to enact in the face of crippling government persecution.

Nevertheless, there is perhaps a danger in too thoroughly romanticizing Burrough and his compatriots, or in seeing them as eager precursors of the modern political state. While self-proclaimed prophets like Burrough unquestionably contributed to the opening of the public sphere that so many scholars have described, other students of the period—David Leverenz among them—have convincingly pointed to a powerful strain of authoritarianism at the heart of radical Protestantism; and Burrough, after all, represents the political overthrow of Cromwell not as rebellion, but as obedience to a higher law and greater authority than the corrupted institutions of mankind.[3] In asserting that it is God, not the Quakers, who will take vengeance against Cromwell, Burrough echoes the claims of many other seventeenth-century prophets who believed themselves, as Paula McDowell has put it, to be "mere physical bodily [channels] for the communication of divine understanding."[4] And the divine understanding that the prophets channeled, however compassionate it might sound, could unquestionably be figured as brutal, absolutist, authoritarian, and oppressive—particularly towards those it saw as unregenerate. For one 1651 writer who viewed England's sins as a disease to be cured only by divine judgment, the worst evil in a "state physician" "is too much pity or Mercifulnesse, loath to put [the patient] to pain, loath to apply a corroding plaister, to have a limb cut off, though it be to saving the whole body."[5] God's cure, that is, was not one which would restore the body of England, rendering it whole and complete, but rather one which would purge and divide, systematically removing infected parts rather than redeeming them; in Burrough's text, Cromwell and his government will be eradicated without compunction because they sinned without compunction, and no Quaker will regret their loss.

For the more conservative writer who depicted the radical prophet crying *"Blood, blood, blood, destroy, O Lord! / The Covenant-breaker, with a two edged sword,"* while simultaneously complaining "of law and bondage," rhetoric such as Burrough's was at best blatantly hypocritical, merely duplicating the forms of power and authority it pretended to reject.[6] Edmund Skipp, the author of *The Worlds Wonder, Or the Quakers Blazing Starr,* claimed that the Quakers as a group were "altogether deluded by Satan, both in their judgments and walkings," their writings little more than the temptations of the devil, and their repudiation of transgression the misguided route to eternal damnation.[7] And while a more sympathetic reading would undoubtedly acknowledge in Burrough's text both a sincere belief and a deep resentment of the physical hardships endured by religious radicals under the Commonwealth, such rhetorical analysis does suggest that while radicals and conservatives, sectarians and government officials, may have yearned for very different kinds of societies, their understanding of the means necessary to achieve them were in many ways similar; their notions, that is, of justice and social order may have contrasted sharply, but the idioms through which they articulated such concepts were often common to both, mutually including images of force, violence, and even dismemberment. Yet to say so, I would argue, is not merely to rehearse a position, quite rightly parodied by James Holstun, that suggests that all "'radicals' are secretly controlled by the conservative ideology they claim to subvert."[8] Rather, it is to insist that in this period, as in most, opposing rhetorics were not simply an articulation of absolute differences but rather deeply interconnected interpretations of common ground that mutually construct each other through the process of debate. Burrough's antiauthoritarian representation of an authoritarian God was in fact partly enabled by representations of absolute human power (sword, wars, vengeance), and the opponents of prophecy just as frequently appealed to the prophetic adumbration of a higher authority in order to launch their attacks against it. *The Worlds Wonder,* despite its ridicule of the Quakers, does not completely reject the form and implications of their prophetic texts. It may well dismiss prophecy as the destructive work of the devil, recapitulating charges that the self-proclaimed prophets of the period were hypocritical, deluded, or even marginally insane, thereby seeking to preserve the institutions of official religion from the incursions of do-it-yourself divines. It also clearly ridicules the most distinctive features of various prophetic—not just Quaker—rhetoric: the frequent appeal to scriptural passages, the obsession with astrology, the interpretation of natural wonders, and predictions concerning the end of the world and the coming of the millennium. And yet, given the very nature of parody, it is Skipp himself who not only raises the specter of prophecy in this pamphlet by incorporating its most common forms into the title page, but also asserts that these prophetic clichés will provide the method by which he himself will judge "the Quakers Blazing Starr," and condemn the rapid rise and popularity of their sect. In short, he does not so much reject prophecy as turn its forms against it, using them—however tongue-in-cheek—to empower his own judgments against the Quakers and their prophetic brethren.

In the course of this chapter, I want to examine the deep interconnection of the genre of prophetic complaint and the attacks upon it, and thus to argue that the debate between radical prophet and conservative opponent represents not simply a battle between two opposing viewpoints—one endorsing prophecy, the other rejecting it—but rather a competition for control of the prophetic voice and for the structure of political and textual authority that it represented in a period when textual and political authority were both clearly threatened. Prophecy itself, after all, as Klein and La Vopa have suggested, was not an essentialist form, but one which both radicals and conservatives reworked and renegotiated, often in very different ways; in so doing, both sides constructed prophetic claims in ways that reflected their own concerns and anxieties about the changes in the nature of authority that the oppositions of the civil wars had precipitated.[9] The result was, as the rest of this chapter will show, an intense competition for the voice and definition of prophetic complaint—a competition that in many ways defined the postwar rewriting of radical prophecy itself.

## I

Prophetic complaint—that prophetic mode which identifies the sins of the ungodly and predicts their impending retribution—was not of course original to the English civil wars, nor was it inherently or necessarily a radical form as it was practiced in prewar England. Far from springing full-grown from the primordial ooze of mid-seventeenth-century religious factionalism, popular prophecy in general had a long history in the British Isles, inhabiting the vast gray area between Christian and pagan that unquestionably influenced English religious discourse, even if it did not leave the vast pools of superstition that Keith Thomas described and subsequent critics have ardently disputed; Howard Dobin and Rupert Taylor have both documented the early history of English prophetic literature as a liminal and a magical discourse.[10] The narrower tradition of English prophetic complaint—distinguished from the more general category of prophecy in part by its impulse towards social reform—has been traced by John Peter to the writings of the early church fathers; for Peter, early Christian adaptations of Roman satire generated a prophetic inheritance that can be traced from late antiquity, through the English Middle Ages, and into popular writings of the English Renaissance.[11]

Almost inevitably, this genre of prophetic complaint, much like the jeremiad that Perry Miller and Sacvan Bercovitch associate with a specifically American prophetic tradition, used the figure of the prophet to articulate causal links between particular acts of disobedience or defiance (transgressions) and the punishments that they predicted.[12] The major prophets of the Old Testament—Daniel, Isaiah, and Jeremiah—had fought (or so they said) to save their people from destruction by making Israel aware of her sins, reforming her, and thus averting the divinely ordained devastation that would be the logical fulfillment of her transgression. Likewise the prophets of the Renaissance identified particular lapses—often the mistreatment of the poor—and suggested that the result of continuing such behavior could only be destruction. Complaints about a general lack of charity, corruption among the rich and powerful, and the violation of particular laws of religious observance all drew threats of destruction, invariably couched as providential inevitability. For one author, the oppression of the poor by papal laws could only result in the eventual decimation of the papal seat and the Roman Catholic Church, just as the Egyptians had paid for their enslavement of God's chosen people with lives surrendered to a divinely manipulated Red Sea.[13]

And in fact, as this example might suggest, the reformist impulse that both Clement Hawes and Phyllis Mack describe was hardly unique to the radical prophecy of the mid-seventeenth century but rather a time-tested formula for English social commentary. Openly acknowledging their formal debt to the Old Testament prophets who had stood guard against false kings and false prophets, the complaints of Renaissance England during the century or so before the civil wars combined exegesis of the prophetic books with poignant social criticism. George Joye, a "sometime fellow of Peter College in Cambridge," translated and edited the Book of Jeremiah for a 1534 edition entitled *Jeremy the Prophet.* In the preface to his text, complete with commentary, he casts himself as a modern-day Jeremiah and creates a line of direct descent from the Pentateuch to Lamentations to his own complaint: as Moses had rejoiced in the destruction of Pharaoh's army, so Jeremiah had pled for the destruction of Babylon, and so he, Joye himself, predicts that God will endorse the newly founded English Church and demolish the bishops of Rome who excavated the "pits of pestilence" by creating laws that beggared the people and oppressed the poor.[14]

In this piece, Joye's support for the English Church and, implicitly, for Henry VIII in his struggle against the pope is neither submerged nor valenced but rather explicitly informs his understanding of the prophet and his text with a political self-consciousness characteristic of prophetic complaint. *The Lamentation of a Christian against the City of London,* written by Henry Brinklow and again clearly modeled on the Lamentations of Jeremiah, similarly defends the English translation of the Bible in an explicitly social context.[15] Arguing that English-language Scripture should be available in every home, Brinklow blames the rich and the aldermen of London for blocking its progress; comparing London's elite to Jeremiah's false prophets, he predicts that the aldermen must either reform themselves or expect to be destroyed for the callousness that informs both their attitude toward the translation of Scripture and their uncharitable treatment of the poor who surface again and again in Renaissance complaint. Politically, ideologically, and socioeconomically motivated, Brinklow's text—like Joye's—does not seek to hide its politics; more often than not, in fact, these Renaissance writers pointed to what they perceived to be the political engagement of the Old Testament prophets as the principal reason for their continued usefulness as rhetorical models.

Early uses of the prophetic voice, however, were not restricted to those engaged in opposition politics, or to those writers who sought to overturn existing institutions; nor, as Joye's own understanding of the function of Jeremiah as a prophet might suggest, was prophecy itself conceived of as an essentially radical form. Certainly the situation of the poor and predictions of the fate likely to befall those who failed in their charitable duties were commonplaces for those who adopted Old Testament models, denouncing the rich and insisting upon a redistribution of wealth, as Brinklow and Joye both do. But in many ways, these writers saw their cries for the punishment of transgressors and oppressors not as an attempt to reject established social order, but rather to insist upon the proper enactment of traditional laws long neglected by the powerful and the corrupt. Joye in particular describes Jeremiah not as a rebel but as a Mosaic antitype—a restorer of order—whose primary function was to enforce the social boundaries defined by Mosaic law. And thus the voice of the prophet often warned of threats to traditional institutions, asking that God destroy those who sought to change by force the power structures of the English government, much as Jeremiah had predicted the coming of the Babylonian army and prayed for their eventual destruction. Joye's *Jeremy* does not seek to undermine the authority of English monarchy, but rather supports Henry VIII against a pope whom he represents as jeopardizing both English autonomy and the consolidation of English power in the figure of the monarch.

Well into the early years of the civil wars, even Cavaliers and loyalists frequently chose to model themselves after the prophets of the Old Testament as a means of crying down the "false priests" of Parliament and the army, identifying explicitly with the figure of the outcast prophet crying in the wilderness or lamenting the fall of a modern-day Jerusalem. Thus for the anonymous but clearly loyalist author of *Ieremiah Revived*, the parliamentary victory of 1648 simply reinforced the idea that God was out to punish England for her intractable civil discord. Explicitly adopting the voice of that particular prophet, the writer lamented the Parliamentary army's capture of Whitehall and Westminster, the habitations of "all that is called God."[16] England, the writer warns, has been brought into slavery by "a heathen sort of people":

> and this the Lord permits . . . because he intends to humble her by afflictions, and chastise her for the multitude of her transgressions. . . . O then that London would purge her stinking ayres with whole gales of heart-breathed sighs, and cleanse her seditious streets with soule wept teares.[17]

From the author's perspective, England has lost her liberty, and her monarch, as a direct result of her own seditious tendencies. Her very willingness to rebel and to permit rebellion against a rightful (that is, divinely ordained) ruler has been a transgression against God's own will and thus she is punished through the very political changes that she had so desired. For this defender of monarchy, the voice of the prophet was not exactly the voice of opposition, but rather a source of both authorial strength and the promise of Jerusalem rebuilt after long captivity.

Even during the 1650s prophecy was not necessarily a sign of the writer's anarchic or leveling intents, as the career of Rhys "Arise" Evans might suggest. Bound early in his life as apprentice to a tailor in Chester, Evans moved to London in 1629, and began to see visions and to prophesy in 1633. Arrested in 1647 for declaring himself to be the reincarnation of Christ, Evans spent considerable time in Newgate, and published pamphlets with such sensationalist and inflammatory titles as *A Voice from Heaven to the Commonwealth of England*, *The Bloody Vision of John Farley Interpreted*, and *The Voice of Michael the Archangel to his Highness the Lord Protector*. Yet despite his hyperbolic rhetoric and seemingly radical stance, Evans was not a detractor from traditional forms of authority. Throughout his career, he professed himself to be a devout member of the Church of England—although he has also been linked with the Fifth Monarchists—and he penned multiple requests, published in mainstream royalist newsletters, for the restoration of Charles II. After the Restoration, he was a staunch supporter of divine-right monarchy, and was touched for scrofula by Charles II. As both royalist and prophet, Anglican and Fifth Monarchist, Evans is a somewhat unusual figure, but the slippery nature of his political allegiances was hardly uncommon in the period, and his use of prophecy in the royalist cause serves as a reminder that not all civil war prophets sought the eradication of monarchy.

Ironically, however, it was this availability of prophecy to multiple political causes that contributed to the pressure on both radicals and royalists to redefine it and to recast the form of textual authority it represented. As early as the 1640s, the profoundly polemical nature of the popular press, as well as early observations upon the commercial potential of print culture, had generated a reading public convinced that representation—in whatever form—was intrinsically a product of political self-interest. In 1641, *The Dolefull Lamentation of Cheap-side Crosse* had argued that the true enemies of peace in England were the politically motivated literary and discursive models of the disputants, which rendered the poles of transgression and obedience continually shifting and ultimately empty signifiers. Thus one polemicist, the author claims,

> will needes make himselfe wise in Gods eternall Counsells, and all his friends shall bee of the Elect, but his foes, and those he bears any grudge unto he accounts them reprobates.[18]

At the same time, as we have seen, competing accounts of particular events during the wars led to wide-scale skepticism concerning the value (and even the existence) of truth itself—a skepticism that ultimately undermined the text's only claim to credibility and thus to a certain textual authority. Prophecy was in many ways especially implicated in this skeptical view of the press, not least because the central claim of prophecy, after all, is a knowledge of God's single and undivided will; by the mid-1650s even the most naive of readers could hardly help but notice that the competing claims of royalist and radical prophets could not all be reconciled, thus seriously undermining the authority and political efficacy of the prophetic complaint itself. And thus during the 1650s and 1660s, both radical prophets and more conservative writers sought to recast an earlier but outdated form of prophetic complaint in the attempt to represent and enact their own textual and social visions.

II

For many of the radical prophets of the civil wars—including many of the writers of prophetic complaint—the primary source of textual authority was not, as it had been for earlier writers, the appeal to the ancient and charitable laws of man that they, like others, perceived as being in some sense already corrupted; instead they sought the pure, unchanging originary law of the divine Word itself. Many radical prophets writing after 1650 claimed that theirs was the voice of God, that they had been specially called and specially gifted to be vessels for a Word that represented the only true law. In a pamphlet entitled *The Good Old Way*, the Quaker Ambrose Rigge asserted that when composing his writings he was "willing to wait upon the Lord, that he might . . . manifest his Will and Mind unto me, what I should write, rather chusing to continue in silence many years, than to set Pen to Paper to declare anything which the Spirit of Truth would not seal unto."[19] Likewise his fellow Quaker William Simpson insisted that his prediction of the destruction of the Anglican Church "was revealed unto me in a *Vision*, in the *Spirit* of *Truth*, which *leads into all truth*, & reveals things to come."[20] Other prophets of the period frequently referred to themselves as messengers and as couriers of the Word rather than as authors in their own right. The anonymous author of *A Voyce out of the Wildernes Crying* (1651), speaking implicitly of his own text, reminds "*The* Parliament *of* England, *and* Councell *of* State" that "God hath wonderfully blessed this Nation above others, in these latter days, . . . in raising up amongst us Holy Men, yea Prophets, whom he hath instructed from above, by his Spirit of truth, to understand his Word, and the great things contained therein: & to declare the same, not only to this Nation of ours, but to all the world."[21] And thus, as couriers, the prophets of the 1650s and 1660s often claimed that they themselves did not so much author texts of their own as transfer divine Word and divine law to the ears and eyes of mortal men.

A cynical perspective, of course, has recognized in such claims to divine inspiration an attempt to capitalize upon the perceived gullibility of a reading public that was at once religious and superstitious, while more sympathetic—but also more patronizing—scholars have spoken of melancholy, delusion, hysteria, and even insanity.[22] In many ways both of these alternatives are ultimately unfair; at best they offer us the limited alternatives of either perceiving those who claimed divine inspiration as archmanipulators or dismissing them as lunatics, with little gray area in between. At the same time, to be diverted by such questions is also in a sense to dismiss the very real rhetorical significance of these writers and their texts. Some few probably were schemers while others may well have been less than sound of mind, and many undoubtedly believed that they did in fact hear the voice of God. But the emphasis they placed upon inspiration—genuine or not—as the motivation behind their writing suggests that all who saw their texts as divinely inspired, the word of God translated into human speech, understood that inspiration as an important means of justifying their religious and political visions in a highly polemicized world.

Perhaps first and foremost, for the prophets of the mid-seventeenth century the appeal to the divine Word meant the ability to eschew the charge of self-interest that threatened so many other polemical voices in the period. As Clement Hawes has aptly demonstrated, one of the effects of the claim to divine inspiration was the perceived ability to eradicate the human subject altogether, seeking power not as the presentation of a self, but rather as the absence of a self—the blank slate on which the word of God could be inscribed.[23] This in turn allowed these prophets to reject the concept of self-interest that so often seemed to threaten the purity of the word and the status of print as a whole. Hence *An Alarme to England* lists self-interest and self-aggrandizement as the cardinal sin for which England will be destroyed. Accusing his countrymen of "[exalting themselves] against God" and "[striving] to exceed each other in bravery," the author condemns self-interest; in contrast, he defines God's chosen by their absolute rejection of self-love, deliberately denying even the possibility of self-interest among a godly people.[24] A few years later, the author of *A Fannaticks Alarm* likewise represents himself as a true prophet based on his status as an objective consultant sent to illuminate the people through his own disinterest. He has been sent, he says, to

> shew Thee the Judgements of God against thy Violent and Inhuman Dealings; to which purpose, I am at this Time, come . . . in Christian Love to deal with Thee; and (to speak after the manner of men) *like a Conscientious Lawyer, to lay before Thee, the worst of thy Case, like an Honest Physician, to shew the True state of thy Body.*[25]

Accusing those to whom he speaks of undo violence and force, he explicitly addresses a people who have no concept of objective truth in the only guise he can—that of a professional seeking not to line his own pockets, as lawyers and doctors were so often accused of doing, but rather laying the facts before his client, however hurtful the results may be to his own practice. Asserting that in speaking for God he can have no human concerns except for the well-being of his people, the author presents the prophetic self—however oxymoronic a concept—as a self of "Christian Love" antithetical to private interests.

Thus in part the appeal to divine inspiration offered a means of transcending the rhetorical and interpretive communities that the radical prophets—like others—felt had failed them during the 1640s because of personal and political interests. Far more then their predecessors, in fact, the radical prophets of the 1650s and 1660s explicitly rejected the communities—both political and rhetorical—of which they were ostensibly a part. Both in their behavior and their writing, radical prophets existed—and often even seemed intentionally to place themselves—on the margins of organized society, which they saw as guilty of gratifying personal and political desire. Many were itinerant preachers and prophets who floated in and out of established communities and in and out of brushes with the law: Abiezer Coppe, the Ranter prophet, was an Oxford dropout who turned first to the Presbyterians, then to the Anabaptists, and finally to the very radical fringes in his search for religious fulfillment. Often, too, their public displays were intended to outrage their contemporaries' sense of social decorum. William Simpson, a native of Lancashire, joined the Quakers in 1656 and devoted his life to preaching and prophesying in the streets, both naked and in sackcloth; public defecation was also not uncommon in the Quaker cause. And the punishments that resulted from such behavior were equally spectacular and equally marginalizing. Ambrose Rigge traveled around southern England during the 1650s and 1660s—seemingly from jail to jail—spreading his prophetic message; by 1665, he had been imprisoned in Rochester, Bristol, Dorchester, Winchester, and Sussex, and whipped, on one inauspicious occasion, by the common hangman at Southampton. *A Lamentation* was written from his cell in Harsham Jail, where he had been imprisoned since 1662 at the request of the local vicar. After the publication of his most famous text, *A Fiery Flying Roll*, in 1650, Coppe was imprisoned first at Coventry, then in Newgate, but these were not his first experiences with the wrong side of the law; he had earlier been incarcerated for preaching naked at Warwick, the town of his birth. Simpson's public demonstrations resulted in his expulsion from the town of Evesham, and he was frequently imprisoned, whipped, pilloried, and stoned in his travels from Cambridge to Colchester to London.

Armed with the word of God, however, these radical prophets saw and represented themselves not merely as victims of an oppressive dominant culture, but as men and women whose sufferings proved the divine and disinterested nature of their texts and thus authorized their visions; the Old Testament prophets, after all, had been identified in part by their suffering, and one who chose willingly to suffer could hardly be accused of harboring a hidden self-interest. Nathanial Hardy's 1658 *Sad Prognostic of Approaching Judgement* thus conceded that often in times of calamity "the *wicked* are *preserved*":

> They *escape* for a *time* that some remarkable *Judgement* may fall upon them, . . . [for] when *God* is *resolved* . . . that he will *destroy* a people, he suffereth the *wicked* to fill up the measure of their sinnes, by killing his *servants.*[26]

Death at the hands of the unrighteous and persecution at the hands of the instruments of social institutions in fact become for Hardy signs of righteousness and religious authority itself, a means of identifying an oppressed community of saints, the servants and messengers of God, as well as a means of ensuring the damnation of the wicked. Likewise, Priscilla Cotton and Mary Cole, writing from Exeter Jail, where they were imprisoned, compared their own condition to that of Old Testament prophets; writing to "the Priests and People of England" the two women complained that "the persecuting Cainish generation would never acknowledge they were such, but in all ages persecuted the just under some false colour, as they of old said, The true Prophets were troublers of Israel."[27] Cotton and Cole, in fact, read their own imprisonment as a sign that they too are prophets, oppressed by corrupt officials and thus the true repository of the Word itself. And thus, too, they imply, the Word, identifiable in part through the oppression of its vessels, raises the true prophet above polemical squabbles and provides his or her utterance with both status and authority in the midst of the Babel of a "Cainish generation."

At the same time, however, claims to divine inspiration did not just enable the assertion of textual authority as a mere self-satisfying vindication of the prophetic text. Rather, they provided a viable mechanism for the social efficacy of prophetic text, which was, as we have seen, inherently instrumental; they provided, that is, the prophetic complaints of the 1650s and 1660s with a way of describing their own agency in the process of social reformation/recreation—the very act in which laws are defined and boundaries are drawn that separate, in some absolute sense, the righteous from the transgressor. In the skeptical climate of the 1650s and 1660s, such explanations were important, in part because, unlike many of their predecessors, the writers of radical prophetic complaint often conceived of social reform not as a process conducted within the structures and institutions of existing society but rather one that demanded the utter dissolution of a present social order and the construction of new, alternative communities. Not all of civil war radical prophecy tended to conceptualize the relationship between crime and punishment as cataclysmic rather than apocalyptic, but that which did focused intently upon the utter national and political dissolution that it claimed would result from the transgressions of the people; war, starvation, and disease—all threatening both physical suffering and national collapse—were the most commonly depicted forms of reprisal. Thus appealing to the precedent of the destruction of the kingdom of Israel, the author of *An Alarme to England* proclaims:

> Let your own consciences bear witness against you, whether at this day, instead of humbling your soule, ye do not rather exalt yourselves against God? Whether instead of mourning in sackcloth and ashes, ye do not rather strive to exceed each other in bravery? Whether those Puppets of pride, your wives, are not suffered by you to weare attire beyond the degree of your callings? Who make a tinkling with their feet, like those the Prophet reproves, who mince it as they go, and move as if they took a strict account of their steps, and yet how often they tread aside! And while these things are so, can ye be so besotted, as not to expect Gods vengeance upon you? Yet surely know, that except ye repent, ye shall be consumed by the sword, by the famine, and by the pestilence.[28]

For this writer sin, represented as the violation of a divine commandment expressed in the form of an earthly law, requires significant reform on the part of a disobedient people. The glorification of feats of bravery in the midst of a war that has been divinely ordained as punishment rather than triumph, like the violation of sumptuary laws represented as the earthly symbol of divine hierarchy, transgresses heavenly law as well as earthly deeds and authority, thus requiring both repentance and a significant change in social behavior. But here the transgressors are not confined to a single oppressive class or institution; rather, society as a whole has become corrupted. All are equally responsible and thus reform can only be accomplished through the eradication of society as it now exists, through decimation by famine, sword, and plague.

Likewise Hester Biddle, writing in 1662, conceives punishment for earthly sins as a kind of divinely ordained national depopulation—an utter and literal dissolution of English society. "Oh *London, London!*" she exclaims,

> The dreadful Lord God of Everlasting strength, which faileth not, his notable, terrible, and dreadful Day is coming upon thee as at noon day, and

> from it thou canst not escape, neither canst thou quench God's Fire which burns as an Oven, which is overtaking thee: Oh the Burden of the Lord concerning this Treacherous and Backsliding City! Oh! Calamity upon Calamity, Misery upon Misery, Plagues upon Plagues, Sickness upon Sickness, and one Disease upon another will the Lord God of Power bring upon thee, and the Lord will destroy thee from being inhabited, unless thou dost repent from the bottom of thine heart.[29]

In this context, sin is not a personal falling away; rather, it is inextricably intertwined with political and civic institutions. The city of London as a whole has rebelled against divine authority by permitting the invasion of Monk and the restoration of Charles II; thus the city as a whole will suffer, as the very streets and buildings are condemned to eternal vacancy. As in the biblical case of Jerusalem, the earthly nature of both crime and punishment is marked by the explicitly physical separation of the English people from their geographical capitol, suggesting that the ultimate punishment is in fact the deprivation of national political identity and social order. Society as the seventeenth century knew it, that is, would soon and finally cease to exist unless its people engaged in immediate and massive reform, and that—the prophet knew all too well—was highly unlikely indeed.

Rather than seeking to reform existing communities, then, such writers used prophetic complaint to create alternative communities comprised of godly individuals. For Ambrose Rigge, England's situation in the early Restoration was the very antitype of the recreation that the story of the flood depicted: "Even as it was in the Dayes of Noah, so it is now in the coming of the Son of Man; for the Earth is filled with Violence, and is corrupted by Iniquity, and the dark corners thereof are full of the habitations of Cruelty, but an Ark is prepared, and a small Remnant are gathered."[30] Just as Noah had been the progenitor of a new civilization, born out of the destruction of a sinful antediluvian society, so Rigge implies, the godly few who will be preserved after the destruction of the English nation will form the nucleus of a new, more obedient community. In so doing, moreover, Rigge echoes earlier writings that relied on the Old Testament story of the captivity and return from Babylon, in which most of Israel was destroyed but a chosen few were preserved to return and form a society more obedient to divine law. Thus too, the author of *England's Distemper* (1651) compares his promise of an England remade and restored to peace to the Book of Jeremiah: the prophet, he reminds us, "speaks of [the] devastation [of Israel and] of their great and glorious restauration, that although they should be carried away captive yet the time of their releasement should be certain, and the years of their bondage should not always endure," lasting only as long as it takes for God to "heal [the] Land by cutting off those distempered members that endanger the health of the Land."[31] Common to these accounts is the picture of a society destroyed, purified, and made anew; Edward Burrough's God assures the people of England in 1656 that his purpose is "to gather the Nations, and to fan them, and to try them, in the wind of my wrath, and to purge them, and to refine them in the furnace of my fire," in order that they may be recreated, reforged, in accordance with His will and His law.[32]

For many of the radical prophets, this reconstruction of community was often conceived of as a process achieved primarily through participation in the emerging public sphere—a self-selection and creation of group identity that took place through the public presentation of text. In the somewhat comical case of the Quaker William Bayly, prophecy becomes a means of rejecting one physical community while embracing another that is created only in the social and economic exchange of text: the depiction of failed ties to family, friends, and neighbors is used to authorize his participation in a wider print culture, thus enabling him to constitute a new community composed entirely of sympathetic readers. In the preface to *A Warning from the Spirit of Truth*, a pamphlet that advertises "a Plain Information and Direction for the Ignorant, who know not the Way of God, nor the Voice of his True Prophet, who is the Light and Life of Men," Bayly complains bitterly of his fortune at the hands of his fellow citizens in Poole:

> The Lord at several times hath moved me . . . to Warn and Exhort the Inhabitants of the Town of Pool . . . whose Message they resisted, & much endeavoured to hinder, both by Haling me Out before I had spoken what the Lord moved me to declare unto them, both in their Publick and Private Meetings; and also, by setting a Watch to keep the Steeple-House Doors against me, which some were bound unto in a Sum of Money, for a certain time, to keep me out of their Meetings, as the *Sheriff* (who was one of them) told me with his own mouth.[33]

The fact that his entire community seems to have joined together to ensure his public silence, however, becomes for Bayly not an indication that something is wrong in his relationships with his neighbors, but a sign that like the Old Testament prophets he has been chosen to spread a divine but unwelcome message, and he goes to great lengths to publish his ostracism, using it as the basis of his authority to print; denied the right to speak, he says, he has no alternative but to find a press so that he may fulfill his function as messenger and create a new community of believers among a reading public.

This self-portrait of the Quaker radical being dragged from the church by a congregation willing to take up a collection to keep him away from their place of worship perhaps unintentionally borders on the humorous, but the story it relates is in many ways emblematic of the much wider investment of religious radicalism in print culture. In fact, as Paula McDowell has shown, the Quakers, perhaps more than any other group in the period, placed a tremendous emphasis upon the production of printed texts, eventually developing a highly organized system for the production and dissemination of pieces written by various Friends.[34] Ranters and Fifth Monarchists, while certainly less well organized, were also extremely prolific. At the same time, I would argue, such elevation of the printed word in many ways represents an even more broadly conceived faith in the creation of community through a kind of collective hermeneutics.

Conceptions of text in the period were hardly limited to the printed word. Whether preached in the church or cried in the street, text was frequently oral; it was often even nonverbal, particularly given the Quaker emphasis on human silence that Richard Bauman has described.[35] Even the transgressive public "pranks" that Clement Hawes cites as a means of escaping a dominant symbolic order can, I think, be understood as constituting representations intended to foster reading and interpretive communities.[36] The Quaker William Simpson, at one point, conceived of his own body as a kind of symbolic text capable of selecting and uniting a godly community through the collective act of correctly interpreting the nakedness he presented to English society; in fact, having recounted the process of "going naked as a sign" in one of his pamphlets, Simpson renders his body doubly subject to symbolic reading, first in its public exposure, then in his discussion of the significance of that event.[37]

Thus seeking to recreate community through the process of writing and interpretation—both highly suspect in the culture of the 1650s—the writers of prophetic complaint used the status of their text as divine Word to explain the process by which text itself (whether verbal or nonverbal) enabled the process of community formation. To the extent to which the writers of seventeenth-century prophetic complaint considered their texts not as human polemic but as faithful translations of the Word that is deed, they understood their writings to serve as crucial moments in which impending judgments could be either averted or confirmed depending upon the response of a reading audience to the truth that the text had to offer. In effect, they constructed social order not as an enactment of their own words, which they claimed did not exist, but as a product of the reader's conformity to the divine distinctions between obedience and transgression that they represented. Thus Daniel Baker, writing from the Worcester city jail in 1660, asks:

> Did the Everlasting, Invisible God of Eternal Life, ever send or execute his visible or invisible Judgements, Vengeance, Plagues, or great Destructions . . . upon Nations, Kingdoms, Cities, Towns, Families, or upon any particular or individual *Man* or *Woman*, before they were sufficiently warned within and without them? O England, England, England, what hast thou done? Wilt thou not yet be warned?[38]

Because, it was believed, a sincere repentance could prevent greater judgments to come, the publication of the evidence of God's anger, both as providential sign and, implicitly, as the text that recorded that sign, was crucial to the future survival of the nation as a whole. Conversely, because it was thought that ignoring indications of divine wrath could only confirm God in His destructive intentions, both sign and text served as a means of separating goats from sheep, good from evil, as the reaction of the reader—based on a willingness to believe that the written word of the text was not the human word of the prophet but in fact the Word—effectively determined his or her own fate, and ultimately the fate of the nation. A lack of response guaranteed destruction—became itself a sign of punishment—and so Baker likewise asks, implicitly begging favor for his own text: "How is it that your hearts are yet so hardened? Is not this the great Plague (to wit) Hardness of Heart . . . the which your wise Builders, Pasters and Teachers have been so often and frequently speaking . . . is not this your plague?"[39] According to Baker, multitudes of unbelieving English people, having been reminded of their sins and of the evidence of God's anger, have turned away and have confirmed themselves in their sinful courses. The result of this choice as he understands it, moreover, is not only that this hardening of hearts becomes a predictor of future suffering, but that in choosing to harden themselves the people have precipitated their own destruction. "Hardness of Heart" is not only a precursor of plague, but is in fact plague itself.

Thus as one who claimed to translate the Word, rather than to present his or her own writing, the prophetic author was represented as an arbiter of the fate of the nation, providing its people with an opportunity to choose, and so dividing the obedient few from the sinful multitude according to the definitions of transgression and obedience that characterized the prophetic representation of divine law. One of the more sensational examples of this theorizing of the authorial function is William Simpson's aforementioned 1659 discussion of the public function of his nakedness, a tract entitled

*From One Who was Moved of the Lord to go a Sign among the Priests & Professors of the Prophets, Apostles, and Christs Words, But dead from their life, and naked from Salvation and Immortality*. Like many of his religious contemporaries, Simpson was especially concerned with national sins—to the eyes of a Quaker, a commodity in no short supply in 1659 as Monk prepared to march on London in the name of Charles II, seemingly overturning whatever slight gains in religious and political freedom had been achieved under the Commonwealth. Many of his pamphlets, in fact, provide warnings to the powerful in England of the publicly transgressive and destructive nature of their behavior. Like others, too, he is obsessed with the inevitability of national judgment, clearly believing that those who do not repent after fair warning deserve communal destruction. Emphasizing the persistence with which God has hitherto warned his people "by words and by writing" that they are "dead from their life, and naked from Salvation and Immortality," he predicts a gruesome day of reckoning to come.

Yet the focus of this pamphlet is ultimately neither the sins of the English people nor the punishments to come, but Simpson's own decision to go naked through the streets of London. Throughout the piece, he claims to have voluntarily foregone the usual encumbrance of clothing on the grounds that God had instructed him to do so, and had selected him to appear before the people of England as a graphic literalization of their unsatisfactory spiritual condition—their rebellion, that is, against divine authority. Writing to all of the "spiritual Aegyptians and black Aethiopians" among his readers, he asserts that "a sign I was made unto you of all your wickednesse and nakednesse in the sight of the Lord God, [because for those] who will not be warned neither by word nor by writing, signes must be given unto you."[40] Thorough as God appears to be, he has by Simpson's account given his people every opportunity to understand their own condition, and the role of the early-modern nudist/prophet/author, as Simpson understands it, is to explicate by word and by gesture. "The darts of the wicked," he relates, "hath been long shot at the righteous, but now they shall be found all naked men without the weapons and armour of the Lord God as spiritual, as naked as I have gone among you."[41] Making of himself both a signifier and a cipher (a signifier, in fact, because he is a cipher, not a self but merely the divine representation of self) and thus serving as a living reminder of the vulnerability of the human body unprotected by righteousness, Simpson understands that the command to go naked is ultimately part of a larger providential plan, and that his role as a human signifier (itself a kind of divine authorship) is a vital link in a logically progressive chain of events that, taken as a whole, comprise God's imposition of divine order upon an implicitly chosen English people.

In this greater scope of divine justice, the function of Simpson's nakedness is much like that of any other visitation—both an indication of God's wrath and a test to separate those worthy of salvation and succession to a new Jerusalem from those condemned to both worldly and eternal destruction. Insisting upon his own significance as a warning device, he remonstrates: "[Y]ou have been warned from the Lord by his servants, by words and by writing, and all this hath not wrought upon you; now the Lord God is sending you signs and wonders, so that mens hearts shall fail with fear " in the sudden recognition of impending doom—a recognition presumably born of visions like a naked William Simpson.[42] At the same time, Simpson insists upon the urgency of both believing and understanding these signs and wonders, as it is the public response to them that will legally determine salvation and damnation; because the people of England "remain stiff-necked and rebellious, and will not take councel at the Lord; so signs in the street also must you have, that you may be left without excuse in the day when the Lord will come to reckon with you."[43] As yet another of the "signs in the street," Simpson himself becomes a kind of human sifter, forever dividing those who can read God's message from those who cannot or will not, thus determining their eternal fates, and ultimately the fate of the nation. And thus the human writer, equally a purveyor of signifiers—linked in fact with the signifier in the figure of Simpson himself—becomes in this case, as in others, an instrument of the enactment of providential order through the proper segregation of obedience (belief) from rebellion (skepticism).

As a text like Ambrose Rigge's *Lamentation over England* might in its turn suggest, moreover, such articulations of the prophetic ability to segregate a reading audience—an ability ascribed as in Simpson's text to the proclaimed absence of the human word—comprised not just a theory of difference and a means of defining distinctions between the saved and the damned but also a vehicle for explicitly elaborating the very standards upon which community boundaries, rhetorical and otherwise, as well as the defining principles of social order, are based. Rigge, like Simpson, was himself concerned with national sins, particularly the oppression of God's messengers, which he condemned in many of his writings. Likewise he was certain that the transgressions of the oppressors would eventually result in the destruction of the nation. In a 1665 pamphlet entitled *A Lamentation over England*, he described and decried the manifold English sins that had inspired the latest example of God's vengeance: the plague that had gripped London in the summer of that year. "Oh *England, England*," he intoned,

> What shall I say unto thee? Or how shall I lay open before thee the *Unutterable Transgressions* and *Iniquities*, of all sorts and natures, that thou mayst be thorowly sensible of the cause for which the God of heaven and earth is now appearing against Thee, with *sore Calamities and great Judgements*? Oh that my head were as water, and mie eyes a fountain of tears, that I might thorowly lament thy *sad condition* into which thou hast driven thy self, through thy wilful resisting the day of thy *Visitations* . . . for from the head even to the foot, thou art a *disjoynted body, full of bruised and gangreen'd sores*, which are so spread in every member that there is now little hope of thy recovery.[44]

Deliberately reading the plague as an outward physical manifestation of England's *"disjoynted"* moral and political body, Rigge blames the pestilence of 1665 upon the treatment of religious radicals after the Restoration. As he argues that God is angry with the newly restored government's treatment of His messengers and prophets, he echoes the sentiments of many who saw the Restoration as a continuation of oppressions experienced under the Commonwealth and a foreclosure of any remaining hope for true religious revolution. Warning that the plague is but a sign of future destruction to be enacted if present sufferings are ignored, the pamphlet predicts a final visitation in which the oppressors will finally be damned and the prophets and believers led into a new Zion.

And thus, like Simpson, Rigge argues that his vision will distinguish between the righteous and the damned, anticipating the purgation of the damned and thus defining a future godly community rebuilt along entirely new principles. Once God has destroyed all sinners (the vast majority of society), then

> *the residue that shall remain, shall return to Zion with songs of deliverance, and allelujahs to the Lord for ever, and sorrow and sighing shall flie away, and they shall receive beauty for ashes, and the oyle of joy for the spirit of heaviness, that they may be called Trees of righteousness, the planting of the Lord.* But thou [English society] shalt mourn as the Dove mourneth, yea thy laughter shall be turned into mourning, and thy joy into heaviness; and thy swarmes of false Prophets who have long *daubed thee with untempered mortar*, and *made merchandise of thee through covetousness*, shall drink deep of the cup of the Lords indignation, who is highly guilty of all the *Cruelty* and *Oppression*, *Pride* and *Iniquity*, for which Gods anger is now kindled, which shall burn them up and leave them neither *root* nor *branch*.[45]

In thus articulating the division between the godly and the disobedient, Rigge invokes the divine law—forbidding harm to God's messengers—that helps to define the society which he envisions. Specifically a protest against the government's treatment of those dissenters who had refused to take the Oath of Allegiance, the crime for which Rigge himself was incarcerated at the time he wrote the piece, the pamphlet defines Zion as the reward intended specifically for those who are believers in the prophetic message. Basing salvation upon belief defined as obedience to divine law, Rigge's pamphlet effectively realizes a society built upon the exclusion of human oppression. Here the transgressors are specifically those who persecute the chosen, and "make strong the fetters and bonds of the Annointed." "Cruelty" and "oppression" on the part of the false prophets are, according to Rigge, the cause of the plague that will destroy the sinful government enforcers while leaving a godly few to inherit the (apparently quite earthly) kingdom of Zion. Those who respect God's people and His prophets, and thus presumably the divine word itself, will invariably "return to Zion with songs of deliverance"; those who oppose His prophets, and thereby His law, shall be burned up altogether. And thus even as the pamphlet seeks to separate the chosen from a fallen populace according to its own definition of obedience and violation of divine covenant, it also delimits an orderly, functioning society that will prosper under God's benevolent eye.

For Rigge, moreover, the standards, laws, and boundaries that define a godly society are fundamentally unnegotiable to the extent that his text (the prophetic text) effectively conflates legislation and execution, enforcing a boundary in the moment at which it is decreed, precisely by making the moment of reading the moment at which the reader's destiny is decided. For Rigge, Simpson, and others like them, the act of reading becomes an act of settling one's fate. The author can only translate the word of God; he or she cannot mitigate, negotiate, make exceptions, or redefine the absolute difference that divine law has established between obedience and transgression. Rigge himself can only predict the absolute separation between the godly and the damned, creating that distinction in real space at the moment he predicts it: his deliberate and repeated use of the verb "shall" invokes a judgment or commandment—a future, in fact—that has already been resolved. He, as another Mosaic antitype, must deliver it to a wandering and reprobate people. And thus his text itself becomes the means of both defining community boundaries and excluding the transgressors from a society of the godly that the text identifies.

Such rhetorical strategies, while popular among the Quaker writers of prophetic complaint, were not simply a product of that particular group but were in fact common to the genre, as it was adopted by the members of other radical sects as well. The Ranters as a movement were considerably less well-defined than the Quakers; they did not persevere as long, nor do they seem to have articulated much in the way of a common agenda, outside of a general rejection of existing forms of civil and religious authority, which they perceived as corrupt and oppressive. The Ranters were also famous, unlike the Quakers, for denying the very existence of sin. In perhaps his most famous text, *A Fiery Flying Roll*, Abiezer Coppe, like other Ranters, asserts that "sin and transgression is finished." And yet this becomes for him not a means of denying divine punishments, but rather of confirming that the ability to judge is God's alone, and thus that his own writing, as it predicts destruction for the proud and the blasphemous, is a manifestation of both divine will and divine judgment.

In fact, while Thomas Corns has asserted that Coppe's texts are more internally subversive and the society they envision more interior than those of his non-Ranter contemporaries, Coppe does resemble other prophets of the period insofar as he presents his particular version of prophetic complaint—his text—as a now-familiar moment of absolute determination, separation, and judgment, violently consummated in the process of creating a new and godly society.[46] Like his Quaker contemporaries, Coppe offers his readers a choice. In that pamphlet he proclaims that "The Eternall God, the mighty Leveler is coming, yea come, even at the door"; and he asks, "[W]hat will you do in that day . . . hie you apace to all the prisons in the kingdom. Bow before those poor, nasty, lousy, ragged wretches; say to them, your humble servants, sirs, (without a compliment), we let you go free and serve you, &c. Do this or (as I live, saith the Lord) thine eyes at least shall be bored out, and thou carried captive into a strange land."[47] In insisting that God has declared that those in power must either set free the prisoners—overturning existing social order—or have their eyes poked out, Coppe would perhaps initially seem to locate judgment in a distant "that day," offering his readers time to decide. Even his use of the question "what will you do?" would appear to offer a choice. But in claiming, as he does syntactically, to quote the divine Word itself ("saith the Lord"), Coppe also plays with time, conflating present and future: God's word and the choices he offers are directly before the reader and the moment of decision is now. In the context of divine proclamation, even Coppe's seemingly open-ended question becomes a demand for an immediate decision that will settle the reader's fate. Thus offering an immediate choice between voluntary conformity with the divine will it claims to embody and a forced annihilation of the old order—which it guarantees through divine proclamation—Coppe's text insists upon the absolute transforming power of its own representation of disobedience to one way or another bring about the order it envisions; the reader has been shown his or her sins and told how to reform them, and will in the act of reading either conform to divine will or be slated for annihilation. And thus Coppe's text, like those of Rigge and Simpson, asserts that the power both to destroy and to create is inherent to the prophetic text itself in its status as divine, not human, Word.

For many of the radical prophets of the mid-seventeenth century, then, the rhetoric of radical prophecy meant both a means of escaping the partisan polemical battles that seemingly characterized the print culture of the civil wars and an effective means of explaining the role of the text in the legislation and creation of voluntarist (if not entirely voluntary) communities. Text was truth because it was Word, and had power because of the particular dynamic it inscribed among divine will, printed text, and human reader. But in escaping one battle, it involved itself in another, this time with embattled royalists and Commonwealthsmen seeking to define their own place in the public discourse of the seventeenth century. For while the republican texts that David Norbrook describes operated on models that valued participation and discourse, radical prophetic complaint was in many ways more closely related to the utopian writing and practice that James Holstun has suggested worked not by including citizens in the creation of a perfect society, but rather by inscribing that society upon them, sometimes against their will.[48] Holstun does distinguish utopian writing from jeremiad, but for readers faced with the choice Coppe offers the alternatives are simple: to be shaped by the prophetic text or written upon more painfully by the Word itself when divine law is executed and retribution enacted. And thus for those who were not included in the godly remainder nor invited to the New Jerusalem, but who sought instead to reestablish political stability on their own terms, radical prophetic complaint could easily seem dangerous and counterproductive: exclusive, rigid, arbitrary, and even hypocritical in its complaints about the rigor and oppressiveness of others. Certainly it was in those terms that they attacked it in the attempt to seize back the authority that it seemed to them to represent. But as they did so, they themselves found it necessary to rewrite the genre rather than discard it, given the power they located in it, and so radical prophetic complaint did not so much reinscribe the official authority it resisted as it did help to create the very forms and structures through which prophecy itself was attacked.

## III

After 1653, few displaced monarchists depicted themselves as outcast prophets rejected by a heedless people—though Arise Evans remains a significant and useful exception—nor did most Commonwealthsmen find it in their interest to associate themselves with the radical margins of religious sectarianism: Quakers, Ranters, or Fifth Monarchists. In fact, presented with a multiplicity of godly futures from which they were manifestly excluded, both groups more often tried to discredit the prophetic voice as the very symbol of chaos and rebellion, accusing self-proclaimed prophets of blasphemy, sexual deviance, adultery, prostitution, and other forms of criminal behavior. The sensational story of Mary Adams, told in *The Ranters Monster,* combined many of these potent themes. Having "blasphemously [affirmed] that she was conceived with child by the Holy Ghost; that from her should spring forth the Savior of the World; and that all those who did not believe in him were damned," Adams, the pamphlet claims, was "deliver'd of the ugliest ill-shapen *Monster* that ever eyes beheld, and afterwards rotted away in prison."[49]

It is in fact from attacks like this one that we often get some of the most vivid—and most lurid—pictures of prophetic frenzy in the period. The Ranters with whom Adams is identified, so prominent in Hill's account of civil war sectarianism as they screech, scream, and fornicate across England, often seem in particular to coalesce as a group primarily in the eyes of their enemies; they were identified by negative portraits that describe them as sexually promiscuous and deliberately sacrilegious. Another attack upon the Ranters—a 1651 pamphlet entitled *The Joviall Crew, or The Devil turnd Ranter*—presents a supposed member of that sect, one Apostatus, proclaiming that "by our only sacred Laws, *every mans wife must be at his friends use*. . . step thou home and bring thence some sleepy potion, which I'le infuse into his cup: so while he sleeps, I'le use his wife before him."[50] Suggesting that the sects have profaned divine law by rendering it a command to adultery, the anonymous author defines ranting as apostasy and promiscuity. Other prophets were depicted as bloodthirsty and violent, as power-hungry money-grubbers, and as prostitutes willing to sell their country in return for the advancement of their own self-interests. Even William Prynne, himself associated with radicalism in the early part of the century but rendered a virtual conservative by the events of the late 1640s, brutally attacked the Quakers in a pamphlet entitled *The Quakers Unmasked* (1655), linking the self-proclaimed quaking inspiration of that particular group with the division of the English people. Proclaiming that England had never had more need to beware of false prophets "then they have at this day," Prynne pleads, "O God thou hast cast us off, thou hast broken us . . . : O turn thy self to us again: Thou hast made the land to tremble; thou hast broken (and divided it). O heal the breaches thereof FOR IT SHAKETH."[51]

In many ways, these pieces would seem to offer a great deal of support for Shaun Irlam's reading of post-1650 attacks on claims to divine inspiration, which suggests that those attacks were simply and inexorably opposed to a prophetic enthusiasm that, by the time they had finished representing it, bore little relation to the actual claims of the prophets themselves. Certainly we would not want to read these portraits as simple exercises in disinterested realism. As scathing satiric renditions of opposition politics and religion, they take great pride and pleasure in grotesque exaggeration and even indulge in a little early modern pornography as they sexually objectify the religious radicals they represent, who as fictional characters enthusiastically objectify each other. But there is also, as James Holstun suggests, a danger in too easily supposing that royalist and Commonwealth representations of religious radicalism were divorced from the reality of prophecy itself. After all, many of the sexual high jinks of which the prophets stand accused—even prostitution and spouse-swapping—have been well-documented by Turner and others, while (as we have seen) the writers of prophetic complaint themselves were hardly politically or rhetorically naive.[52] Thus more applicable perhaps is Dennis Todd's study of monstrosity in early-eighteenth-century England, which (though concerned with events a bit later than the birth of Mary Adams's toad-child) certainly suggests ways in which stories such as hers could serve as important sites for the working out of social anxieties and struggles for power and control.[53] Similarly, I would suggest, we need to look at the attacks upon religious radicalism as responses that focused on certain salient features of radical prophecy and interpreted those features in the attempt to negotiate and articulate their own concerns and anxieties.

By the mid-1650s, not the least of those concerns was the increasing implication of both royalists and Commonwealthsmen in the very polemical battle that these attacks represent. The rhetoric of pre-war Stuart government, after all, had hardly emphasized dialogue or advocated the polemical involvement of the ruler with his subjects; having done away with parliamentary sessions, the personal rule in particular was as symbolically nondiscursive as England with its constitutional monarchy could get. Norbrook's analysis of the Augustanism of the Protectorate, moreover, suggests that while Cromwell pointedly and repeatedly refused to take the title of king, he and many of his supporters still understood political power as concentrated in a single, divinely ordained figure who should be set before the public, not negotiated by it. Such nondialogic stances, however, also clearly became increasingly untenable in the world of the 1650s. And while Norbrook has suggested the challenge to Augustanism that republican writing represented, Lois Potter, in *Secret Rites and Secret Writing*, has similarly explored some of the problems that dispossessed royalists faced as they sought to compete in the world of public polemic. Documenting the royalist involvement in political propaganda from 1642 on, starting with the highly organized propaganda machine that developed around the king in Oxford, Potter points to a significant royalist dilemma: involvement in the polemical marketplace meant at best a confusion of motives, a perceived inability to claim a purity of principle when payment meant, as she puts it, that some "were at least partly in it for the money," while silence meant defeat and even implied complicity with rebellion.[54] Royalist participation in the "pamphlet wars," moreover, was hardly limited to starving hacks, but often extended to titled and landed figures who fifteen years earlier might well have eschewed publication as beneath them. And thus by 1650 the disinterested and nonnegotiable stance of the early Stuarts had necessarily given way to a proliferation of competing rhetorical responses to the opening of print culture.

And in fact, as the period began to reassess not only textual but political authority as a result of the explosion of polemic, it became more difficult simply to return to old models. Steven Zwicker has written that in the period between 1649 and 1689 "polemic engulfed the literary and tempered all the idioms of culture," suggesting that changes in notions of textual authority that the polemical battles of the period necessitated precipitated innovations in discourse that themselves affected the ways in which political power could be and was described.[55] Andrew Marvell's "Horatian Ode," searching as it does for new metaphors to contextualize the emerging power of Oliver Cromwell, and even Milton's *Paradise Lost,* redefining (as John Steadman has so convincingly shown) the classical notion of virtue and with it earlier Renaissance ideas about leadership and authority, both testify to the perceived inadequacy of old models of power after 1650 and the need to determine new rationales for political and textual authority.[56] The richness of the 1650s as a wellspring of early modern political and economic theory likewise indicates the deliberateness with which writers reevaluated and reconceived traditional formulations of power and authority. And often these reevaluations sought explicitly to ground themselves, however uncomfortably, in the discursive and economic world that print culture had created.

For many, in fact, the only means of authorizing text in a skeptical environment was in fact to concede the universality of individual interest; the power of the text was thus understood to lie in its open admission of its own interested agenda.[57] Suspicion of self-interest of course did not disappear; in 1661, the author of a response to *A Coffin for the Good old Cause* entitled his pamphlet *The Coffin Opened: Or, Self-Interest Discovered,* figuring the moral contamination of self-interest as the literal corruption of the body after death, and thus legitimating his own condemnation of his political enemies. But even George Wither, though he elsewhere warned of the dangers of self-interest, argued in 1645 that an author who has not actively demonstrated a desire to protect his own interests has little credence as a public voice:

> For, he that makes no concience to prevent
> His private ruine, shall be seldom heard
> In any publike matter, with regard.[58]

By 1650, that is, the conditions of both print and civil warfare had necessarily rendered self-interest an important ingredient in the public representation of authority.

Ironically, one of the most conservative political texts that sought to redefine the basis of political authority after 1649 may have gone the furthest toward resetting the bases of political authority in terms of self-interest. Thomas Hobbes's *Leviathan*, written in the late 1640s and very early 1650s, has long been taken as a political manifesto declaring a crisis of political authority and the need to establish both a new locus and a new foundation for political power. Hobbes, moreover, provides a particularly useful insight into the reconceptualization of authority during the civil wars, in part because, as David Johnston has aptly demonstrated, *Leviathan* understands itself as a response to the polemical crises that the civil wars precipitated.[59] Hobbes's project, that is, depends not upon the mere assertion of authority to a rhetorical community of believers, but rather upon the evidence of authority—understood specifically as a function not of truth but of representation—and upon the ability of that evidence to appeal specifically to self-interest, the established enemy of social order and national unity. In chapter 10 of *Leviathan*, "Of Power, Worth, Dignity, Honour, and Worthinesse," Hobbes asserts that

> the power of a Man, (to take it Universally,) is his present means, to obtain some future Apparent Good. . . . The Greatest of humane Powers, is that which is compounded of the Powers of most men, united by consent, in one person, Naturall, or Civill, that has the use of all their Powers depending on his will; such as is the Power of a Common-wealth: Or depending on the wills of each particular: such as is the Power of a Faction . . . Reputation of power, is Power; because it draweth with it the adhaerence of those that need protection.[60]

According to this understanding of civil government, the reputation of power, that is, the representation of power, is in fact the essence of power itself. Men band together in societies for the purpose of protection; and therefore the reputation of the ability to protect is sufficient to grant political authority, as the private interests of individuals lead them to barter away the freedom of the state of nature in the hopes of buying a reprieve from the nasty, brutish, and short life span of those unintegrated into civil society. Hobbes's construction of power thus in fact transforms political authority into cultural sign, recasting it as textual authority, even as the real conditions of the civil war press suggested the increasing power of propaganda in constituting or debilitating institutionalized political power.

For Hobbes, moreover, the ability to represent oneself as powerful is in fact to have authority, not because of any belief in the magically divine power of representation, but because of the implicit self-interest of an audience eager to ally itself with the representation of power for the purpose of self-preservation. As a result, because society according to Hobbes is not so much a product of divinely granted authority as it is the result of the collective self-interest of autonomous individuals, the process of creating social order becomes for him a process not of submission but of exchange; the right to rule is derived from negotiations in which the individual agrees to trade private freedoms for the very representation of power that serves as the most precious commodity of authority. Like the riches that Hobbes also cites as a source of potential political authority, representations can be bartered according to a negotiated system of needs, thus serving as the basis for social contract.[61] Given the presumed inevitability in *Leviathan* of self-interest in the construction of any community, power is of necessity a market commodity. And as representation becomes in this system not an absolute truth but a bartering token whose value can thus be negotiated upon the open market, power is inevitably rendered in terms of text, and of reading.

As a result, in *Leviathan* the value and authority of the representation of power, the source of power itself, becomes dependent upon the interpretation of a reading public—a rhetorical community constructed not upon the basis of common belief but through their own often competing self-interests, not only as the material that constitutes it is bought and sold, but as the versions of truth that it has to offer are weighed and evaluated according to the needs of a reading public that must either endorse or reject the representations it has to offer. Thus definitions like the distinctions rendered by radical prophets between social order and disobedience, virtue and sin, cannot be absolute but must result from a constant process of negotiation between writer and reader, whose interests can never be assumed to be in any sense identical; Hobbes's famous fears about both the potential abuse of language and its resulting effect upon social order themselves confess, however reluctantly, that meaning is inevitably socially constructed through a process of negotiation that must proceed by carefully agreed-upon rules if communication is to be both orderly and successful. Thus representation itself becomes for Hobbes inevitably, if not entirely happily, part of a system of evaluative exchange that both constitutes authority—real and textual—and ultimately defines social order, not as a system of arbitrary oppositions, but as a process of ongoing negotiation.

Certainly *Leviathan* was a controversial text in its own day, but that controversial status in part suggests the anxiety with which conservatives greeted even their own attempts to reassess political authority in terms of self-interest, and the very deep ambivalence with which those seeking to reconstitute order after 1653 regarded the strategies to which they turned in their efforts to represent power and reestablish civil and religious boundaries. In such a climate attacks upon radical prophetic complaint, with its claims to disinterestedness and to the absolute authority of the divine text, suggest the extent to which, for both royalists and Commonwealthsmen, prophecy focused their concerns and became a means of articulating and thus exorcising their own anxieties about the changing nature of political and textual authority. In fact, those attacks often located in the prophetic other that which its opponents most feared in themselves, and thus the prophetic text was often constructed by its enemies through seemingly counterintuitive claims that the supposedly objective prophets—unselfish vessels for the word of God—were in fact motivated by the same self-interests as everyone else, and thus drawn back into the same polemical mire that beset other political and religious writings of the period.

Thus the author of *A Satyr Against Hypocrites* (1655) depicts prophetic speakers taking turns at a sectarian meetinghouse:

> Up stept another [speaker] then, how sowre his face is!
> How grim he lookt, for he was one oth' *Classis*,
> And here he cries, *Blood, blood, blood, destroy, O Lord!*
> *The Covenant-breaker, with a two-edged sword.*
> Now comes another, of another strain,
> And he of law and bondage doth complain.[62]

Here a first speaker, full of fire and brimstone, begs like Abiezer Coppe for the destruction of all of his mortal enemies—those who have transgressed the law and covenant of sectarian religion; he is followed, ironically, by a speaker bewailing the enforcement of Commonwealth laws and regulations that render the radicals themselves transgressors liable to punishment. By depicting these speaker/prophets as both brutally bloodthirsty, willing to seize the nation by force, and ideologically inconsistent, the author suggests a genuine anxiety about the rhetorical claims of the prophetic text, while ridiculing the narrowness of a religious and political absolutism that can tolerate only its own definition of social boundaries and social hegemony. Hinting that the hypocrisy of the speakers, evident in their highly partial diatribe against law and order, undermines their credibility as vessels for God's word, the author radically questions the supposed efficacy of prophetic speech. In the process, *A Satyr* also accuses the prophetic word of a latent personal interest. The fact that the first speaker confidently advances a violent totalitarianism, while the second decries offensive laws suggests that definitions of law and transgression are manipulated by the prophets to fit their own political and religious agendas. The titular reference to hypocrisy likewise suggests that their pretense to an objective transmission of divine law hides a catalog of self-interests discovered by their reluctance to conform to any laws but their own.

Even the more sensational attacks upon radical criminality and sexuality reveal similar concerns, as self-interest was frequently coded by such attacks as a matter of economics or as the sexual behavior that so troubled the opponents of the sects. Such attacks implied, in effect, that the prophets were really working for their own financial or sensual advantage. One common claim was that prophetic disinterestedness concealed deeper financial motives. Often associating prophets with artisans and tradesmen "tainted" by their occupational interest in profit, such attacks deliberately and often erroneously aligned the period's prophets with social and cultural "lowness," in order to suggest a motive for economic self-interest. Thus the author of *A Satyr Against Hypocrites* complains that "every *Mechanick* either wanting stock / Or wit to keep his trade must have a flock."[63] Implying that prophecy is a trade like any other, such attacks intimated that prophetic inspiration was more a matter of business management than divine utterance. Even more popular, and probably better selling, were the claims that the radical sexuality of many sectarians was a product not of theology or inspiration but of personal sexual interest, the satisfaction of the individual libido. *The Joviall Crew*'s Apostatus quite explicitly uses the rhetoric of God and religion to fulfill his own sexual desires, literally taking advantage of his position by drugging one of his supposed brethren in order to enjoy that so-called brother's wife. Mary Adams's monstrous birth, a baby born with no arms and no legs but with "claws like a toad," is likewise directly associated with her "ranting," defined by the hint of sexual indiscretion in her blasphemous claim to be a modern Virgin Mary, and thus represented as a punishment for her blasphemy, her abuse of the divine Word as a means of covering or concealing her own sexual interest and gratification.[64]

Frequently these discourses of economic and sexual interest were actually conflated in a disturbing vision of prophetic prostitution. One of the most famous of all attacks upon the radical sectarians of the civil wars, *Peters Patern*, presents a mock sermon in which a radical preacher warns his congregation of their duty in the eyes of God, while unconsciously revealing the personal motives that underlie his seemingly religious demeanor. "There is a duty," he claims,

> that lies upon every professour, we find evident by this, that there is in all men not only a labouring and panting, but also a tye upon them to look after self-preservation. . . . Therefore when Necessity, the best Schoolmistresse of the Godly, that maketh Magpies to speak and Spaniels to fetch and carry, had made [the German *Gusman*] to consider his duty, he was not slack in the exercise thereof, so that betaking himself to the religious calling of a Thief, he stole the Cooks silver Goblet, the Grocers Royals, and couzened the Cardinal of his Barrel of Conserves. Moreover my beloved, this Duty of self-preservation caus'd our dear Sister *Agatha* as you may read in the first book of our pious *Francion*, not only to bethink her self, but to bestirr her stumps also; Finding herself therefore to be of a well shap'd body, and of comly feature, and lovely in the eyes of men, she became an Harlot, and was unto the brethren a great comfort in the frail distresses of Human nature: hereby she was stored with wealth, and increased in worldly enjoyments. This Duty it is that obligeth Butchers to preach, and Coblers to pray.[65]

Here we find prophets and preachers who speak, not by divine inspiration, but for economic advantage—prophets who are thus driven not so much to enact God's will as to better their own financial state and increase their "comfort." The very Word itself, this piece implies, has been stolen and pimped to conceal the self-interested motivations of those "Butchers" and "Coblers" who assume it. And in this context, the claims of the prophetic text to a certain social efficacy are made to backfire. Because they are the product of human self-interest and the prostituted Word, the society they create is one of thieves and harlots: low, coarse, and vulnerable to all of the internally corrupting diseases associated with early modern prostitution. Suggesting that the prophetic word was not, then, the all-powerful Word of God, but rather a word corrupted, already rotting from within, and thus both hollow and impotent, such images sought anxiously to defuse the powerful and apparently disturbing rhetoric of the radical prophetic text.

Yet these satires did not merely represent, I would argue, an effort to construct prophecy as ridiculous or harmless. For as they accused radical prophetic complaint of the very crime, self-interest, that prophecy itself explicitly rejected, these attacks articulated the very terms in which conservatives nervously regarded their own polemical prostitution. *Peters Patern,* as a parody of prophetic discourse, suggests that it is not simply prophecy itself, but language—its text and therefore its public presentation—that is under fire. Such parodies were common in the period, and their characteristic use of radical religious language was a popular means of satirizing the idiosyncratic nature of radical prophecy. But behind the surface ridicule of form and style lies a concern—very Hobbesian, in fact—with the misuse and abuse of words and texts themselves, as the literal prostitution of the female radical metonymizes the illicit appropriation of language for personal gain. For the speaker of *Peters Patern*, words such as "religious," "duty," and "comfort," meaningful in the context of religious observation, have become a convenient means of concealing his own self-interested behavior—a behavior manifest not only in his sexual and criminal activities, but in his verbal justification of the cause itself. In the many parodies written throughout the 1650s and early 1660s, conservatives thus sought to focus their own anxieties about the changing nature of text and public speech on the one group that essentially denied its own human involvement in the public sphere, partly as a means of discrediting the very concept of textual authority (its own disinterestedness) on which the prophetic text insisted, but also as a means of verbalizing their distaste of the very polemical struggles in which they themselves were implicated.

And as they did so, we must concede, conservative attacks on radical prophecy also engaged in their own acts of misappropriation. The speaker in *Peters Patern* is not the only one in that text to use language to his own advantage; the author, after all, is equally guilty of misrepresenting the language of radical religion and twisting its discourse to meet his own highly polemicized ends. In the process, moreover, the author engages in the same act of self-justification—the same attempt to conceal self-interest—as the corrupted speaker, using the speaker's misuse of language as a rationale for his own attack and suggesting that his own piece in effect passes a kind of judgment on the speaker in much the same way that the religious language the speaker invokes asserted its own ability to judge. Margaret Doody has suggested in *The Daring Muse* that the mimicry of opposition language so common in the period served as an important means of expressing one's own beliefs and allowing the opposition to condemn itself.[66] But parody also, I would argue, allowed text in the midst of a crisis of authority to parasitize the power of its victim, not simply discrediting the opposition text but rather using the potency of language and rhetorical strategies it implies to empower the parodic text: if *Peters Patern* condemns the misuse of religious language, it also authorizes itself in part through the religious language it uses. Thus too, a piece like *A Satyr*, while it savages the hypocritical misuse of the language of divine judgment, suggests its own ability to judge in part through the implicit power of the language of judgment to which it is juxtaposed. If the speaker in that text misuses language, he can do so only because there exists—in the implicit originary language that has been abused—a genuine prophetic discourse to which the author implicitly juxtaposes not only the hypocritical language of his opponent but his own more genuine judgment. And thus the prophetic voice, while ridiculed, is also retained in the language of the attack as a genuine source of power, even as it is redefined in the process of layering and allusion to which it is subjected.

In fact, just as the rhetoric of radical prophecy owed much to the authoritarian politics it seemingly rejected, conservative attacks upon radical prophecy may be understood to depend upon the very relationship between text and political authority that radical prophecy proposed, in their attempts to come to terms with their own anxieties about the complicity of conservative text in a polemical marketplace. While conservatives worried about the implicit acceptance of personal and political interest that their engagement in the pamphlet wars implied, they found in their appropriation of radical prophecy a source of textual authority and efficacy. Because the language of prophecy is retained and refracted in texts like *Peters Patern* and *A Satyr,* it provides those texts with access to a theory of judgment and an understanding of the textual foundations of recreated community that were useful and even necessary in the aftermath of the death of Charles I. And as the language of the prophetic texts informed the very attacks against them, it thus ironically encouraged the attackers themselves to reconceptualize both textual and political authority. In engaging religio-prophetic language as an implicit source of power, the authors of *Peters Patern* and *A Satyr* necessarily reworked their own notions of authority, already in flux. And thus prophecy and its opponents did not so much exist in opposition as flourish in symbiosis.

That interdependence, moreover, did not simply vanish after the Restoration, but rather continued to grow and develop. If the unrest of the 1640s and 1650s provided an environment in which prophetic and conservative voices could interact, offering one the freedom to speak and confronting the other with the need to reevaluate the nature of representation, the Restoration did little to mitigate the tensions inherent to the relationship between them. Prophecy remained an important discourse through the early eighteenth century, particularly at moments of cultural crisis. Arguably, in fact, radical prophetic activity actually increased during the early years of the Restoration as men like Ambrose Rigge found themselves more heavily persecuted by a restored government than they had been under the Commonwealth. And even if the Quakers as a group grew more passive after 1670, while other groups seemingly disappeared, uncooperative individuals unwilling to accept an institutional fate proved rather more difficult; McDowell, for instance, points to the case of Quakeress Joan Whitrowe, active during the 1680s and 1690s, whose discussions of God's judgments proved too radical even for the Quaker press itself. Even alongside the French enthusiasts of the early eighteenth century, genuine English descendants of the civil war prophets wailed and predicted doom. The popularity of prognostication, astrology, and providential logic between 1710 and 1720, moreover, suggests that even if prophetic and providential rhetoric disappeared from much of the polite literature of the period, it thrived in the slough of popular culture, and thus remained available as a living discourse. At the same time, as the work of J. C. D. Clark has suggested, the Restoration did not mean so much a settlement of monarchical authority as a new reason to agonize over its shape and form—and a new desire to preserve the institution of monarchy. That in turn meant continuing anxieties about the nature of political power, exacerbated by frequent challenges to an ever-changing political authority: challenges represented by the Exclusion Crisis, the Glorious Revolution, the death of Queen Mary, and the settlement of the Hanoverian succession. And thus prophecy and political anxiety in fact traveled closely together through the last years of the seventeenth century and the opening decades of the eighteenth century.

In such a context, the rewriting of prophetic complaint—particularly, though not exclusively, by royalists—persistently located anxieties and ambivalence about new modes of social and cultural authority within the prophetic voice itself, much as the attacks of the 1650s had done, perpetuating the stereotype of the self-proclaimed prophet as oversexed, underethical, amoral, and above all acutely self-interested. Relegating fears about the corruption of authority to the prophetic other, they effectively exonerated royalists, who were depicted as knowing satirists wittily condemning the imperfect process in which they were (at the worst) compelled by the flawed nature of the human condition to participate. At the same time, they offered a voice, in the figure of the prophet, which presumed to transcend that human condition, and with it the anxieties, ambivalence, and interests to which all flesh was seemingly heir. Representing the very form of unnegotiated authority that it had arguably denied royalist and Commonwealth voices, the appeal to prophecy made possible claims about the nature and creation of social order that were otherwise unavailable.

And yet, even as the ability of the prophetic text to articulate the absolute difference between obedience and transgression, loyalty and sin, provided one basis of authority for postwar rewritings of prophecy, those rewritings also adapted the prophetic voice, which they neither entirely embraced nor entirely rejected, changing it in ways that reflected the certainty, however grim, that the form of difference it proposed was not conducive to either political or textual authority in a period that obsessively feared a return to violence and always respected the disruptive power of force. Often imbuing the prophetic voice with the volition and capacity to authorize the same process of negotiation that royalists often unwillingly embraced as a necessary alternative to the potentially anarchic rhetoric of absolute division, these texts reconstituted the prophetic voice according to the rhetorical needs of a group of writers who wished to preserve their own textual authority but also sought, however reluctantly, to render that authority the nonoppositional product of openly self-interested exchange.

One of the earliest texts to employ such a large-scale rewriting of the prophetic voice was Samuel Butler's *Hudibras*. Rendering its unsightly, unwieldy, and distinctly inept "hero" both a Presbyterian and a prognosticating pseudoprophet, Butler's poem overtly parodies both prophet and Commonwealthsmen in its bathetic vision of order and knight/preacher errancy during the interregnum. In fact, deliberately and persistently linking prophecy with the low-culture world of the tradesmen, mechanicals, and rabble who inhabit the poem, Butler perpetuates the stereotypes of the 1650s as he seemingly tries to purge lingering fears of disorder from a newly established Restoration order. And yet, like many of the popular parodies of the prophetic voice that appeared during the confusion that beset England between the death of Cromwell and the restoration of Charles II, Butler's text also conflates prophetic and satiric voices; it is unwilling or unable to profess a restored monarchical authority without conceding the extent to which that authority was in fact implicated in the forces—often explicitly economic and self-interested—that opposed it. In so doing, it provides a powerful early example of the use of the prophetic voice to renegotiate the shape of both power and opposition after the Restoration. And thus it is to *Hudibras*, prophetic parody, bathos, mechanicals, and the economic negotiation of both politics and culture that we now must turn.

# 2

# Joining with Self-Interests: Royalist Reconstruction and the Popular Press

With the restoration of Charles II in 1660, reinstated royalists began the complicated task of reconstructing and re-presenting monarchical authority. During the early 1660s, the signs of Stuart monarchy were painstakingly rebuilt. His majesty's ships were carefully renamed—the *Naseby*, for one, became the *Royal Charles*—and Cromwell's remains were theatrically displayed as a reminder that the power of the king reached even beyond death. Estates of prominent commonwealth officials were seized (or often retaken) and redone according the wishes and the iconographies of their new royalist owners.

Yet throughout the early 1660s, the optimism of this thorough rewriting of English political signs was beset by a consciousness that England was still persistently divided by many of the same political and ideological controversies that had originally led to social upheaval. Many of the prominent leaders of the Commonwealth had been executed at the Restoration, but others had been pardoned by the Act of Indemnity and left as potent reminders of the civil conflict so recently past—remaining both as symbols of the forces that had sought to destroy hereditary monarchy and as remembrancers of the price of loyalty and the unfairness of political necessity for those royalists whose estates were not returned at the Restoration. Censorship was restored under Roger L'Estrange in an attempt to regain control of the presses, but royalists were able to do little more than the Commonwealth had to silence the voices of radical unrest.

Radical prophets—in particular, men and women like William Bayly, Ambrose Rigge, and Christopher Taylor—continued to predict the demise of the English nation. Between 1658 and 1662, the prophets of the civil wars protested stridently against what they perceived to be the regression of monarchy returned; Milton's *Readie and Easie Way* provides the most famous example of anti-Restoration prophecy, but it was merely the most eloquent of a flood of disgusted and energetic outpourings with titles like *The Last Trump*, *Yet One Warning More*, and *A Fannaticks Alarm, Given to the Mayor in his Quarters. By one of the Sons of Zion, become Boanerges. To Thunder out the Judgements of God against Oppression and Oppressors*. The radical prophetic voices that survived the Restoration were often made even more vocal by the enforcement of new measures designed to oppress them. Ambrose Rigge, for one, was deeply embittered by his treatment during the early Restoration, and in fact published many of his most radical prophetic works after 1660. For many of these self-proclaimed prophets, in fact, the plague of 1665 came as a welcome sign that God was finally beginning to punish the English nation for its persistent repression of His most loyal prophetic voices. All in all, the much-celebrated hegemony of monarchy restored seemed precarious at best in the years immediately following 1660.

It was in the midst of the first great Restoration outpouring of prophetic text in and around 1660, protesting Parliament's change of heart and the prospect of monarchy restored, that Samuel Butler published the first part of what remains his most famous work, the parodic poem *Hudibras*. During that period, Butler was himself involved in the reconstruction of the returned estate of the royalist Richard Vaughan, and *Hudibras* is a piece that—at least at first glance—would seem a textual parallel to the author's architectural activities, seeking to purge the last vestiges of anxiety from the English collective consciousness by ridiculing both Commonwealthsman and radical prophet into ineptitude and impotence. George Wasserman has described Butler's use of the mock-heroic as a distinctly political attempt to discredit the nonroyalist forces of the civil wars as grotesque, corporeal, undeniably unspiritual, and therefore both hypocritical and unreliable.[1] Hudibras himself is at once Parliamentarian, Presbyterian, and prophet: the sign of both law and order under the Commonwealth and a rather more eccentric prophetic radicalism. Often thought to be modeled upon the figure of Sir Samuel Luke, Presbyterian and member of the Long Parliament, Hudibras is a justice of the peace, a member of the Parliamentary army, and a committeeman. He is also a prophet in the finest tradition, possessed of a beard that can tell the future, linking national destiny to providential signs and typological readings:

> This hairy Meteor did denounce
> The fall of Scepters and of Crowns;
> With grizzly type did represent
> Declining age of government;

And tell with Hieroglyphic Spade,
Its own grave and the State's were made.[2]

Above all, however, Hudibras is a moron—ignorant, incompetent, cowardly, and consummately self-interested—and thus incapable as either Presbyterian or prophet of posing any threat to a monarchical government restored. Fears of chaos renewed, the poem would seem to suggest, are unfounded in the face of such enemies as these.

Yet even as Butler's poem would seem to create the very antitheses and oppositions that Wasserman and others have described as typical of early-Restoration royalist texts, it also simultaneously, inexorably works against those very polarities. Having rhetorically constructed both the terms of political and cultural difference and a rationale for political and cultural exclusion, *Hudibras* immediately seeks to confuse, to conflate, and to disassemble, apparently altogether conscious of its own distrust of the polemical and defining written word. In citing Butler's literary and philosophical objections to heroic poetry, John Wilders has argued that the poet "disliked the style and conventions of such poetry because they were artificial, but also rejected its ideals as trivial and foolish . . . when judged by practical, realistic standards"—standards presumably the result of two decades of decidedly unromantic civil conflict.[3] And in fact the mock-heroic nature of *Hudibras*, together with its attack upon the vocabulary of a romance tradition that had effectively sought to transform the world into the very image of strength, courage, and martial prowess, suggests that attempts to polarize ideological difference into rigid oppositions exposed values seemingly no longer viable or accessible in a post–civil war context.

Thus at the end of the first part of the poem, an overflowing Hudibras is quite literally contained—placed in the stocks by an annoyed opposition—but if anything Butler's description of this contest should suggest that the world of *Hudibras*, rather like the real world of the early Restoration, is one in which the word of the law (the careful distinction between order and disorder, obedience and rebellion) has ceased to satisfactorily define the boundaries of political, cultural, and religious transgression. Hudibras himself, ineffectual knight-errant that he is, is the sole representative of the law in the poem; his sword of justice is rusty, his rational ability to judge, we are told, is more than lacking. And if such a depiction seems directed specifically against a past of Presbyterian rule, we might recall that the rabble, while certainly entertaining and associated with the vaguely royalist exercise of bearbaiting, are hardly a more attractive alternative to the decrepit knight. They themselves are depicted with little compassion as tradesmen and tradeswomen who are both literal and ideological prostitutes. In Butler's poem, in fact, the antiheroic vision has seemingly rendered military battle (the forceful eradication of opposition) forever trivial, irrelevant, grotesque, and chaotic, even while its reminders of the belatedness of the prophetic voice leave the terms of sin, transgression, and obedience hopelessly inadequate to the conditions of Restoration culture.

Ultimately, in fact, Butler's thorough deconstruction of the terms of both political and cultural opposition suggests that *Hudibras* does not so much exemplify royalist attempts to create and thereby exclude the political "other" as it does typify a royalist dilemma born of the realities of contemporary polemical conflict. In the early years after the Commonwealth, as we have seen, royalists faced with the need to rebuild political authority were forced to come to terms with the fact that absolutist understandings of both discourse and law had apparently lost their efficacy, trapped in rigid and seemingly destructive dialectics. For writers such as Butler, the challenge was to renegotiate the very terms of social structure in a way that, however reluctantly, found alternatives to strict oppositions and absolutist polemics.

Somewhat ironically, one solution attempted in *Hudibras* and other royalist texts published between 1658 and 1660 uses the rhetorical debasement of low culture, which Wasserman cites as an example of cultural authoritarianism, to modify the prophetic voice—itself often connected in the royalist mind, as we have seen, with seemingly destructive absolute oppositions.[4] Relocating the prophetic voice in the context of a rapidly commercializing print culture, *Hudibras* in fact posits an alternative social order based upon the rhetoric of economic exchange rather than that of absolute authority. And in the process, it redefines the way in which text affected real social and political space in the commercialized world of post-Restoration politics.

## I

By 1660, the prophetic vision that Hudibras's beard so grotesquely represents had become for royalists a symbol of opposition rhetoric in general and, more specifically, a representative of a potential polemical crisis whose danger lay not so much in the quality of opposition rhetoric but in its very state of being. Repeatedly, after 1658, royalist writers deliberately conflated Commonwealth authors and politicians with the radical prophetic voices of the civil wars. Prominent members of the Commonwealth government, men like John Bradshaw and John Lambert, together with their largely Presbyterian constituency, were represented as lamenting prophets, weeping for the destruction of their briefly held Jerusalem and searching for the sins that had brought down God's judgment upon their once seemingly elect state. In *The Lamentation of a Bad Market*, a piece that purported to have been printed "at the charge of John Lambert, Charles Fleetwood, and Arthur Hesilrig, and —— Hewson the Cobler" (all prominent Commonwealth leaders), one royalist author thus purposely depicts Commonwealth supporters as fanatic would-be prophets foretelling their own execution.[5] "Oh Lucifer! Lucifer!" one of the speakers cries,

> Why hast thou forsaken us, and left thine own people in the day of Adversity? . . . Friends, seeing we have begun [to examine our sins], let us search ourselves to the bottom, and recount what we were in the days of old: Were we not the despised of the Nation? Were we not contented with the meanest Cottages to cover our heads, the like Food to sustain ourselves, and the poorest Weeds to clothe ourselves? In those days we took no thought, neither were our heads busied with National Occurances, the Secrets of Kingdoms, Kings and Princes, the acquaintance of Powers, and Exercise of Powers, Ruling and Dominion, Government in Church and State. . . . O' that we had never known or been instructed in the Rudiments of Ambition.[6]

A prophet of Lucifer rather than God, the speaker engages in a parodic version of the radical prophecy of the period; seeking not to identify the sins of the nation in order to predict a future destruction, but rather decrying the personal transgressions of himself and his followers, he cites the reasons for a commonwealth gone bad, rescued from itself by the Babylonian saviors of the monarchy restored. Rendering prophecy not a serious ideological or religious activity, but a sign of mistaken political rhetoric, the pamphlet uses the prophetic voice to signal the failure of the political and religious opposition to Restoration monarchy.

As *The Lamentation* might suggest, moreover, one rhetorical effect of the conflation of Commonwealth and prophetic voices was to make available to attacks upon the Commonwealth the rich body of imagery that had marked negative representations of prophecy during the 1650s; to align Commonwealthsmen with prophets was to accuse them of the same lasciviousness, social marginalization, and even insanity with which they themselves had labeled the self-proclaimed prophets of the period. In particular, as we have seen, Commonwealth and royalist attacks upon prophetic writing decried the prophetic voice on the grounds of its purported cultural lowness—its engagement with a world of mechanicals, thieves, and prostitutes—and its represented entrenchment in an ethos built around financial self-interest. Likewise royalist attacks upon the Commonwealth used the association of prophecy and "Good old Cause" to accuse Commonwealth politicians of similar attachments. The speaker of *The Lamentation* points out at great length the low origins of his followers, their familiarity with cottages and rags, and their subsequent unsuitability for political office and national responsibility. Similarly, a mock will (purportedly that of the regicide and Commonwealth leader John Bradshaw), part of a pamphlet entitled *Bradshaw's Ghost*, lumps together Bradshaw's "Goods and Chattels, Lands and Hereditaments" with his "Religion, Charity and Mercy," effectively equating them; all are to go together to his "dearly beloved Pimp, Mr. Nedham," suggesting among other things that Bradshaw's prominent role in the execution of Charles I was a debasing act of prostitution.[7]

To the extent to which these royalist attacks lumped prophet and Commonwealthsman into an indiscriminate morass of low culture, moreover, they deliberately linked both parties with a process of explicitly mechanical production, itself a condition of the commercialization of polemic and decried by the period as ungentlemanly and self-interested. Frequently supporters of Charles II attacked the enduring legacy of the "Good old Cause" on the grounds that its primary public spokesmen were craftsmen—producers of commercial products. Thus the author of *The Lamentation of a Bad Market* equates Commonwealth polemic, represented by the persona of the allegedly prophetic speaker, with the production of shoes, clothing, and other manufactures. The actors of *The Lamentation* are "Coblers and Brewers," "[marching] under the severall Banners of [their] Professions, and several Occupations, Trades and Vocations."[8] More than one royalist pamphlet of the day referred to those who opposed a monarchy restored as swineherds, driving pigs to market—and a bad market at that. Aligning both prophets and prominent Commonwealth politicians with the trades from which many of them in fact had come, these attacks render political opposition, and perhaps more importantly the spokesmen for a political opposition, members of artisan culture and the producers of real material product.

As Wasserman has suggested, Butler's *Hudibras* works in much the same way, linking in its own turn the image of Commonwealthsman and prophet—conflated in the figure of Hudibras himself—with the signs of so-called low culture and mechanical production. Hudibras is not merely inspired by his beard to an ineptitude characteristic, Butler suggests, of parliamentarian JPs, but is also a mechanical of sorts, incapable of properly and judiciously executing the office of a gentleman because of his links to the culture of trade and commercial interest. The actions of Butler's knight, along with his possessions, repeatedly belie his gentle birth, relating him almost obsessively to the conditions of artisan culture. Thus using the basket-hilt of his sword both to cook dinner and to "[melt] lead for Bullets / To shoot at Foes, and sometimes Pullets," Hudibras abdicates his position both as magistrate and soldier, aligning himself instead with the explicitly commercial occupation of cook and the lowly stature of servant. (*Hudibras* 1.1.353–54). His dagger, likewise, alludes to the debasing efforts of its master, implicitly reducing his social status through the narrative of its own dubious lineage:

> It would scrape Trenchers, or chip Bread,
> Toast Cheese or Bacon, though it were
> To bait a Mouse-trap, 'twould not care.
> 'Twould make clean shoes, and in the earth
> Set Leeks and Onions, and so forth.
> It had been Prentice to a Brewer,
> Where this and more it did endure.
> But left the Trade, as many more
> Have lately done on the same score.
> (*Hudibras* 1.1.380–88)

Thus discrediting its owner through its own disregard for honorable employment, the dagger becomes a figure not only for Hudibras but for all those members of the Commonwealth and all the radical religious separatists whose public actions have purportedly demonstrated their lower-class origins. At the same time, the poem's repeated emphasis upon gluttonous and debasing appetite serves to suggest the extent to which self-interest determines all of the knight's great actions. Fighting his most desperate battles not against his royalist enemies but against the rats that seek to invade the larders of his pant legs, Hudibras's heroism is ultimately the figurative product of his own miserly appetite—signified in the giant storage locker that his body has become—not the result of any "higher" intellectual dedication to political or religious principle. More than once in the poem he is quite literally reduced to the level of the tradesmen/townspeople he seeks to subdue—primarily because of his poor horsemanship, the very sign of his failure as a member of the country gentry.

Hudibras's incompetence, symbolic of both his political allegiance and his religious inspiration, would thus in many ways seem to provide the perfect cultural rationale for his exclusion from political and religious power, and his exile from the influential workings of Restoration society, as Wasserman has claimed; and in fact, the battery of attacks upon the conflated representation of Commonwealth and prophetic voices would seem to suggest that royalist writers in general did see cultural lowness as a legitimate reason for exclusion from political power. At the same time, however, the obsessive linking of opposition spokesmen with mechanical culture and the production of material objects would also seem to suggest that one of the perceived problems with opposition rhetoric was not merely its represented cultural inadequacy but rather its very polemicism—marked by an engagement in a commercial press that seemingly confused writing and production, and thus produced (in all senses of the word) real and often disorienting social change. Earlier writers had recorded in the burgeoning popular press of the 1640s and 1650s a crisis that was not merely epistemological, as Michael McKeon has argued, but also both social and economic, disrupting order within the artisan class while insidiously effacing distinctions between gentleman and mechanical. With the sudden fall of Archbishop Laud in 1640, the subsequent dissolution of both the ecclesiastical high commission and the Star Chamber in the summer of 1641, and the resulting, almost instantaneous, breakdown in the enforcement of censorship, the sudden absence of institutional control had sparked a flood of broadsides and pamphlets in 1641–42 large enough to elicit complaints from a Stationers Company that saw itself under siege from a multitude of upstart printers. In their "humble Remonstrance" to Parliament in April 1643, the Stationers Company pleaded that

> the affairs of the Presse have grown very scandalous and enormius, and all redresse is almost impossible, if power be not given by some binding order to reduce Presses and Apprentices to the proportion of those times which did precede these last four years. This is so farre from an Innovation that tis the removall of a dangerous Innovation, and without this removall, the Company of Stationers being like a feeld overpestred with too much stock, must needs grow indigent, and indigence must needs make it run into trespasses, and break out into divers unlawfull shifts; as Cattle use to do, when their pasture begins wholly to fail. Besides the same disorder which undoes Stationers by too great multitude of Presses and Apprentices among themselves, causes also Strangers, as Drapers, Carmen, and others to break in upon them, and set up Presses in divers obscure corners of the City and suburbs; so that not only the ruine of the Company is the more hastened by it, but also the mischief—which the State suffers by the irregularity of all, is the lesse remediable.[9]

In citing potential "mischief" to the state as one possible threat generated by the wide-scale productions of "Drapers, Carmen, and others," the Stationers Company raises the epistemological specter of competing truths, and cites the repercussions of such a loss of rhetorical monopoly for a government that had traditionally located a part of its authority in its dual ability to speak for itself and silence the seditious utterances of others. Yet in a world in which the effect of the written word was unavoidably tied to its commercial value and for which the access to rhetorical appeal had traditionally served as a symbol of status and authority, as well as a carefully controlled route to real political power, the fears that the Stationers Company reveals, like those of later royalist pamphlets, were also deeply located in the context of more concrete social and economic manifestations of disorder. Their concerns are expressed primarily as a vision of an economic chaos that is itself part of a larger cultural and professional revolution, in which the new opportunity to print that had been granted to classes and occupations traditionally denied access to the mechanisms of widespread dissemination threatened not only a literary revolt but also a real and immediate disturbance in the order of the artisan class itself. The portrait painted by the Stationers of a London in which every tradesman and apprentice finds a safely obscure dark corner from which to publish doggerel, sedition, and libel is one in which professional as well as cultural hierarchies are obfuscated and even elided by deregulation and the possibility of anonymity.

In and around 1660, royalist writers attacking both prophets and Commonwealth writers and politicians equally betray very real fears about the extent to which the perceived danger to order restored after the civil wars lay in the very engagement of polemical culture in the world of production and commerce. In the opening lines of the first part of *Hudibras*, Butler himself succinctly outlined the terms of polemical crisis for a nation still uncertain of its political fate. Explicitly reviving the civil chaos of the 1640s as both embarrassing past and potential future, the poet laments a time when

> . . . civil Fury first grew high,
> And men fell out they knew not why;
> When hard words, *Jealousies* and *Fears*,
> Set Folks together by the ears,
> And made them fight, like mad or drunk,
> For Dame *Religion* as for Punk,
> Whose honesty they all durst swear for,
> Though not a man of them knew wherefore:
> When *Gospel-trumpeter*, surrounded
> With long-eared rout, to Battel sounded,
> And Pulpit, Drum Ecclesiastick,
> Was beat with fist, instead of a stick.
>
> (*Hudibras* 1.1.1–12)

As he painfully recalls the period of "hard words," religious drum-beating, and prophesying which had led England into civil war, Butler (perhaps wishfully) represents the apparently substantial and meaningful issues that had precipitated real violence and bloodshed as mere chimeras, produced by those two great loci of seventeenth-century spin-doctoring: press and pulpit. As illusory constructs that are meaningless because they convey only noise, represented principles dissolve when exposed to the enlightened eye of the resisting reader as Butler himself creates it. Yet at the same time, as Butler also concedes, those same words, however void of sense, have force precisely because they have no content beyond their own existence—nothing to communicate beyond their own status as a commercial product. Their power, that is, is ontological rather than epistemological.

Thus polemic, according to the early complaints of the Stationers Company and the later complaints of Butler himself, has the power both to disrupt and to reorder society as a very condition of its being. As a mechanical process that is itself implicated in the nexus of economic relations that define seventeenth-century artisan culture, print culture as it changes to accommodate new polemic both necessitates changes in economic relations and produces a material product whose presence is real and undeniable, thus inevitably affecting the world around it. Much like the utterances of the radical prophets to whom Hudibras is frequently compared, Butler's "hard words" exert power because they are not simply abstract signifiers but substantial weapons given material being by a print culture that eagerly propagates the anarchic engagement in commercial print that they represent. As such, they not only serve as reminders of political dangers past but also evoke the uncertainty of a restored monarchy in a society that could not simply relegate commercial polemic, absolutist rhetoric, and the perceived prostitution of "Dame Religion" to the shameful errors of recent history.

And thus for many royalists writing between 1658 and 1662 one of the most commonly expressed fears about their political opponents (particularly those who had emerged as spokesmen in pulpit, press, and political office) was that they confused intellectual endeavor and material product, threatening the very structure of social order. Their problem with opposition polemic as a whole, radical and commonwealth, was that it seemed to understand itself as a kind of material product of artisan culture, deliberately perpetuating the rhetoric of absolute opposition by insisting upon the ability to propagate the undeniable stuff of political difference—making opposition real by manufacturing substance. In his *Characters*, Butler himself describes fanatics as those who "cheat themselves with Words, mistaking them for Things,"[10] unable to separate word from material product; ultimately, he implies, both the fault and the danger of radical rhetoric was that it asserted its own real material presence. At the same time, because the speaker of *The Lamentation* and his compatriots are also explicitly artisans (cobblers and brewers) they have, the royalist author implies, the capacity to make the word (true or not) into real substance—merely transferring their energies from one form of manufacture to another with disastrous results. Likewise the mock wills that purportedly transform the regicide Bradshaw's ideological inheritance into "Goods and Chattels" imply that the problem with a commonwealth legacy is that it has achieved a real material being, not least in the print culture that it controlled during the 1650s, and thus it is capable (as real and inheritable substance) of continuing to disorder society and threaten the restored monarchy.[11]

In fact, as these attacks on Bradshaw might suggest, for royalists in 1660 the relentless manufacture of the opposition word seemingly threatened not only social chaos but also the very workings of effective structures of law and authority themselves. Ironically, the all too visible experience of a frustrated commonwealth that had sought with great diligence to punish and contain the material word of radical prophecy must have suggested, if nothing else, the extent to which the forceful execution of arbitrary distinctions could only perpetuate chaos when faced with the propagation of material text. Prophets had been arrested, whipped, and pilloried—publicly deterred by force from speaking, writing, or publishing. Yet such efforts had done little to prevent these writers from continuing to publicly prophesy and lament. Instead, they gained strength and authority from the often cruel treatment they received at the hands of the government.

And thus royalists frequently argued that the very undeniable materiality of the word rendered void any attempts to make absolute cultural (and therefore political) distinctions. In many of the royalist writings of 1659–60, political opposition defies the attempts of the law to enforce social and cultural boundaries and blurs the distinction between legality and illegality, precisely because of its very materiality, the persistent and undeniable proof of its existence. When the regicide Bradshaw leaves his "Goods and Chattels" to his "pimp" Nedham in *Bradshaw's Ghost*, political opposition is reduced to the illegal act of prostitution, but it is an illegal act that is not prosecuted but rather, oddly enough, upheld by the legal document (the last will and testament) that contains it. It is an act that transmits and propagates itself because of a material presence that cannot be refuted, resulting not in the creation of the new order that royalists so fervently desired, but rather in the spread of anarchy and chaos.

For royalists at the Restoration, then, the perceived danger of a polemicized press was not merely the potential inversion of precarious social hierarchies but also the potential propagation of "hard words" within a commercial system that was understood by royalists to reward the perpetuation of oppositional conflict, making real and efficacious the disorder that that polemic represented. And thus, the deliberate conflation of Commonwealthsmen, mechanicals, and prophets also suggests the inadequacy, even danger, that an absolutist polemic represents within a commercial infrastructure, in which it is given force and efficacy not by the claims to divine inspiration that had authorized the writings of the civil war radical prophets, but rather by the power of economic interest that renders it material and thus in some sense real. Within Butler's poem, it is this awareness of the failure of absolutist constructions of legal and political authority that Hudibras himself represents. As a text that actively seeks to generate support for a restored government, *Hudibras* works hard to undermine understandings of language that the poem persistently attributes to those opposing an implicitly royalist rationalism—understandings that invariably insist, as the civil war prophets had done, upon the materiality and substantial force of the written and spoken word. The distinctly Presbyterian (and profoundly corporeal) hero of the poem is himself attacked as one who mistakenly seeks to employ language as a transmogrifying weapon, "[undertaking] to prove by force / Of Argument . . . that a *Lord* may be an Owl"; for Butler, the folly of Hudibras's logic lies as much in its assumptions about its own ability to foster change as in its superfluity (*Hudibras* 1.1.71–74). Likewise Ralph, a Quaker gifted with self-proclaimed knowledge of the divine Word, understands not only the practice of bearbaiting, but also the very word "bear-baiting" as "carnal, and of man's creating," preposterously opposing the practice because he does not like the "fleshy" word that signifies it (*Hudibras* 1.1.800). Even the form of the poem itself—its structural juxtaposition of vocabulary and content—suggests the potentially misleading nature of assumptions about the real efficacy of language, as its heroes repeatedly and erroneously assume that their heroic destiny lies in their access to the languages and images of both romance and the Old Testament.

And thus the law that Hudibras represents as justice of the peace and legal guardian of the ordered boundaries that separate obedience from transgression is one effectively based upon absolute oppositions. As a defender of the Presbyterian religion he is one of those who

> Compound for Sins, they are inclined to,
> By damning those they have no mind to;
> Still so perverse and opposite,
> As if they worshipped God for spight.

> . . . . . . . . . . . . . . . .
> All Piety consists therein
> In them, in other men all Sin.
>
> (*Hudibras* 1.1.213–22)

Like the civil war prophets to whom his beard alludes, creating absolute and arbitrary distinction between right and wrong, obedience and sin, Hudibras is the embodiment of a law that operates, like the texts of the civil wars prophets, through the forcible exclusion of arbitrarily defined opposition. Both prophet and law at once, Hudibras represents a concept of social and political order based upon the ability to assert and enforce absolute, objective, exclusionary, and ultimately arbitrary distinctions between friend and foe, self and other.

Yet ultimately, within the world of *Hudibras,* it is this essentially artisan-like dedication to a language, a rhetoric, and a law that Hudibras himself sees as at once material, absolute, and effective that threatens chaos within the larger community. Much as Hudibras's manufactured bulk debases his claims to legal authority, revealing his hypocrisy and interest, the multicolored "tile" that adorns his face suggests the confusion and unreliability inherent in the prophetic word through its own ridiculous claims to the status of divine signifier. Even more significantly, perhaps, it is Hudibras who insists upon translating verbal argument into (potentially) deadly battle. He puts his pistol to Talgol's head, thus proving himself to be

> . . . of that stubborn Crew
> Of Errant saints, whom all men grant
> To be the true Church *Militant*:
> Such as do build their faith upon
> The holy text of *Pike* and *Gun*.
>
> (*Hudibras*, 1.1.190–94)

Unable to resist equating doctrine and force, Hudibras—the very representative of the word of law—becomes the source of chaos precisely because he cannot allow abstractions to exist independent of their material embodiment, but must continue to produce them, to make them real.

As Butler's implicit representation of his own understanding of the nature of opposition discourse might well suggest, then, royalists seeking in 1660 to reimpose some kind of political order were ultimately compelled to face the fact that merely degrading a political opposition by rendering it gross and transgressive material, the very stuff of low culture, would not make it go away, particularly in light of the overwhelming evidence that even a restoration was not going to heal all political breaches. If anything, they thought that attempts to transform language into force could only perpetuate violence. And thus, given their distrust of rhetorical strategies that insisted upon the absolute transforming power of the word, royalist writers were also forced to come to grips with the limitations of their own equally arbitrary claims that cultural lowness was a sign of political failure. For these authors, the viability of reconstructed authority and stability under the Restoration settlement depended upon finding some alternative to the "hard words" of the civil wars.

## II

Ironically, and somewhat ambivalently, one solution to the perceived rhetorical crisis faced by royalists in 1660 lay in the parodic conjunction and adaptation of the very prophetic and economic discourses that these same royalists so actively denounced. In a series of *PMLA* articles printed during the 1930s, C. M. Webster showed just how many of the royalist attacks upon those who opposed a restoration were written as parodies of prophetic discourse—specifically parodies of a radical religious rhetoric that erroneously but deliberately conflated the nasal preaching of Presbyterian ministers with the cataclysmic rhetoric of radical prophecy.[12] *A Satyr Against Hypocrits*, *Peters Patern*, *The Lamentation of a Sinner*, and *Hudibras* itself all fit into a distinctive pattern of English royalist parody, and all, as we have already seen, use the language of trade and manufacture to debase a political opposition.

As the titles of such pamphlets as *The Lamentation of a Sinner* and *The Lamentation of a Bad Market* might suggest, moreover, one of the most popular forms of prophetic parody from the mid-seventeenth century on was the parodic lament. Taking as their model not the explicitly prophetic utterances of the Old Testament prophets—themselves considered divine and thus in some sense incorruptible and unassailable—but rather Lamentations, the explicitly human text of the prophet Jeremiah, these texts undercut the authenticity of self-proclaimed prophetic speech through often brutally unflattering examinations of the prophet's human persona. Much as Lamentations had recorded Jeremiah's distress after the divinely ordained destruction of Jerusalem at the hands of the Babylonian army, the parodic lament of the seventeenth century depicted speakers appropriating the prophetic persona to uses at once secular, bathetic, and above all else self-interested, bewailing everything from bothersome peddlers to stale beer and troublesome wives. While Pollard and Redgrave list only one adaptation of Lamentations published before 1640, Wing records a veritable explosion: *The*

*Lamentation of Cloris*, *The Lamentation of Mary Butcher, now . . . in Worcester City-Gaol*, *The Lamentation of Mr. Pages Wife*, *The Lamentation of Seven Journey Men Taylors*, and *The Lamentable Complaints of Hop the Brewer*, just to name a few. Most of these were effectively burlesque, purposefully debasing the human remorse of the prophet in order to expose what the writers saw as hypocrisy, self-interest, and a deliberate misdirection of reformist attempts in the personally motivated whinings of others.

In the early 1640s, the represented aim of these so-called lamentations was not so much the ridicule of a radical prophetic persona—not yet the perceived source of chaos it would become in the mid-1650s—as the more general debunking of self-interested complaint. Yet even at that early stage, such texts incorporated much of the economic language so typical of later royalist polemical attacks, deriding reformist discourse by suggesting the debasing economic complicity of the complainant. *The Lamentable Complaints of Nick Froth the Tapster and Rulefrost the Cook Concerning the restraint lately set forth against drinking, potting and pipeing on the Sabbath Day, and against selling meate* (1641), for example, records the complaints of a tapster and a cook against a parliamentary law forbidding the sale of meat and liquor on Sundays. Their objection, predictably, is not that these new laws have brought God's vengeance upon the nation for its sinfulness but that the regulations have rather destroyed their trade by depriving them of their most profitable sales day of the week: the Sabbath. At one crucial juncture, the cook tries to console the tapster, urging the good intentions of the bill, but the distraught tapster, shaken, replies with an appeal not to the good of the society but to his own self-interest:

> Alack you know all my profit doth arise onely upon Sundays . . . I got more by uttering halfe a Barrell in time of Divine Service, than I could by a whole Barrel at any other time, for my customers were glad to take anything for money, and thinke themselves much engaged to me.[13]

Far from being filled with a concern born of devotion to God's Word and repentance for its violation, both cook and tapster express only fear for their own economic future. Proud of the economic shrewdness with which he is able to take advantage of the weaknesses of others, the cook, like the butcher before him, eventually reveals his complicity in the gradual erosion of the English moral character, thus explicitly undermining the force of his own complaint and rendering himself rhetorically ineffective. At the same time, his self-interested lament serves as an attack on the pious sham of religious ritual, exposing the more general corruption of a nation in which divine services are attended only unwillingly by a nation of nonbelievers—many of whom are all too willing to be waylaid and exploited by the local pub.

This early example of an increasingly popular genre does not, of course, specifically attack an opposition polemic; if cook and tapster are in part ridiculed for their language, they are no more to blame than the institutions that enable their transgressions. As English society became increasingly polarized during the civil wars, however, the language of economic self-interest so basic to these parodic lamentations came to offer not only a means of discrediting perceived opposition hypocrisy but also a vehicle for both valuing and evaluating the sins of a political opposition. Having come to see economic self-interest as an irremovable opponent, detractors of non-Anglican religion frequently acknowledged, as Hobbes had before them, that the relationship between politics and public order was essentially economic, defined not by divine sanction but by the rules of a marketplace that places a negotiated value upon political ideology. *A Lamentation of the Ruling Lay-Elders*, an anti-Presbyterian pamphlet of 1647, purports to be a lament of the Presbyterian lay-elders for the terrible judgment evident in "the death of their late foster-father Sir John Presbyter."[14] Predicting the impending doom of the Presbyterian cause as a direct result of the sins of the elders, the speakers reach a series of resolutions that will atone for earlier sins, including promises to "forbear the frequenting of all Taverns, Alehouses, Brothels, and the like," vowing instead that the presbyters will spend their money to buy a private brothel.[15] Much as the financial motives of cook and tapster had revealed the self-interested debasement of their complaint, the elders' misappropriation of church funds to support illicit activities suggests their own irreligious and hypocritical values. At the same time, however, their willingness to exchange currency (financial, religious, and cultural) for a brothel (the symbol in these texts of both moral and ideological debasement) offers an estimation of their religious and political worth that relies not only upon their motivations, but also upon a direct appraisal of the quality of their material purchases—their competence, that is, as buyers and sellers.

For royalists in and around 1660, faced with the need to reconstitute political authority in the context of seemingly irresolvable antipathies, texts such as *The Lamentation of the Ruling Lay-Elders* offered a useful model, suggesting in essence how parody might offer a means of diffusing the danger of political opposition, seemingly so uncontrollable by mere debasement. In his *Thematics*, Tomashevsky described parody as a ferreting out of formalist dead wood, a rhetorical phoenix, building living text out of the ashes of reified discourse. "[Literary] devices," he explains, "are born, grow old, and die. To the extent that their use becomes automatic, they lose their efficacy and cease to be included on the list of acceptable techniques."[16] Rhetorical worthlessness thus becomes prey to parody, whose usual function, as he explains it, "is to ridicule an opposing literary group, blasting its aesthetic system and exposing it."[17] For royalists, ironically, it was the very laws of the trade in which it was implicated that rendered opposition discourse dead, and thus subject to the workings of parody. Opposition polemic, represented in royalist texts as a product of artisan culture, was—according to royalist logic—a product subject to the same laws of the marketplace as any other manufacture, and thus, they suggested, its debased nature therefore guaranteed its failure. As royalist attacks upon the Good old Cause explicitly conflated prophet, tradesman, and Commonwealth politician, they not only defined cultural difference but also enabled the claim that opposition writing, resulting in a characteristically material prophetic product, was simply a process of debasing human labor—one that produced a valueless product that would bankrupt its owner, or worse.

Thus as the very title of *The Lamentation of a Bad Market* would suggest, royalists ultimately argued that it was the forces of human economies, the laws of economic transaction, rather than divine intervention, that would ultimately render the "stuff" of radical political opposition worthless and unsaleable, and so not a threat to the restoration of social order. Referring to those who opposed a monarchy restored as swineherds driving pigs to a bad market, the pamphlet implies that in bringing their arguments to a politically polarized print market, the speakers have foretold their defeat through their own economic failure. Likewise, in *The Lamentation of a Sinner* (another purported will of John Bradshaw), prophecy becomes a process of manual labor enabled by an economic transaction, the inheritance of material goods, which can result only in the shame of the prophet and the annihilation of his cause; there Bradshaw leaves "ten pound for the erecting of two poles, on which each of Vanes and Needhams Heads may be placed, for to demonstrate (truer than any Weathercock) which way the wind blows"—to predict, that is, the gruesome demise of the Good old Cause.[18] The destruction of the political and religious values advocated by Bradshaw—the ideological inheritance of his followers—ironically comes to rest in their own economic transmission and subsequent realization as explicitly transgressive material product.

As *The Lamentation of a Sinner* suggests, moreover, it is precisely the misguided labor of opposition writing, as it renders potentially valuable (that is, effective) text quite literally dead, that also transforms that text into the mechanism of its own punishment in a way that the external imposition of legal authority could not. When Butler tells his readers of "a *Tobacco-Man*, that wrapped *Spanish* Tobacco in a Paper of Verses which Benlows had written against the Pope, which by a natural Antipathy, that his wit has to any Thing that's Catholic, spoiled the Tobacco, for it presently turned Mundungus," he gives us a vision of a polemical writing whose very material status as a kind of textual byproduct renders the product that it encloses worthless as well; in a world driven by economic advantage, it is a liability, bringing about its own demise.[19] Doggedly driving pigs to a bad market can only, we assume, result in cheap bacon and failed swineherds. Likewise, writing laborious polemic seems a sure recipe for political disaster—one that obviates the need to legislate difference in a world in which such legislation seemed practically impossible.

At the same time, understanding the parodic text as a form that effectively subjected polemical rhetoric to the laws of the commercial marketplace offered not only a means of precipitating the self-debasement of a political other but also a means of redefining social order on the basis of opposition rather than through its eradication. In fact, one of the perceived advantages of the parodic text, given the apparent economic complicity of the written word, was that it ultimately offered a means of establishing order that did not insist upon the represented exclusion of either political or cultural opposition (a recognized impossibility by 1660) but rather relied upon its very embodied presence for the recreation of stability—an understanding reflected in the period's changing definitions of parody itself. When Ben Jonson had used the word in the folio version of *Every Man in his Humour*, he had evoked merely a kind of general debasement and an enhancement of natural bathos, as Kno'well defends his doggerel poetry by claiming that the verse is "A Parodie, a Parodie! With a kind of miraculous gift to make it absurder than it was."[20] By the late Restoration, however, John Dryden was able to articulate a much more specific understanding of the imitative structures of meaning inherent in parodic text, explaining in the 1697 dedication to his translation of Juvenal's satires that

> from some fragments of the Sillii . . . we may find that they were Satyric Poems, full of parodies; that is, of Verses Patch'd up from great Poets, and turn'd into another Sence than their author intended them. Such, amongst the Romans, is the famous *Cento* of Ausonius; where the words are Virgil's, but, by applying them to another sense, they are made a relation of a wedding-night; and the act of consummation fulsomely described in the very words of the most modest among all poets. Of the same manner are our songs, which are turned into burlesque, and the serious words of the author perverted into a ridiculous meaning.[21]

For Dryden, parody is not merely a debased imitation, a travesty, as it was for Jonson, but a radical transformation of both the structure and sense of the work of art to a satiric end. If Dryden does not suggest that parody necessarily mocks the speaker or author of the original words, he does insist that it creates new meaning out of the juxtaposition of familiar formal structures. By the late Restoration, that is to say, the parodic form insisted that the value of the parodic royalist text could only be created out of the dross material of that opposition which it devalues and thus that transgression, opposition, and antagonism are in fact the very raw materials of new and reinvigorated order.

The royalist authors of 1660 did not, of course, have Dryden's definition available to focus either their satires or their texts. Yet many of these pieces reflect precisely this same notion of the negotiated revaluation of the parodic text at the expense of the devaluation of that which it parodies. Thus in the mock wills and testaments of John Bradshaw, for example, the legal nature of the documents purportedly represented ensures the self-destruction of the depicted heirs by allowing for the necessary transmission of worthless ideological property. Yet in this case form can hardy be said to contain content, since it is actually disorderly material that it inevitably propagates in the process of transferral. Rather, in fact, the real authority of these supposedly legal texts, the law itself, becomes legitimate only as the economic transfer it describes is fulfilled to the detriment of the Good old Cause. The royalist parody depends for its power—and its very status as parody—upon the representation of Commonwealth goods; without their necessary demonstration of opposing political principles, the royalist text would have no value to a buying royalist audience nor, as Tomashevsky would suggest, any structural significance, any power to order experience. In the case of these writings, the depiction of legal text serves not to assert the overarching power of law and order, but rather to suggest the extent to which disorder, division, and opposition are in fact both implicit and complicit in the creation of structure and stability.

Thus in *Hudibras,* too, we see evidence of a royalist understanding of the social role of polemic as a kind of merchandise, to be bought and sold not at the whims of the publisher, but by the more uncertain, yet potentially more decisive, force of public opinion. As a Hudibras preparing for conflict, or rather trying to avoid it, chides the townspeople for bearbaiting, which he clearly believes to be an essentially royalist betrayal, Butler depicts a possibility of order restored that depends not on monarchical politics, but on a world of trade and manufacture whose very success relies upon the fact that it is actually too low to be politically engaged. In a protracted speech, Hudibras speaks fondly of a time when

Tinkers bawl'd aloud to settle
*Church-Discipline*, for patching *Kettle*.
No *Sow-gelder* did blow his horn
To geld a Cat, but cry'd *Reform*.
The *Oyster-women* lock'd their fish up,
And trudg'd away, to cry *No Bishop*.
The *Mousetrap-men* laid *Save-alls* by,
And 'gainst *Ev'l Counsellors* did cry.
*Botchers* left old cloaths in the lurch,
And fell to turn and patch the *Church*.
Some cry'd the *Covenant* instead
Of *Pudding-pies* and *Ginger-bread*:
And some for *Broom, old Boots and Shoes*,
Baul'd out to *purge the Common's House*:
Instead of *Kitchin-stuff*, some cry
A *Gospel-preaching-Ministry*;
And some for *Old Suits*, *Coats*, or *Cloak*,
No *Surplices*, nor *Service-book*.
A strange harmonious inclination
Of all degrees to *Reformation*.

"And is this all?," Hudibras asks:

Is this [bearbaiting] the end
To which these *carr'ings on* did tend?
Had *Publick Faith* like a young heire
For this tak'n up all sorts of Ware,
And run int' ev'ry Tradesman's book
Til both turn'd Bankrupts, and are broke?
(*Hudibras* 1.2.535–60)

Here, self-interest is its own punishment, as those convinced by the teachings of this endless list of mechanicals and tradesmen turned prophets are seen as spendthrifts throwing away money on worthless goods, running themselves and their cause into bankruptcy. Implying that he is the last in this great parodic line, Hudibras suggests that he is similarly bankrupt; and like the speaker in *The Lamentation of a Bad Market* he is unable to find a buying public. His speech falls on the deaf ears of two audiences who refuse to buy his polemical wares; neither the represented townspeople nor a real Restoration audience, Butler implies, are convinced by his "[skill] in Analytick" (*Hudibras* 1.1.67). Ultimately, the questionable injustice of a Presbyterian rule—setting Crowdero in the stocks—is transformed into its defeat when Hudibras is set in that lowly prison in Crowdero's place.

And yet, as the transitory and unstable nature of even self-inflicted punishment in the poem might suggest, *Hudibras* also demonstrates that ideological battles in the period could no longer be permanently won simply through the debasement of others, nor does debasement of an opposition guarantee stability. What order does exist comes into being only at the level of a text that does not so much contain disorder as it does render it viable, and thus socially valuable. The paunchy knight's transient defeat does not simply represent a triumph of idealism over revolting corporeality; Butler, as we have seen, was hardly an idealist, and the temporary transformation of injustice into justice is effected only through the actions of a crowd marked by the same gross materiality and self-interest as Hudibras himself. Led by Trulla, a prostitute, both a sign of Hudibras's transgression (his Presbyterian prostitution) and the mechanism of his punishment, they overcome in a vision of justice that, however ambiguous, relies upon their own politically and culturally transgressive nature—their willingness and ability to overcome swords and guns with cudgels, rocks, and even wooden legs. Likewise, in the third part of *Hudibras*, published considerably later but retaining some of the characteristics of the earlier text, it is Sidrophel—himself a charlatan and social outcast—who is called upon to punish Hudibras for his false dedication and his lies. Neither cultural baseness not political opposition, the poem thus claims, can be overcome by an idealized order imposed from above. Instead their regulation depends upon their inclusion in a larger order that enables a consistent interplay, negotiation, and even uneasy alliance (though never an identity) between the forces of hegemony and cohesion and the depicted representatives of social, cultural, political, and religious chaos.

And thus Butler's text, too, presents its reader with a model of order that is always, almost obsessively, dependent upon that which defies it for its very shape and substance. Butler's famous Hudibrasticks, providing the text with the only genuine form it has, yet often considered a kind of childish poetic affectation, take their power from the very baseness that Butler so often decries. Butler's prosody, in fact, depends upon the assumption, so often ridiculed within his poem, that words are things—that what is important about them is not merely their content but their real material presence as both printed text and audible sound—literally understood as material presence by the scientific theory of the day. The best-known rhyme in all of *Hudibras*—describing how "Pulpit, Drum Ecclesiastic / Was beat with fist, instead of a stick"—relies for its effect upon our awareness that poetry does have a kind of reality in its aural presence that defies abstract meaning, at the same time as it creates meaning out of the ridiculous juxtaposition of clearly dissonant sounds (*Hudibras* 1.1.11–12). Butler's poetic structure can become painfully annoying as it repeatedly transgresses the basic rules of prosody, continually jarring our sensibility with merciless oppositions where there should be harmony. And yet by Butler's poetic logic, those very oppositions become the stuff of a kind of order—an order dependent upon the necessary and unavoidable presence of both the material word and irreconcilable difference. Even as order is defined within the poem through opposing parties, neither of which can ultimately eradicate the other, the structure of the poem itself relies not on harmony or hegemony, but on the careful, consistent, and occasionally disruptive tension between forces unalignable by any poetic authority. At the same time, because the poem is parody, intended to ridicule through self-debasement, poetic authority must ultimately be contingent upon its representation of such emphatically hard words, relying for its success upon the deliberate and sustained embodiment of that which it repudiates.

Ultimately, Butler's poem suggests that in both real and textual space a royalist restoration sought to generate a new political order out of disorder, confusion, opposition, and chaos, the only materials truly available to political authority in and around 1660. Insisting on a model of political competition that relied not on exclusionary politics, cultural or otherwise, but on a system of free-market exchange that necessitated constant negotiation between opposites (hitherto merely opponents), *Hudibras* and other royalist parodies of the period suggest that by 1660 royalists had come, however unwillingly, to accept that the stabilization of early Restoration society would not be managed through the eradication of political opposition, or through any arbitrary declaration that the opposition was politically or culturally inferior, but through the negotiation of political value in a process of political and ideological exchange. Royalists, that is, had come to see polemical conflict not as a battle of force but as a kind of economic competition, in which value is necessarily relative and defined in essence through interaction, not isolation.

And thus they acknowledged that they themselves were implicated in that same low realm of the marketplace, understanding their own fate, as well as that of their opponents, to be at the hands of a buying public. By 1659 royalist politicians had openly declared that a restoration could be effected only by joining with and satisfying the self-interests of those with political influence; one royalist pamphleteer remarked in that year that Charles Stuart was presently "dispossest, but [might] attain if he [could] tend to join with self-interests."[22] Likewise, *The Lamentation of a Bad Market* is effectively a represented commonwealth lament over the loss of an audience—an audience that has both literally and metaphorically bought a royalist rather than a commonwealth product and thus sympathizes not with the speaker's appeal to Satan, but with the promised punishment that the lack of a receptive ear, supernatural or otherwise, inevitably ensures. The tremendous commercial and political success of the first part of *Hudibras*, and Butler's subsequent attempts to capitalize upon that success with second and third volumes, itself provides evidence of the extent to which these ideological heirs of the coterie Cavaliers saw their political future both literally and metaphorically in the hands of a public market.

Thus while a represented marketplace provided a means of punishing an opposition—or rather allowing it to punish itself—it also offered an arena in which a royalist order newly created out of the dross of political division could compete for both symbolic value (meaning) and real political power. Butler's legacy, despite the relative failure of the later parts of *Hudibras*, lay in his definitive proof that royalist writers could openly and successfully vie for public favor, outselling their political and religious opponents though they could neither suppress them nor eradicate them root and branch. Royalists, of course, continued to try to eliminate opposition to the Restoration throne. Censorship under L'Estrange was more deliberate and more aggressive that it had been under the Commonwealth, and the conditions faced by imprisoned radicals were at least as severe as they had been during the 1650s. Yet it was censorship that died during the Restoration, and toleration (both religious and political) that slowly prevailed. The success of John Dryden, explicitly a commercial propagandist, and the development of the two-party system were in fact the rightful heirs of Butler and his anonymous parodic contemporaries, speaking stability without containment and order in opposition, and always conscious of the illusory nature of the rhetoric of hegemony, particularly in a society whose underlying tensions had been so recently and so brutally revealed.

# 3

# Interpreting Providence: The Politics of Prophecy in Restoration Polemic

It was perhaps well that royalists had early on sought strategies for coping with the rhetoric of irreconcilable political opposition, for by the mid-1660s it was clear that the Restoration settlement was a qualified failure. The king's inability to deliver quickly enough upon the promises of religious toleration specified in the Declaration of Breda had already led to increasing animosity between court and Dissenters, many of whom proclaimed their opposition in a language no less virulent than that of the civil wars.[1] At the same time, reports of the licentiousness of the court worried royalists and Dissenters alike, offering a spectacle of royalty out of touch with the morals and sympathies of a Protestant nation dominated by a powerful city full of artisans and shopkeepers.[2]

For Charles II the Fire of London in particular was a minor public relations nightmare, leading as it did to rumors that he was largely indifferent toward both the fate of London and the suffering of his people. Years later, the earl of Clarendon (only vaguely sympathizing with the king) remembered that Charles had capitulated far too easily to the callous levity of those around him even while the fire still burned. Clarendon points in particular to the undue influence of a courtier named May (presumably Baptist May, the keeper of the privy purse) who had

> presumed to assure the king, "that this [fire] was the greatest blessing that God had ever conferred upon him, his restoration only excepted: for the walls and gates being now burned and thrown down of that rebellious city . . . his majesty would never suffer them to repair and build them up again . . . but would keep all open, that his troops might enter upon them whenever he thought necessary for his service, there being no other way to govern that rude multitude but by force."

"The wit and pleasantness of [that joke]," Clarendon reports, "was repeated in all companies, infinitely to the king's disservice, and corrupted the affections of the citizens and of the country, who used and assumed the same liberty to publish the profaneness and atheism of the court."[3]

Michael McKeon and Elizabeth Skerpan have both suggested the political importance of appealing favorably to "the affections of the citizens" in Restoration polemic, and it is tempting to read this episode as the simple result of an ignorant unconcern with public reaction and popular feelings.[4] Certainly it seems evident that the court underestimated the public impact of the fire. For many of the disaffected citizens whom Clarendon reports, that catastrophe was tragic in the loss of life and property it had caused, while it also raised fears of an entirely supernatural kind, providing evidence to those who were so inclined that God's anger was once again directed against the English nation. In Clarendon's eyes, public opinion had turned against the king in part because of the court's public demonstration of its parasitic selfishness—finding its own security in the losses sustained by those it supposedly protected—and in part because such indifference suggested an insensitive and atheistic contempt for the power of divinity. Our own reaction to the interpretation of the fire as a "blessing" might well be to attribute a limited understanding of human suffering and anxiety to the nobleman in question.

Yet to the extent that the fire did make concerns about the meaning of God's providential will for England both visibly public and vitally urgent, it required of the court not only sympathy with a suffering public but also the careful and responsible public interpretation of divine action—tricky hermeneutic territory for a royalism that sought to balance a sensitivity to providential history against the perceived danger of prophetic rhetoric. In viewing the fire as a "blessing," May displays an arrogance and a militancy completely out of touch with the realities of Restoration politics as we have seen them in *Hudibras* and other texts of the early 1660s, for as he does so, he ironically echoes a tradition of radical prophecy that maintained that the suffering of God's people would eventually result in the destruction of their enemies and the purification of a godly few. Most Restoration royalists, including apparently Clarendon, were still insistently skeptical of such readings, particularly since six years of restored government had made it clearer than ever that opposition was not going to go away. For royalists faced with an uncertain and unstable political situation, new strategies for interpreting providence were pressing urgencies in the year of wonders. Part of May's problem, in Clarendon's eyes and in the eyes of an anxious public, was that he had gotten the politics of prophecy wrong.

This chapter will examine what it meant for Restoration royalists to get the reading of providence right, as what were in fact deeply partisan strategies for the public interpretation of providence emerged in the popular press of the mid-1660s. In many royalist accounts of the fire, these were strategies that openly rejected attempts such as May's to exclude or destroy old opponents. Cynthia Wall's study of texts written after the fire has suggested that even early accounts of the disaster represent it as an event that realized changing concepts of space, text, and society. In the wake of the fire, royalists seized the opportunity to envision a new modeled society that made space for their former enemies and could thus survive precisely because it acknowledged and accounted for the inevitable, even necessary, presence of difference, rather than simply insisting upon a uniform hegemony.[5] Enabled, as we shall see, by that part of traditional providential rhetoric that insisted at some level that a society was always in opposition to itself, those texts suggested important revisions to the more general strategies of Restoration polemic, providing useful alternatives to less flexible models of political opposition.

Nowhere, perhaps, are such strategies so famously articulated as in John Dryden's *Annus Mirabilis,* a poem that synthesizes anxieties about prophetic rhetoric with the very economic and financial definitions of success that attacks on prophecy had traditionally decried. Completed in the fall of 1666, that poem has frequently been dismissed (rather like *Astrea Redux*) as an early, imperfect, and somewhat sycophantic piece of royalist propaganda, with its portrait of a benevolent paternal monarchy and nascent British imperialism.[6] And yet, I would argue, it is precisely because *Annus Mirabilis* is written so expressly in the royalist cause that it says much about the state of royalist polemic in the wake of 1666. Added after the fact, in all probability, to a poem initially about the second Anglo-Dutch war, Dryden's fire does much to moderate the relative jingoism of the earlier sections of the poem. Denying the efficacy of attempts to externalize conflict in the cause of national hegemony, the rebellious and seemingly sui generis flames serve as a potent reminder of the uncertainty of political order. At the same time, the portrait of monarchy that Dryden presents at the end of that poem, clearly designed as a response to antimonarchical propaganda, creates a vision of kingship forced to admit the necessity of negotiation in the face of ineradicable difference as it transforms Charles from martial leader to humble and penitent reader of divine providence. Dryden's nationalism is often specifically economic, while it evokes the same ethos of trade that earlier royalists had identified as a potent if double-edged rhetorical weapon, seemingly locating the authority and evidence of restored monarchy in the commercial prosperity of the country.

Yet while it points to Dryden's poem as both an exemplary royalist depiction of monarchy in the early Restoration and a touchstone for Dryden's own later adaptations of royalist politics, this chapter is equally concerned with popular representations of the fire that remain, despite Wall's recent study, largely unexplored. Assuming that the interest of *Annus Mirabilis* lies not so much in its transcendence of popular polemic as in its engagement with it, my purpose here is to locate the vision of monarchy that Dryden presents in the context of a larger royalist recuperation of Charles II in the wake of the fire, illuminating in the process a range of reactions to prophetic reading that provide crucial insights into the adaptive strategies of a restored but precarious royalism in the early Restoration.

I

Prophetic writing had typically been a mainstay of the popular press through the civil wars and into the earliest years of the Restoration, but in the wake of the remarkable events of 1665–66, English writers of all political persuasions sought evidence of a divine plan with a new intensity. The result was a new—and not always radical—proliferation of providential writing. The year 1666 had been billed long in advance as a year of wonders by millennialist writers, and the conjunction of the plague of 1665, the second Anglo-Dutch war, and the Great Fire seemed to bear out the idea of a certain divine obsession with England. In such an unstable climate, moreover, public and even official providential readings were often perceived as crucial to national well-being because they provided an assurance of divine and hence worldly order in what might otherwise have seemed overwhelming chaos. Unsure of what the confluence of God's three greatest scourges—sword, fire, and plague—might mean for a country still emerging from the ruins of a civil war and beset by enemies abroad, many (like May) read the signs of providence in the hopes of identifying some underlying pattern that might give meaning to the nation's trauma. Even royalist writers who recounted the progress of the fire once again began to suggest causal links between national actions and providential retribution, rendering the fire as a sign from God. The author of *A Short Narrative of the Late Dreadful Fire in London* publishes his account "so men may see the dreadful effects of providence . . . and call off their hearts and confidences, from [acquisitions], to God," while a poem *Upon the Late Lamentable Fire in London* aligns the fire with flood, drought, and pestilence—all forms of divine judgment—depicting the enactment of divine will as a never-ending, sin-precipitated series of disasters:

While Men in sin grew wiser yet,
And various in their wickedness
God himself did think it fit
Their punishment should be no less,
The Air itself which makes our breath,
Became an instrument of death,
If still Offences of a deeper die
Offend his purer eye,
He gives an other Judgement birth,
Fire comes from Heav'n, or Fire from Earth
Thus the four Elements take turns,
He Drowns, he Swallows us alive, he Plagues,
[or else he Burns.[7]

Such a view of heaven's influence may seem less than comforting, but in drawing a definite connection between crime and punishment, it did provide a recognizable pattern in a barrage of seemingly random misfortunes. Guaranteeing a controlling intelligence that was rational and knowable, it offered the assurance that experience was meaningful, however cold a comfort that might turn out to be.

At the same time that such writings offered hope of a divine plan in the midst of chaos, however, in the highly factionalized world of the early Restoration they were seldom disinterested quests for religious truth, or at least they did not often separate religious truth from political party. Both the plague and the Great Fire in particular were frequently read as divine comments upon political opposition in the wake of the Restoration settlement, as royalists and Dissenters alike proclaimed proof in these events of God's displeasure with their opponents and His desire to reunite England under their own political banner.

Dissenters, on the one hand, often depicted the horrors of the plague as a sign of ongoing political struggle, representing it not only as a perceived punishment for royalist acts against Nonconformists but also as a kind of divine rebellion against the restored monarchy—one that would this time at last succeed in eliminating royalist oppression. Condemning England for the brutal treatment of his Quaker brethren during the Restoration, Richard Crane, for one, declared the plague to be God's own continuation of the civil wars; for Crane plague was the form in which He was "come to plead the cause of his poor, oppressed, despised, and afflicted ones . . . who thou [England] hast destined for destruction and counted unworthy to live in thee." Plague was also for Crane a sign that God was about to destroy those who have "resisted the Spirit of the Lord, and despised his counsel, and evil intreated and persecuted his Servants, Messangers, and Children," as Crane seeks not so much to explain the tragedy of plague as to enlist a militant providence in the Dissenting cause.[8] For Ambrose Rigge too, as we have seen, the plague was an indication of divine displeasure at the post-Restoration treatment of Dissenters, retribution for the mistreatment of God's chosen people, and a sign of continuing struggle between spiritual orthodoxy and religious radicalism.[9]

Predominantly royalist accounts of the Great Fire, on the other hand, most often depicted that tragedy as a form of closure upon the civil conflict of the previous twenty-five years—retribution enacted not against the restored government but against its opponents. The fire was thus described by many royalist writers as a form of civil insurrection; it was "Rebel-Flames"—an invader from within who "straight doth spread / His bloudy Banners, which still Menace dread, / Wasting where e're he comes"—a rebel suppressible only by the king himself, but definitely suppressible.[10] These same writings often insisted upon the purgative effect of the fire as a symbol of the settled authority of the Restoration government, burning off the sins of wartime rebellion. One account of the burning of St. Paul's—destroyed on the second night of the fire—describes a ritual cleansing of the stain left by its use as a stable during the civil wars:

> When Horses thus *Paul's* Temple once defile,
> How soon becomes it then a flaming Pile?
> For which Profaneness, well might heaven be urg'd,
> To have it thus by Fire again be purg'd.
> Once the Messias in a Manger lay,
> Where th'Eastern Sages did him homage pay;
> Where some prophane ones thought he might be found
> Still in a Stable though with Glory crown'd.
> Those wilder Beasts, to *Ephesus* once brought,
> With which the Doctor of Gentiles fought,
> Did not *Diana's* Temple so defile,
> (Though it became so soon a burning Pile)
> As those beasts stain the Temple of his Name,
> That now doth perish by as great a Flame.[11]

For this author the fire purges not just the literal filth left behind by stabled livestock but also the doctrinal impurity represented here by a misguided (even ludicrous) attempt to return to the primitivism of the very earliest Christian worship (the magi themselves), suggesting an end to religious factionalism and political division.

For Dryden, too, in *Annus Mirabilis*, the fire is a symbol of religious and political rebellion, the internal threat that in its own way is far more dangerous to English stability and prosperity than the seeming threat posed in the poem by the Dutch navy. Thus the fire is a “dire Usurper” attacking “Palaces and Temples”—the architectural signs of England’s political and religious institutions: The “main body of the marching foe / Against th’Imperial Palace is design’d,” as the fire in the end makes straight for the king himself.[12] In a grotesque parody of satanic ritual,

> The Ghosts of Traitors, from the *Bridge* descend,
> With bold Fanatick Spectres to rejoyce:
> About the fire in a Dance they bend,
> And sing their Sabbath Notes with feeble voice.
> (*AM*, ll. 889-92)

Yet even here the fire has a purgative force. As a calamity that can be resisted—that can be and has been, by the time Dryden writes his poem, extinguished—it seemingly provides a kind of closure to the very evils that it symbolizes. Thus here too the burning of St. Paul’s is represented as a miraculous stripping away of the profanity of Commonwealth rule:

> The dareing flames peep’t in and saw from far,
> The awful beauties of the Sacred Quire:
> But, since it was prophan’d by Civil War,
> Heav’n thought it fit to have it purg’d by fire.
> (*AM*, ll. 1101–4)

As the king overcomes the fire, he subdues a rebellion that has purportedly cleansed itself, opening the way to political stability and religious conformity.

Inspired by such visions of a purified hegemony, many royalist authors (including Dryden) also went to great lengths to depict these events as divine trials, from which London in particular would emerge as a miraculous phoenix rising reborn from ashes and ruin, a model of political stability, and a potent imperial power. *Londonenses Lachrymae*, for example, asserts that the fire was a punishment for the rebellion of radicals during the civil wars and promises a placid future to follow purgation:

> Now *Loyal London* has full Ransome paid
> For that *Defection* the *Disloyal* made:
> Whose *Ashes* hatch’d by a kind *Monarch’s* breath,
> Shall rise a fairer *Phoenix* after Death.[13]

*Annus Mirabilis*, as well, predicts a London rebuilt, purged of the defiling effects of civil conflict and more glorious than before its destruction. Dryden proclaims:

Methinks already, from this Chymick flame,
I see a City of more precious mold:
Rich as the Town which gives the Indies name,
With Silver pav'd, and all divine with Gold.
(*AM*, ll. 1169–72)

Yet such claims were often recognized as tenuous at best. Because the rhetoric of royalist providential writing itself was almost diametrically opposed to that of its Dissenting counterpart, it in effect belied the very optimistic portrait of a land cleansed of political opposition that royalist authors sought to create; the differences in these interpretations of human tragedy indicated to all that as much as royalists may have wished for faction to go away—even optimistically depicted it going away—it nevertheless would not. The author of *The Conflagration of London*, fully aware of the persistence of factionalism, qualifies his emblem of England reborn and reunified (a phoenix on the top of St. Paul's) by admitting that "*Few hope*, 'twill *soon* be *verified there*."[14] If political necessity insisted upon a vision of England renewed and reunited, the reality of an uncertain political situation forced the repeated if reluctant confession that such a rhetoric was all too often wishful thinking.

One result of this painful disparity between hope and reality was that royalists ultimately rethought the nature of providential polemic itself, very much in opposition to recognizably radical strategies for interpreting providence. They particularly rejected, as the royalists of 1660 had before them, a radical understanding of the specific relationship between text and divine will that was to bring that resurrection about—an understanding that, as we have seen, had traditionally relied upon the ability of the text to establish absolute oppositions that it resolved by using words themselves as weapons of annihilation. Dissenting prophecy in general had explicitly tied its effectiveness as a polemic to its highly vocal insistence that it represented direct access to the divine Word—and to claims that it was the enactment of divine law capable of reordering the world in its own image, independent of human self-interests. Insisting that plague would only lead to more extreme forms of punishment unless royalists stopped hampering and imprisoning dissenting preachers and instead permitted them to practice their religion as they chose, dissenting texts claimed to offer a choice between voluntary conformity with the divine will that they said they embodied, and a forced eradication of the old order, which they effectively guaranteed. William Bayly, for example, asserts that "all your Lyes shall be swept away," for "The Terrible, terrible, terrible dreadful day of the Lord God is at hand."[15] When it came to interpreting seeming acts of providence in a political context, the emphasis of these radical readings was upon the absolute transforming power of the text to one way or another bring about the divine order it envisioned.

Royalists, on the other hand, were poignantly conscious of the inadequacy of absolutist rhetoric to the Restoration political situation, and all too sensitive to the potential emptiness of the phoenix's nest. They were also acutely aware of the dangers that such a rhetoric of force, regardless of its political affiliation, could conceivably present to the stability of the Restoration settlement. After all, Clarendon's criticism of May, himself a supporter of the king, attacks not only that gentleman's callousness but also his inability to recognize that force (both military and rhetorical) can only perpetuate struggle and resist closure in the most obvious ways: the city literally remains open because the walls have been destroyed, while the absence of the walls permits a continuation of civil struggle and a renewed use of force against political opposition. Dryden too, in *Annus Mirabilis*, seems wary of both the rhetoric and enactment of force as a means of solving internal divisions, relegating their use to the much vitiated king of France, that "Eunuch Guardian" whose subjects "from Birth did forc'd Dominion take" (*AM*, ll. 157, 175). Forceful attempts to fight the fire, blowing up all that lies in its path with the same gunpowder earlier used to fight the Dutch, are in vain as the fire transcends and trespasses all attempts to bound it, multiplying "*Hydra*-like" every time it is directly assaulted (*AM*, l. 993). Force, it seems, can only propagate opposition, not supply resolution.

Faced with such concerns, royalist interpretations of the fire often sought to diffuse the insistence of Dissenting readings of providence upon continued conflict by attacking the revolutionary potential of the prophetic form itself. Parodic attacks upon a radical prophetic rhetoric, as we have seen, had been standard fare for royalist polemic during the late 1650s and early 1660s in texts like *The Lamentation of a Bad Market* (1660), and while accounts of the fire seldom resorted to parody, they often favored more direct means of attack. One narrative of the fire's destruction of the statues in the Royal Exchange triumphantly reports that

> The *dreadful Wrack* now all together slings;
> *Crowns*, *Scepters*, and the *Trunks* of *Kings*.
> And, like your *Statues*, *Kings*, said she, you must
> Once *mingled* be with *common Dust*.
> But Heavens Charles his *Fate* delay! may slow
> Arrive his Age, and *slower go*.
> And *you*, who dream't o'the Fall of Kings at last
> Grow wise, now *Sixty-Six* is past.

> Come off (at least) like Oracles; and say,
> Your *Credit's* sav'd; *These Kings* [the statues] *are they*.[16]

Such advice to the would-be prophet renders prophecy suspect through the accusation that it is more accurate after the fact than before, suggesting that the guilty prognosticators have been forced to retract their unsupportable predictions, which were themselves originally motivated not by divine inspiration but by transparent political interest. While certainly an attack upon specifically antimonarchical apocalyptic writing, these allegations also effectively seek to condemn the whole prophetic enterprise.

Yet as they began to question the very source of authority that such radical texts claimed for their social vision, those royalist appeals which did seek to predict and enable the future were ultimately faced with the problem of their own rejection of direct human access to divine knowledge, and hence with the confessed limitations of their own texts to bring about the change that they desired. Without a professed access to divine inspiration, royalist claims that the imminent rebirth of London would be a direct result of their foretelling it could at best carry little weight. The royalist quest of the mid-1660s then was to find new strategies for reading and writing providence in order to realize their imperial visions, and it was in this context that they ultimately rethought the basic form of prophecy itself.

## II

Where traditional strategies for interpreting providence had frequently relied on claims to divine inspiration, royalist texts after the Fire of London increasingly emphasized the process of reading God's providence rather than the state of knowing it. One common solution to the royalist dilemma was in fact to suggest that the power of the text lay not in its ability to translate the divine Word into human social structure but in the ability of the human writer to represent (or recreate) divine logic (providential history) by building a system of social signifiers. These accounts made the claim that human text did not reshape the world by force, but rather enabled hegemony by creating a unified interpretive community capable of reading and responding to the signs of providence with a single understanding.

Basic to this explicitly human capacity to remake the world was the notion of compunction—a combination of repentance and humility that linked the past sins of the reader with present visitation, thus serving as a human interpretation (rather than translation or enactment) of divine order, while still encouraging divine blessing. Using the Jeremiah of Lamentations as a model for their readings, royalist writers often indicated that the only hope for England's survival lay in correctly identifying those sins for which the fire was a perceived retribution. Jeremiah, watching the destruction of Jerusalem, could ensure the survival of his people and defuse the wrath of an angry God only by identifying and bewailing, without the help of divine inspiration, those past national sins that were the reasons for the destruction of Jerusalem (turning away from God, elevation of false preachers and such). Likewise, the writer's ability to bring about the rebirth of the English nation was seen to rely precisely on his or her ability to identify the cause of God's anger and relate it effectively to the condition of the English people.

Thus Nathanial Hardy, for one, having asked his readers to feel sympathy with the suffering of the city, asserts that sorrow itself is not enough to remove God's wrath:

> All this while, I have only set before you the *sadness* of the *Ruine*, together with the doleful effects which attend it; but now give me leave to *enlarge* and increase your *sorrow*, by minding you of the *causes*, as well as the *effects*, entreating you to consider *by whom*, and *for what* it is, that this great *desolation* is befallen this *great City*. . . . [It] was no other than the angry and *revengeful hand of God* which caused the *Fire* (with the *wind*) to bring upon the *City* such a *generally destructive Calamity*. Upon this consideration, it will be fit for us, as we look upon the *burning* to be the *effect* of *Gods wrath* to bewail the sins which have incensed it, and thereby procured this Conflagration: So that whereas all this while I have called upon you for tears of compassion, I must now exhort you to tears of compunction.[17]

Having duly inspired his readers to feel affective kinship with those who have suffered in the fire, he suggests that even more important is the consideration of a causal link between human transgression and divine retribution. For Hardy and others, concerned with the future primarily as it arose from a purely human relationship to the past, only this kind of reading of England's sins (enacted in the experience of compunction) could conceivably lead to renewed order and rebirth.

As Hardy's expressed consciousness of his position as an author and a public preacher makes clear, moreover, in the intensely political arena of the Restoration merely reading with compunction was not enough. In a world where divine signs were political capital, the process of interpreting providence was unrelentingly public, and so not simply a process of reading, but also one of writing and of signifying. Thus equally central to this kind of providential reading was the ability of the human text, and often the human body, to represent the signs of compunction and so publicly demonstrate before others and before God that His providence had been read rightly. In many of these works, metaphors of spectatorship create powerful social bonds, as they link a community of providential readers and weepers. The author of *The Conflagration of London* stresses the importance of seeing the fire more clearly than even a picture can describe it, insisting that

> *Londons Flames* should so be set to *view*,
> That those who *see*, in part may *feel* 'm too;
> And even those that *cannot see*, may find
> Th'*eye*'s not th'*only Glass* that *Burns the mind.*
>
> . . . . . . . . . . . . . . . . .
>
> *Poetry* is an *Intellectual Mint,*
> That stamps a *Picture* with a *spirit* in't;
> Whose *secret Magick* Senses want supplyes,
> And makes *Spectators* where it finds no *Eyes.*[18]

Similarly, Samuel Wiseman's *A Short and Serious Narrative of Londons Fatal Fire* describes the fire as a kind of dramatic spectacle, from which the lessons of compunction will come:

> Forth the dark Caverns of the dismal Earth,
> A boisterous bellowing Wind rous'd and sprung forth,
> And to disturb this quiet Silence came,
> And with its shuffling feet spurn'd up a flame
> From some few glowing Sparks, and made them be
> Apt Actors for a purpos'd Tragedy.[19]

Tragedy was itself in the literary theory of the day a form that represented (even, in the case of the drama, embodied) not just sorrow, but an idealized, orderly relationship between sin and retribution, thus creating an orderly society.[20] Here the writer seems to suggest that the very process of watching such a representation of compunction is itself redemptive—as is, he would seem to imply, the process of representing it in his own text. Even Hardy's discussion of compunction is set in the context of Christ's own spectatorship, as it urges the reader to "tread in the *footsteps* of our *Saviours* deportment toward *Jerusalem, Who when he came near, beheld the City, and wept over it.*"[21] For these writers who encouraged watching, redemption (the rebuilding of community) was not merely a matter of feeling the effects of providence but of publicly interpreting (reading) and signifying providence itself correctly, both in the eyes of God and, as Clarendon makes clear, in the eyes of an imagined and politically interested audience.

Thus for many of these writers, tears of compunction often became the proper response to affliction, not merely as the socially binding signs of human compassion, though sympathy and affection are clearly important in all of these texts, but as signs of the same moral link between crime and punishment that was providential history. As they modeled themselves after the weeping Jeremiah of Lamentations, the authors of many accounts used tears to represent an acknowledgment of the individual's share not only in suffering but also in the sins that had inspired the fire. Wiseman's "London's Lamentation to her Regardless Passengers" (appended to *A Short and Serious Narrative*) presents the reader with the voice of a demolished London, urging passersby to weep as a sign of their recognition of their guilt; "Why do you slight me thus," London asks, "and pass me by,"

> Spurn my neglected, dusty Misery?
> You that have laid me in the fatal Urn
> Of SIN, and seen me there to ashes burn:
> You that with crimson Crimes, like Cables great,
> Pull'd Vengeance on me, and my happy state
> Have made thus wretched, can you pass me by,
> And yet not at my Ruines wet your eye?[22]

Seemingly only tears laced with the acknowledgment of complicity in the connection between sin and punishment—tears that signify, that is, the compunction of the weeper—will serve to produce the desired effect. Similarly, the author of *Londonenses Lachrymae* describes himself as a weeper, and having shown that his tears are born of the recognition that "sin was the Common Cause, no faction freed" that will abate England's suffering and lead to her eventual rebirth, he urges himself on to further weeping as a means of authorizing his expressed belief that London will rise again, for "no less than *Noah's* flood / Can quench flames kindled by a *Martyr's* blood."[23] Both these texts thus imply the key role of those signs of compunction in London's eventual rebirth.

For the writer of *The Conflagration*, moreover, the depicted spectacle of tears even renders the text (and thus, by association, the represented rebirth of England) substantial, makes it real. Penning his own lamentation he asks to be pictured on the frontispiece of his poem in a way that associates him both with the Jeremiah of Lamentations and with the history of human tragedy:

> The *Poet* in a *Cypress-wreath* insert;
> (The *Lawrel* is a badg of a *Desert*
> Which he *pretends not to:* besides he *wears*
> An *heart* more suiting to an *Age of Tears:*)
> *Pale*, like the *City's Ashes*, make his *Looks*,
> (Too many *wear* its *Fires:*) by, let his *Books*
> (*Jeremy's Threnes*, *Salvian*, *Gildas*, and
> The *Tristia* of the *Banish'd Poet*) stand:
> Let his *Eyes drop* into his *Ink*, and thence
> *Supply* his *Quill*, and *mingle* with his *sense*.[24]

Here, tears are the appropriate response to tragedy, and as such they make the text substantial (much as drama is a form that embodies) by making up its substance—the ink that becomes the words. And thus tears give the writer's text the power to make renewal possible.

In an age in which faction, difference, and opposition had been institutionalized through the very process of representation in ways that suggested that they were not going to go away, at the level of either the symbolic or the real, these tears of compunction were important in part because they represented the ability to create national prosperity through divine blessing by representing opposition rather than destroying it—without, even, the intent of destroying it. Tears of compunction embody and make present not only repentance and humility (punishment) but also sin (transgression, and thus political opposition). To weep tears of compunction is to represent oneself, and one's country, as a political extension of that self, as a sinner by condition as well as by circumstance. "As both *Prince* and *People*," Hardy proclaims, "will find *themselves* concerned in the *sad effects* of the *flame*, so all have *reason* to charge themselves with the kindling of it," and, by an odd sleight of hand, rebel, loyalist, and king are all thrown together into a united state of disobedience.[25] And thus, much as the parodies of 1660 had depended upon the worthless material of opposition text to create meaning within their own, the very process of representing God's providence, as it serves to provide order, depends upon past transgression for the creation of that order, and perhaps more importantly relies upon owning and sharing past transgression rather than rejecting it. In a world in which pamphlet warfare had become a very real vehicle for the effecting of change, the translation of sin and faction to the realm of the symbolic does not necessarily make them safe, but the penitent writer, accepting his own internal struggle, can make of them a working grammar—a functional logic. The real social and economic rebirth that reading and writing ensures—the accomplishment of a new royalist order—is thus (however ironically and however reluctantly) utterly dependent upon the necessary embodiment of factionalism itself, much as the purgative effect of the fire is repeatedly, if paradoxically, connected to its signification of internal division. The hermeneutics of reading providence, a new and specifically royalist prophecy, thus made possible the claim that dissent could be productive rather than destructive, providing a crucial alternative to often transparent images of affective social ties and cultural organicism. That claim in turn, as the last part of this chapter will show, made possible a new royalist polemic for the political recuperation of Charles II—a polemic perhaps most fully realized by the historiographer-royal to-be in the lines of *Annus Mirabilis*.

III

In the months following the fire, many royalist authors sought to redeem Charles II, clearly responding to the kinds of unfavorable reports of the king's behavior that are mentioned by Clarendon. The author of *Observations Both Historical and Moral*, for example, praises Charles for "making rounds about the city, in all parts of it where the danger and mischief was greatest"; "we cannot but observe," he insists,

> to the confutation of His Majesties Enemies, who endeavour to perswade the World abroad of great parties and Disaffection at home against His Majesties Government, that a greater instance of the affection of the City could never be given, than hath now been given in this sad and deplorable accident . . . even those persons whose Losses rendred their Condition most desperate . . . beholding those frequent instances of his Majesties care of His People, forgot their own misery, and filled the Streets with their Prayers for His Majesty, whose Trouble they seemed to compassionate before their own.[26]

Another author urges the citizens of London to

> admire the goodness of our KING,
> Whose tender Heart bore SUBJECTS suffering![27]

Such images clearly sought to counter the reports of Clarendon's memory—images of a distanced and callous court, circulated "infinitely to the king's disservice," while equally eager depictions of a grateful London offer optimistic promise of the political and social stability to be expected under such a monarch.

Frequently, moreover, such recuperations represented the goodness of the king as a function of his effectiveness as a mediator with divine providence.

His competence as a ruler is, in many of these accounts, measured by his ability to read the fire correctly as a sign of God's anger, and to make of himself the public and embodied text that Hardy and others saw as the necessary condition of England's redemption. Ascribing the end of the fire solely to the efforts of the king and his brother James to turn the divine will to renewed favor with England, the author of *A Short and Serious Narrative* insists that

> The active Prudence, and industrious Cares,
> Th'uncessant Labors, and the fervent Pray'rs
> Of those two Royal Brothers CHARLES and JAMES,
> At last effected Conquest 'bove the Flames!
> The worthy Tears that trickle from the Eye
> Of his afflicted Sacred Majesty
> Prevail'd with Heaven, whose fierce avenging Arm
> MERCY with-holds; Strong Invocations charm
> His ireful Indignation, Intreaties urge
> Appeased Heaven to fling by his Scourge.[28]

This is a vision of a nurturing and benevolent king, whose tears reflect not only the suffering of the people but also their efforts, as he works alongside them in a common cause (although some suggested that his engineering attempts to stop the fire did more harm than good). Both his right to rule and his affective merits, however, here ultimately stem from his ability to intervene for his people—an ability located precisely in his willingness to weep and thus represent England's understanding that the fire was not a blessing but a scourge, and to acknowledge openly that the only means of averting God's anger lay in a public demonstration of reading and repentance. As we might by now expect, only by becoming the living symbol of compunction can the king truly assert his fitness to rule. Thus much as new textual strategies for the public interpretation of providence had offered an alternative to affective theories of social order, they also came in these portraits of Charles to develop a new explanation of kingly authority.

Nowhere perhaps was that new representation of authority, with all of its social and political implications, more fully developed than in Dryden's *Annus Mirabilis*. Since the publication of Michael McKeon's *Politics and Poetics in Restoration England*, that poem has been recognized as Dryden's early attempt, predicted in many ways by *Astrea Redux*, to redefine political (and particularly monarchical) authority in a post–civil war context. *Annus Mirabilis* is a poem, in McKeon's eyes, about "civil, royal, and national virtue": although factionalism is always present and evident in

Dryden's poem, he claims, the future of London, and indeed of England as a whole, depends upon the ability of both king and people to perceive "the generality of [London's] cause"—creating a community bound by common interest and leading ultimately to national unity and imperial power.[29] For McKeon, who primarily elevates the poem's familial metaphors, *Annus Mirabilis* succeeds as royalist polemic by casting the king as a benevolent father to whom England owes both filial and conjugal duties, uniting prince and people in a family unit whose common good is the primary aim of all concerned while articulating in the process an explicitly royalist theory of obedience and power.

Unquestionably the familial dynamics that McKeon recognizes in *Annus Mirabilis* do exist. Charles II is at various points in Dryden's poem both father and husband to a people ultimately loyal but occasionally in need of paternal leadership and discipline. Yet by also representing Charles as a public reader of providence, Dryden offers a vision of a royalist future based not simply upon the blessed hegemony of domestic affection but also upon the negotiation of ineradicable difference, thus providing a pragmatic alternative to ideals of hegemony that are represented as simultaneously attractive and unrealistic. England may well be a potentially affectionate family in Dryden's poem, but the world of *Annus Mirabilis* seldom if ever offers the possibility of stable unity or harmony—much like the real world of Restoration politics itself. In *Annus Mirabilis*, victory over one's enemies is always temporary and sure to be overturned. The ghosts of Henry IV and William the Silent watch their descendants batter the English, while English victory over the Dutch in the second Anglo-Dutch War is immediately displaced by the Fire of London. Total hegemony, moreover, is not necessarily a good thing. In Dryden's poem the fire is emphatically a divine punishment for English overconfidence in their own ability to eliminate opposition, while the fact that the Dutch are unopposed begins the war in the first place. Dryden shows us a world, then, where political difference is not only inevitable but necessary (if not exactly pleasant) because hegemony inevitably decays into violence.

In this world the goal is not to strive for unity, but to enable stable opposition. And it is in that context, I believe, that Dryden offers a picture of Charles as providential reader, responding both to the fire and to the larger problems that divide his realm. The fire eventually goes out only after Charles prays passionately, acknowledging both his own sins and the sins of the nation, reading the lessons of providence, and asking for divine mercy. As he "Out-weeps an Hermite, and out-prays a Saint" in sympathy with the suffering People, he asks of God:

Be thou my Judge, with what unwearied care
  I . . . have labour'd for my People's good:
To bind the bruises of a Civil War,
  And stop the issues of their wasting blood.

Thou who hast taught me to forgive the ill,
  And recompense, as friends, the good misled;
If mercy be a Precept of thy will,
  Return that mercy on thy Servant's head.

Or, if my heedless Youth has stept astray,
  Too soon forgetful of thy gracious hand:
On me alone thy just displeasure lay,
  But take thy judgments from this mourning Land.

We all have sinn'd, and thou hast laid us low,
  As humble Earth from whence at first we came:
Like flying shades before the clouds we show,
  And shrink like Parchment in consuming flame.

O let it be enough what thou hast done.
(*AM*, ll. 1042, 1049–65)

As elsewhere, the fire is a "dire Usurper" provided by Heaven "To scourge [the] Country with a lawless sway," thus presenting a threat against which Charles must prove his own right to rule by restoring order (or, in the terms of Dryden's particular metaphor, law) (*AM*, ll. 849–50). The fire, moreover, does not go out of its own accord, or because of any sudden national reformation; rather, it is extinguished only through the intervention of the monarch who begs mercy for his people. Because of his entreaties the fire is transformed from rebel to purge, wiping from St. Paul's the stain of civil strife that that structure had hitherto embodied. In the end, then, it is Charles who changes destruction into purgation, and thus enables the final vision of an England reborn and prosperous under the influence of a benevolent monarch and a "constant Trade-wind" that "will securely blow, / And gently lay us on the spicy shore" (*AM*, ll. 1215–16).

In *Annus Mirabilis*, moreover, London is saved, the promise of a reborn kingdom fulfilled, by a weeping king whose tears are explicitly tears of compunction as well as compassion. As we have seen in the passage quoted above, Charles ultimately earns divine forgiveness not through sacrifice but through his willingness to represent, in his tears and in his person, the suffering of all of his subjects and the nation's recognition that the horrors of the fire are a punishment for England's sins—his ability to represent, in a conflation of symbolic and political orders, both the sins and sinners of the nation. When he acknowledges that "we all have sinned," he in effect charges himself, as Hardy says, "with the kindling of [the fire]"; he becomes himself a representative sinner, embodying not merely repentance, but also transgression—the very opposition that threatens his throne. By reading the fire as a sign that he himself may have "stept astray" and by asking to be punished in return, he quite literally comes to embody the tragic link between crime and suffering, and makes of himself the public spectacle of compunction. Kingly authority, for Dryden, resides not merely in the ability to mediate divine wrath, but also in the capacity to simultaneously represent obedience and transgression, thereby holding them in stable opposition.

As in other accounts of the fire, the display of compunction does not, however, simply unite the transgressor and the obedient. It also creates a space where both are necessary to the future of England—a future explicitly defined in the baldly and boldly economic terms that Butler on his part had so tentatively embraced. In Dryden's poem, in fact, economy and imperialism become metaphors for processes of negotiation and exchange which enable a powerful and stable state. Success, after all, in *Annus Mirabilis*, is measured by the ability to sustain difference while avoiding the full-scale use of force; thus the primary goal of the poem, as well as its principal metaphor, is circulation, the renewal of trade, a measurable economic endeavor that both depends upon differences (one does not, after all, trade with one's self) and suffers visibly from war. Embracing the commercial order implicit in Butler's poem, *Annus Mirabilis* equates that financial interest with the ineradicable presence of opposition. The sign of future English prosperity, we are told, will be marauding pirate fleets, while the end of the poem reminds us that "to the Eastern wealth through storms we go" (*AM*, l. 1213). Likewise, to represent all of his people, Charles must publicly represent himself, and thus his kingdom, as one that is internally divided—as a private self, he, like others, publicly transgresses against the better interest of his nation and thus against his kingly self. And it is ultimately his apparent ability to accept the inevitability of ongoing disobedience—even in his own being—that in the end provides a visible model for divine mercy, and thus saves London. Publicly enacting internal division in the spectacle of compunction that he presents, he begs:

> O pass not, Lord, an absolute decree,
>   Or bind thy sentence unconditional:
> But in thy sentence our remorse foresee,
>   And in that foresight, this thy doom recall.
>
> (*AM*, ll. 1073–76)

Acknowledging the inevitability of transgression, he makes future remorse the sole condition of redemption, and thus he embodies both the uncompromising presence of disobedience and the process of its transformation—politically and publicly enabling a narrative of productive opposition. God in his turn renders past sins the painful but necessary precursors of all progress; alluding to the divinely enabled process of rebuilding once crowded, now devastated London streets, Dryden laments that "onely ruine must enlarge our ways" (*AM*, l. 1108). Thus both God and Dryden create a divinely sanctioned order that at once reinforces the authority of a royalist government by emphasizing new prosperity, and also reminds the reader that opposition and transgression have a crucial place at the heart of both society and empire.

In Dryden's poem, then, as in the larger world of Restoration polemic, the act of reading providence rightly is in a sense the act of reading and preserving political difference, of keeping it present and making it real. Charles rules well because he has become the living symbol of compunction through his tears, openly translating the representation of the spiritual self into the political sign it had always in some sense been. And like other royalist texts of the period, Dryden's poem seeks to offer some relief to a troubled nation through the embodiment of the very problems that plagued it. Turning to divine providence for new models of political authority, these often underappreciated texts sought ways of negotiating, rather than removing, the new realities of political difference. And thus whereas both seventeenth-century providential thought and Restoration royalism had, by some accounts, failed by the end of the seventeenth century, they had by then nonetheless helped to rework the fundamental understanding of political opposition and make possible a notion of government based on stable party difference that had a clear and lasting impact.

Rendering distinction, division, and multiplicity the vital preconditions of both market value and successful trade, the royalist texts of the 1660s thus transformed dissent into productive difference and political opposition into English prosperity. Rewriting and reappropriating prophetic text, they reinterpreted the strident oppositions created by the prophetic voices of the 1650s and 1660s as the very foundation of a prosperous society whose institutional metaphors were essentially economic rather than military. Such optimistic, if nevertheless ambivalent, representations of a negotiated social cohesion were not, however, destined to last unchanged and unchallenged. By the late 1670s, with the emergence of party politics, the dynamics of Restoration politics had begun to change, as conciliatory debate once again hardened into something that all too uncomfortably resembled reified opposition. And as the exigencies of Restoration political life changed, so too did royalist polemical strategies, royalist conceptualizations of hegemony, and ultimately the rewriting of prophecy itself. By 1680, the realities of English politics demanded even from Dryden a radical rethinking of the dynamic relationship between loyalty and transgression which he had presented in *Annus Mirabilis*. With the publication of *Mac Flecknoe* in 1682, Dryden proffered new explanations of social hegemony and irremediably altered the perceived relationship between politics and representation.

# 4

# "High on a Throne of his own Labours rear'd": *Mac Flecknoe,* Prophecy, and Cultural Myth

The emergence of the earl of Shaftesbury after 1673 as a dynamic focal point for a sustained political opposition to the authority of the crown effected radical changes in both English politics and English polemic. While it would undoubtedly be an overstatement to credit him with the single-handed development of a Whig agenda and an English party system, it is no less certain that Shaftesbury's prominence—first as the leader of the Country Party, later as the force behind the Green Ribbon Club, the leader of "the mobile party," and the primary spokesman for the Exclusion Bill—above all fostered a sense that the potentially fertile discord of the early Restoration had coalesced into a resistance that was unified and coherent, but also increasingly rigid, reified, and ostensibly philosophically opposed to the uneasy cooperation of the 1660s.[1] Royalist accounts of the growing dissonance between Whig and Tory, court and country, in fact, frequently depict the reemergence of hard-line oppositions inherited from the civil wars in the political battles of the mid-1670s. David Ogg reports that "the most common accusation against [the Whigs] was that they reincarnated the men of 1641," while one 1679 broadside entitled simply *The Lamentation* asserted that the main aim of Whig politicians was to bring back the Commonwealth and once again "rejoyce at *Charles*' Fall."[2] As factions rapidly developed into partylike structures, and as these nascent parties increasingly located their own origins and those of their enemies in the conflicts of the 1640s and 1650s, political opposition appeared, at least, to be constructed less as a negotiable reaction to present circumstance and more as a historically defined and determined set of political preconditions.

These political changes, in themselves significant, put tremendous pressure upon a polemical press whose representations of political difference bore increasing responsibility in the eyes of the nation for the political health of the state. Polemic, as we have seen, had always been a source of potential confusion and chaos for the seventeenth century, seemingly legitimating competing claims to both truth and power and thus offering a disconcerting glimpse of political, social, and epistemological relativism. Rigid representations of political opposition seemingly possessed the power to render England permanently fractured. Yet after 1675, the very availability of a discourse that constructed emerging and dislocating divisions between Tory and Whig in terms of earlier, known oppositions between Crown and Parliament also paradoxically offered a means of making party oppositions comprehensible. By defining party politics in terms of prior divisions that, while they had not been eradicated, had at least been made productive, political polemic seemingly had the potential, if used to the national advantage, to define the rules and boundaries of party opposition, organizing political interest into some recognizable form. It was small consolation, but nevertheless welcome reassurance in the midst of political confusion. And such an understanding of the function of polemic, in its turn, placed a tremendous responsibility on both author and representation, granting to cultural representations of the political arena the power either to create a form of institutional stability and hegemony or, alternatively, to generate utter chaos.

As poet laureate and historiographer royal during these precarious years, John Dryden was the principal literary spokesman for a royalism (and a conservatism) thus beset by very different challenges than those which had produced *Annus Mirabilis* in the mid-1660s. *The Medall*, Dryden's direct and uncompromising attack upon Shaftesbury himself; *Mac Flecknoe*, his bitter denunciation of Whig playwright Thomas Shadwell; and *Absalom and Achitophel*—all represent a royalist satiric voice that leaves behind the comparatively gentle and optimistic conscience of the early Restoration in response to a new polemical landscape. *Absalom and Achitophel* has traditionally been the writing to which scholars have turned in their attempts to define Dryden's royalism in the early 1680s, presenting as it does both politics at the highest level of state and a vision of satanic heroism drawn from that most canonical of seventeenth-century texts, *Paradise Lost*. And yet, I would argue, it is in many ways *Mac Flecknoe* that serves as a particularly useful text for understanding royalist polemical strategies in the 1670s and 1680s, precisely because its defining metaphors are not merely political, but also cultural and ultimately concerned with the problems of representing (and thus, in a sense, creating) social institutions in a politically divided society ever more reliant upon the commercialized production of representation itself.

Like *Hudibras* and *Annus Mirabilis*, both concerned in their own right with the issue of social hegemony and political authority, *Mac Flecknoe* turns to the figure of the prophet as a means of exploring rhetorical strategies for the consolidation of social order. However petty, self-interested, and aggressively unspiritual *Mac Flecknoe* may be, Shadwell is the "last great prophet of tautology," a prophet whose reign, we are told, had been "prophesied long since" by "ancient Dekker."[3] Thomas Dekker, the playwright famously ridiculed by Ben Jonson, was also the author of pamphlets that proclaimed the destruction of England for its manifold sins in titles like "Gods Tokens of his fearful Judgements"; and if Shadwell is "a scourge of wit, and flayle of sense" (*MF*, 89), he is thus equally the long-awaited judgment upon his people and upon himself. At the same time, Dryden also perceived a close generic relationship between prophecy and satire, as had others before him. He would later locate the origins of satire in the Roman equivalent of English civil war prophecy, developed by actors who "were first brought from Etruria to Rome, on occasion of a pestilence, when the Romans were admonished to avert the anger of the Gods by plays"; those players, he would claim, "with a gross and rustic kind of raillery, reproached each other with their failings," assuming, that is, the role of the castigating prophet.[4] As within *Mac Flecknoe*, the words of the prophet Shadwell (who is also one of "Gods Tokens") form the very fabric of Dryden's own satire (or raillery), for while Flecknoe, for instance, is figured as John the Baptist, "sent before but to prepare [the] way" for a Christlike Shadwell (*MF*, 32), he is also, in spite of himself, Jeremiah denouncing the false priest, speaking an inspired truth that he need not comprehend.

At the same time as Dryden writes a prophetic tradition into *Mac Flecknoe,* the principal organizing metaphor of the poem is the theater; the poem is, we might say, about theater and thus about a realm that is just as much a cultural domain as a political one. Theater, however, does not simply leave prophecy behind. Rather, the theatrical metaphors of the poem provide Dryden's text with the very authority that the prophetic voice had so manifestly and deliberately lacked in *Annus Mirabilis*—enabling text, as cultural product, to exert the real efficacy that the radical prophecy of the civil wars itself had claimed and that nascent party divisions seemingly necessitated. Like the theater it depicts and the prophecy it derides, Dryden's poem is essentially performative—persistently materializing the texts it represents. The titular identification of "the true-blue-protestant poet, T.S." as the object of satiric attack emphasizes theater, rather than monarchy, as the poem's informing discourse (the tenor of its metaphor), and in the process it effectively frames the poem in the confines of the stage. Flecknoe's kingdom is, in fact, the stage presided over by its playwright king, and its limits are those of the theater: the stage itself is associated with "the walls which fair Augusta bind" (*MF*, 64). Within this world, text (like prophecy and like script) is literally formed into real substance: Shadwell's productions clog the streets like refuse, and the subjects who flock to his coronation are books transformed to men by Dryden's own figures of speech.

The point, however, is not merely that text, as the literary product of an explicitly commercial order, takes on a physical substance in this poem. *Mac Flecknoe* also argues that literary representation determines the very institutions—both political and cultural—from which society is formed. Margaret Doody and Michael Seidel have both argued that the poem reflects late-seventeenth-century political attitudes toward imperialism and succession, respectively, but *Mac Flecknoe*, like both prophecy and polemic, is also clearly concerned with depicting the textual origins of political authority.[5] The symbol of Flecknoe's authority is a pile of his own "labours"—at once both literary and excremental (*MF*, 107)—and his incompetence as a playwright is realized at the social and political level in his failure as a king: Dryden insistently relates the decline of the kingdom he depicts to the inability of its monarchs to "represent" their state on the stage, embodying poor script in the form of an imperfect world. Moreover, while George McFadden has suggested that the poem puts forth a set of coherent literary standards in its attack upon poor writing in general, Dryden clearly sees those cultural standards—which he implicitly claims to maintain in his own poem—as the only hope for the restoration of order to a chaotic society whose fate is perceived to rest in the hands of those who represent it.[6] Within the poem disorder springs primarily from dull poetry and tautological poets, while the ability to establish order comes (if only in Dryden's own poetic project) with the satiric correction of literary disarray. *Mac Flecknoe*, that is, ultimately seeks to develop a new hegemony, based not upon the represented ability to exert control, but upon the ability to control representation through a carefully elaborated set of laws—now not divine or even political, but rather literary.

Thus *Mac Flecknoe*, I would argue, offers a powerful and coherent myth of the creation (and destruction) of social, political, and cultural order, as Dryden depicts a state that is formed, however badly, by text—a state decaying through the transformation of the human word that both sinks in bathos to the physical structure of material remains and embodies excrescence in a grotesque parody of metaphysical transcendence. As a text engaged in both political and literary criticism, Dryden's poem is above all interested in the laws (political, aesthetic, and often religious) that regulate literary production, social institutions, and the metamorphic process that binds text and society together. Explicitly seeking to delineate the boundaries between poetic conformity and literary transgression, *Mac Flecknoe* both depicts the destructive nature of literary disobedience and suggests the social importance of revitalizing structures of hegemony, disguised as and transformed into cultural myths. It is thus with the laws of cultural hegemony, as Dryden represents them, that this chapter will be concerned, both as *Mac Flecknoe* seeks to establish and uphold them, asserting its own mythmaking as the authority by which they are maintained, and as the poem (in its obsessive representation of the violation of those laws) often threatens to collapse into chaos. In the process, it offers a glimpse of Dryden's own developing anxieties concerning the relationship between literary products and social institutions—registering one seventeenth-century recognition of the complexities and potential dangers inherent in the social text.

## I

The notion of the metamorphosis of the word and the efficacy of the text in the creation of social order was hardly new to Dryden, having been—as we have seen—a popular image among radical writers of the 1640s, 1650s and 1660s, many of whom described the revelation of God's Word as a kind of theater.[7] But for Dryden, at least in *Mac Flecknoe*, the fact that prophecy had been read and used as the embodiment of the social order dictated by "the law"—as, that is, the interpretation, application, and practical fulfillment of a theoretical model—meant that it is precisely the ability of the prophet/monarch/playwright to establish and execute (to stage, in fact) the distinction between order and transgression that can construct (or destroy) the state, depending upon the variable talent and discretion of the author, much as print culture itself was perceived to hold the political fate of the nation in its hands. As the word becomes "real," the failures of the monarch and his representations to maintain a certain literary standard, imposed by Dryden himself, are revealed in the process of physical decay to which, the opening lines of the poem suggest, the original imperfections of man universally subject him and his works. And it is precisely the insistence of Flecknoe upon blessing when he should, we feel, be castigating or at least lamenting (like Jeremiah after the destruction of Jerusalem), imposing in some way the structure of the law, that ultimately dictates the excremental future of his kingdom, while it dooms him to the underworld/privy and the "Hell" of the Restoration stage. Collapse, chaos, and revolution all are the suggested social repercussions of the improvident efforts of the prophet/playwright, as Dryden assesses the social impact of literary representation.

The deliberate figuration of language as an essentially material medium capable of real efficacy is a trope, however, whose principal source may seem at first glance unlikely for a Restoration Tory, later-to-be Catholic, grounded as it was in the language of prophetic absolutism and discursive force that royalists had earlier worked so hard to defuse and redefine. Ironically, however, it was Whigs rather than Tories who by the late 1670s proved the most virulent detractors of prophetic discourse—despite the fact that many radical prophets, Ambrose Rigge among them, continued to write and publish. The 1670s saw a reaction against prophetic discourse primarily on the basis of an essentially Whiggish economic progressivism—a reaction that often led to the surprising association of complaint itself with Tory conservatives. Typical, for example, of the objections against complaint was a pamphlet attributed to John Houghton and entitled *England's Great Happiness or A Dialogue Between Content and Complaint Wherein Is demonstrated that a great part of our Complaints are causeless* (1677). At first glance, this author sounds much like many royalists who had attacked radical Jeremiahs during the civil wars on the grounds of their seemingly arbitrary claims to divine inspiration. He warns his reader in "The Author to his Book" that

> You must take care, you don't ill fare
> From those men that are furious
> . . . . . . . . . . . . .
> Against all things that reason brings
> To contradict their humours;
> And scarce are pleas'd, unless they're eas'd
> By spreading forth false rumours.[8]

The author's rejection of these "false rumours," however, quickly goes beyond problems of religious skepticism to challenge the central identification between complaint and national prosperity that had traditionally defined prophetic discourse, as we have seen in the case of *Annus Mirabilis*. Whereas earlier radical and Dissenting writers had often insisted that national destiny hinged upon self-flagellation in the name of divine providence, Content, quoting liberally from biblical texts against murmuring, urges Complaint to "remember that you are a rational creature, don't make your own and others lives uncomfortable by refusing to enjoy those Blessings Providence hath heaped upon you."[9] Insisting that those blessings which are viewed by fanatics and sectarians as "great Complaints," in fact, when "rightly considered are some of our main temporal advantages . . . [a] great encrease whereof would make us so rich as to be the envy of the whole world," the pamphlet suggests that complaint has been outmoded by a new construction of national prosperity based on trade, self-interest, and the individual accumulation of wealth.[10] Content openly declares that he judges all things purely by individual interest, and an overconcern with divine providence would here seem to retard rather than advance the nation. Tossing aside in this way issues that had been a mainstay of religious radicalism during the 1650s and 1660s—luxury and excessive living on the part of the rich, the enclosure acts, mismanagement of national resources, and ill treatment of the poor—the author speaks for a great many in Restoration England who had had a taste of imperial power under Cromwell, and were eager for a new age in which a combination of laissez-faire economics and imperial politics could leave behind the vocal misgivings of radical sectarians.

Just as ironically, moreover, it was those who ostensibly sought to preserve authority—with all of its signs and trappings—who during the 1670s increasingly turned to providential logic and to prophetic discourse as means of exerting control over a people depicted as sinful and recalcitrant. Despite the progressivist rejection of complaint, prophecy actually experienced a kind of official revival throughout the 1670s, particularly in the form of jeremiad, "that particular prophetic genre which both "[calls a] nation to repent for violation of its covenant with God" and threatens its imminent destruction if it does not.[11] That revival, not surprisingly, reached its height in the anxiety surrounding the Popish Plot and the Exclusion Crisis. Thus as John Spurr has suggested, the prophetic mode was adopted by the Anglican Church, among others, as a ritualized vocabulary of obedience and an instrument of cultural control, and as part of the regular liturgical cycle the text of the Book of Jeremiah, for example, was used on 5 November and 30 January to memorialize traumatic threats to the political status quo:

> [T]he aldermen of Cambridge, and thousands of other loyal Englishmen like them, were giving thanks for a "miracle of resurrection" of church and state [after the civil wars], the most admirable of "the wonderful revolutions and intricate riddles of God's providence" in which the hand of God could be seen "punishing us justly for our sins, yet relieving us mercifully from our sufferings."[12]

Often explicitly opposed to an overemphasis upon commercial prosperity, pamphlets and ballads were published that asserted their right to complain, in a political environment in which men were again prepared to risk violence and conflict in the name of political interest after the relative calm of the early 1660s. As early as 1668, the postscript to *Vox & Lachrymae Anglorum, or The true Englishman's Complaint* threatened that "if [Clarendon's] Practise justify our Fears, / He'll set's again together by the Ears."[13] Frequently these texts used God's judgment as both an analogue to and an excuse for a purely human show of force, while their claims to interpret the law (both divine and human) and set the boundaries of social acceptability served as a means of historicizing and institutionalizing the absolute and essentially arbitrary terms of contemporary political conflict. A lord mayor's proclamation of 1679, for example, uses the logic of divine judgment to rationalize threatened violence:

> [T]the Lord Mayor having taken into his serious Consideration the many dreadful Afflictions, which this City hath of late years suffered, by a raging plague, a most unheard of devouring fire, and otherwise: And justly fearing that the same have been occasioned by the many hainous crying Sins and Provocations to the Divine Majesty: And his Lordship also considering the present dangers of greater mischiefs and misery which seem still to threaten this City, if the execution of the Righteous Judgements of God Almighty be not prevented by an universal timely Repentance and Reformation: he hath therefore thought it one duty of his Office . . . first, to pray and perswade all and every the Inhabitants thereof to reform in themselves and families all Sins and Enormities whereof they know themselves to be guilty: And if neither the fear of the Great God nor of his Impending Judgements shall prevail upon them, he shall be obliged to let them know, that as he is their Chief Magistrate, he ought not to bear the Sword in vain.

Here the security of the city from divine punishment is ultimately determined by an appeal to law that is represented principally as a use of force, and the purely human swipe of the magisterial sword both averts and yet replaces the greater fiery sword so often depicted as the symbol of God's vengeance.

Much as this proclamation translates the terms of divine order into the representation of a predominately legal division between ruler and ruled (or obedient and unruly), moreover, complaint also became a means of establishing the laws of party politics, particularly among moderate to conservative Anglican supporters of the monarchy. Attacks upon the duke of Buckingham dating from the early 1670s defined opposition to him in terms of his earlier "treason," reminding readers that he had "[sworn] Allegiance to the rotten Rump," and was now "re-killing dead Kings by monstrous Slanders."[14] In much the same way, *The Lamentation* explains the politics of the Popish Plot as a reconfiguration of the basic divisions of the civil wars:

Great *Charles*, we do lament thy Fate,
For thou the Object art of late
Of Popish and of factious Hate.

These Winds from distant Quarters come,
From North and South, *Scotland* and *Rome;*
Yet both Concentre in thy Doom.

. . . . . . . . . . . . .

Each of them Plots to have the Sway,
And struggle only, that it may
Be brought about in their own way.

'Tis neither Love nor Loyalty,
That make Phanaticks talk so high
'Gainst Popish Plots and Treachery,

For they'l rejoyce at *Charles'* Fall,
And hope, once more, to have at all;
If Common-Wealth they could Recal.

The Papists hope will ne're be gone,
While they can set the Factions on,
And by them get their business done.

This "lament" over the projected fate of the king—lamentable as it threatens to repeat that of his father, for whom the Restoration was exhorted to "weep . . . for the Murther of a Father, the Father of our People and Country," as "the Prophet *Jeremiah's* grief swelled to that height as to wish his *head all waters,* and his *eys a fountain of tears, that he might weep day and night for the slain of the Daughter* of his *People*"[15]—cements the alliance of father and son in suggesting the equally continuous descent of their enemies. The ballad goes on to insist, in fact, that the safe negotiation of present political division is utterly dependent upon its representation in terms of past polarities. Thus lament in this broadside suggests the absolute, unchangeable, and hence nonnegotiable nature of party opposition, if ultimately containing that division in its claim to properly identify the source of the threat to the king. It resists the confusion of political oppositions in favor of a rigidly and historically defined polarity between Whig and Tory that offers to preserve political order and social harmony in the face of threatened chaos, paradoxically symbolized by Shaftesbury and the emergent Whig party.

Similarly, in *Mac Flecknoe*, the claims of the prophet to realize a viable legal order form the basis of what can only be described as a politics of culture—itself conceived as a source of political and social stability. On the one hand, Flecknoe's (Shadwell's) kingdom decays because the essentially economic transformation of the word into text fails to fulfill the structures of the law, even as it forms the substance of the kingdom. Whereas Butler had reluctantly accepted the marketplace as a viable locus for political negotiation, Flecknoe's kingdom is overwhelmingly ordered (or disordered) by a Whiggish market economy, linked to that rhetoric which earlier royalists had so reluctantly embraced, but here explicitly opposed to the maintenance of strict standards of (cultural) obedience and transgression. In the anarchic world of *Mac Flecknoe* both theatrical and poetic product are linked inextricably to a commercial order and a process of production that is inevitably destructive, leading to bad text and thus to a bad state. Theater is joined to brothel: the "Nursery" in Flecknoe's kingdom is a place for training both young actors and young prostitutes. Text is meant for sale: at Shadwell's coronation, his subjects/works emerge from "dusty shops" in the commercial streets of London. Moreover, just as these associations with the literary marketplace are essentially negative ones, the process of production in this system yields only excrement. Much as Baudrillard has claimed that the process of artistic production in a capitalist society inevitably alienates the product from the act of creation, the productions of Shadwell and Flecknoe are dead, dismembered, and essentially meaningless: "scattered limbs," "Martyrs of pies, and relics of the bum" (*MF*, 99, 101), and of course the ubiquitous fecal matter of Flecknoe's kingdom.[16] Excretion, here at least, embodies both production and alienation, effectively equating them. Text itself is cut off from both integration and interpretation, shredded and unread, salvageable only, the poem implies, by the strict enforcement of critical laws rather than market values.

At the same time, the true prophecy of Flecknoe resides in the satiric strategy of Dryden's poem as it executes the essentially arbitrary, exclusionary law of literary criticism according to which there is an absolute disjunction of aesthetic and transgressive, wit and dullness, and an articulated distinction (relatively new to the late seventeenth century) between popular and polite cultures. These distinctions themselves, moreover, are represented as explicitly political divisions: Shadwell, after all, is the "true-blue protestant poet." And just as Flecknoe asserts explicitly literary criteria (stupidity, dullness, and "thoughtless majesty" [*MF*, 26]) for rulership, he also describes the maintenance of literary standards in terms of the arbitrary use of force, much as the lord mayor's proclamation had done: Shadwell's duty, after all, is to "wage immortal war with wit" (*MF*, 12).

Yet as the skepticism of *The Lamentation* might also suggest, it is precisely the difference that Dryden's poem thus elaborates between the divine efficacy of prophecy and the human execution of satire that in the end also necessitates some further form of textual arbitration. In *Mac Flecknoe*, for instance, the potential inefficacy of the purely human word generates the paradox that has frustrated so many Dryden scholars, for while Dryden establishes refinement as a criterion for literary judgment and accuses Shadwell of transgressing in his crudeness, his own verse, we must admit, revels in these very faults. The rules of neoclassical criticism leave us little to say about Flecknoe's description of the progress of the "new Arion":

> Echoes from Pissing Alley Sh—— call,
> And Sh—— they resound from Aston Hall.
> About thy boat the little fishes throng,
> As at the morning toast that floats along.
>
> (*MF*, 47–50)

The problem with human law, as earlier royalists had clearly pointed out, is that it is both arbitrary and, as the earthly reflection of divine law, potentially inaccurate, subjected to the vagaries of political and personal interest. As we have seen, however, this is a difficulty of which the late seventeenth century was acutely aware—one which Dryden himself, in fact, had been forced to negotiate in *Annus Mirabilis*, and thus one that brings us back, albeit by a roundabout route, to conceptions of theater in the 1670s, and their relations to the religious, political, and economic matter of Dryden's poem.

## II

Throughout the seventeenth century, theater served as a popular metaphor for divine revelation—so popular, in fact, that it was parodied in the beginning of Herrick's *Poor Robins Visions,* where the speaker complains of his vision that "this Tragedy was so long a playing."[17] It had also been used as a figure for the political arena. Sources ranging from Pepys's *Diary* to Marvell's *Rehearsal Transprosed* suggest the perceived interrelation of monarchy and theater, as well as a specific politics of that analogy. The royalist Pepys praises the spectacle of restored monarchy, while the Nonconformist Marvell worries about the power of the player-king from the "Horatian Ode" to the *Rehearsal Transprosed.* For the 1670s, however, theater also came to be thought of as an answer to the very problem of the arbitration of human law that is so clearly raised by Dryden's aesthetics.

If the inevitably arbitrary nature of the human word had created problems of textual authority for royalist writers seeking some form of negotiation among interests in the 1660s, the need to find some new model for that authority was even more pressing for writers, particularly royalists, seeking to reassert hegemony in the later 1670s. As the terms of transgression, of the violation of law, had been both politicized and humanized by the institutional struggles of the early Restoration, the arbitrary nature of the interpretation of divine or "universal" law had become particularly evident to those seventeenth-century Englishmen without an easy faith in either God's signs of displeasure or the interpretive power of human institutions:

> For, as a late *Author* well observes, *Every Opinion makes a Sect; every Sect, a Faction; and every Faction (when it is able) a War; and every such War is the Cause of God.*[18]

Jean-François Lyotard has suggested that all of history is a series of propagandistic statements that must be arbitrated in order for meaning to be determined. After forty years of prophetic polemic, the late-seventeenth-century conception of divine judgment could be remarkably similar.

Simon Ford's *A Discourse Concerning God's Judgements* (1678) was thus typical of an age obsessed by almanacs, wonders, and a last powerful gasp of "providential histories." Working carefully against traditions that read the world as organized by a divine grammar, Ford seeks to provide a strictly human grammar by which to make God's judgments, the signs of transgression, meaningful. To this end he divides those judgments into two kinds, laws (words) and dooms (execution), from which he concludes that human law (for Ford, the human word) is often, but not always, the execution of God's judgment: "[W]e too often render our selves guilty of *prophaning God's Name*, (of which his great works are a considerable part) by stamping our own fond conceits with his *Image* and *Superscription.*"[19] Rejecting both the erected wit and the metaphysical potential of human language as a form of false coinage, he provides a code of instructions for reading God's judgments in conjunction with the story of an unfortunate man who seems to have died from gangrene. Interpretation becomes, then, a system of exchange subject, like any monetary system, to both the regulations of official coinage and the possibility of counterfeit, and thus seems dependent upon the authority to mint, but is never entirely ensured or reliable. Thus it is with this caution that Ford lays out a series of conditions by which those judgments may (in all probability) be known. They must be greater than anything man can inflict, and relate to some identifiable crime, and although the application of judgments is best made privately "in our own Bosoms,"[20] the public confession of a criminal is a good sign that his destruction is God's punishment, and that the human word had successfully represented the divine will according to a meaningful syntax of crime and punishment.

Thus, Ford's text—rather like Dryden's own *Annus Mirabilis*—attempts to portray a system capable of reading the signs of transgression despite the inherent difficulties of that act. Whereas *Annus Mirabilis,* however, had elevated both personal and public evidence of compunction as a means of defining social hegemony, Ford's concern is rather with the execution of human law and the ability of punishment to replace and represent an inscrutable providence. Thus he focuses upon publicly demonstrated signs of disobedience rather than upon the definition of sin, suggesting that for him, as for others like him, the violation of either divine or human law is significant primarily as a mechanism of production that creates the signs of its own being—signs that ultimately go on to create or inform a social order. In the *Discourse*, wrongdoing itself becomes the means by which God's judgments are to be known, at the same time as it precipitates the providential signs that must be interpreted: a crime and a confession by the criminal are the best means of identifying God's judgments, themselves the signs of human trespass. Transgression, for Ford, is not merely that against which the social order is defined, nor is it a means of making comprehensible a divinely ordained plan. Rather, it becomes the source of a symbolic order that ensures human order by making the human representation of punishment meaningful within a social syntax, in a world in which providence itself has become uncertain and unknowable.

It was in part as a result of the interpretive dilemma that Ford articulates that the stage, along with the scaffold, emerged during the 1670s as a perceived forum for arbitrating both the competing claims of false prophets and misguided lamenters and the politics of the succession. As early as "An Essay of Dramatic Poesy" (1668), Dryden had made reference to the Aristotelian commonplace of tragic irony or poetic justice as a criterion for good drama, suggesting that the audience expected the play to provide such a judgment, and in his *Tragedies of the Last Age*, first published in 1677, Thomas Rymer argues the moral superiority of drama over history on the grounds that poetic justice is potentially more perfect and thus more instructive than the seeming vagaries of divine providence. He writes of those past poet/playwrights that

> finding in History, the same *end* happen to the *righteous* and to the *unjust*, *vertue* often oppress, and *wickedness* on the Throne: they saw these particular *yesterday-truths* were imperfect and unproper to illustrate the *universal* and *eternal truths* by them intended. Finding also that this *unequal* distribution of rewards and punishments did perplex the *wisest*, and by the

> *Atheist* was made a scandal to the *Divine Providence*. They concluded, that a *Poet* must of necessity see *justice* exactly administred, if he intended to please.[21]

Earthly politics, Rymer concedes, are often apparently unfair and imperfect; more importantly, perhaps, they provide the opportunity for those (atheists) motivated by irreligious interests to question and confuse man's interpretation of the workings of providence. Drama, on the other hand, freed from the restrictions of history, has the power to clarify the perplexing evidence of divine judgment by seeing "*justice* exactly administred"; it serves as a kind of higher interpretive truth, determining (or overdetermining) the link between crime and punishment that Ford found so problematic. At the same time, for Rymer, who was a strong proponent of the Restoration belief that drama was meant to teach by example, it is the perfected and *"eternal truths"* of the playwright that serve as the most effective pedagogy. Thus it is the privileged arena of the stage, he implies, that can most effectively heal the "real" political and religious evils of oppression and wickedness that have already been amended within the text, returning order and stability to the state.

While Rymer's analysis provides a theoretical model to explain the privileged position of the stage in Restoration society, at a more popular level a broadside of 1679 entitled *A New Satyricall Ballad Of The Licentiousness of the Times* points to the stage as the only locus of truth amid the chaos of libels and false prophetic claims that, it insists, characterize Restoration politics:

> The devil has left his puritanical dress,
> And now like a Hawker attends on the Press,
> That he might through the Town Sedition disperse,
> In Pamphlets, and Ballads, in prose and in Verse.
>
> . . . . . . . . . . . . . . . . .
>
> They howl and they yowl aloud through the whole Town,
> The rights of Succession and Claims to the Crown,
> And snarling and grumbling like Fools at each other,
> Raise Contests and Factions betwixt Son and Brother.
>
> . . . . . . . . . . . . . . . . . .
>
> But it is not enough to see what is past,
> For these very Men become Prophets at last,
> And with the same eyes can see what is meant,
> To be Acted and done in the next Parliament.
>
> . . . . . . . . . . . . . . . .
>
> Petition the Players to come on the Stage,
> There to represent the vice of the Age,

> That people may see in Stage looking-Glasses,
> Fools of all sorts, and those pollitick Asses.
>
> . . . . . . . . . . . . . . . .
>
> Men may prate and may write, but 'tis not their Rimes,
> That can any way change or alter the Times,
> It is now grown an Epidemical Disease,
> For people to talk and to write what they please.

For this author, the theater reveals the folly of politically interested prophetic claims in part through the elevation of the mimetic ("Stage looking-Glasses") over the supposedly inspired word of commercial polemic, as the language of the ballad sets true vision—the recognition of vice in public spectacle—against politically interested assertions of privileged sight. Moreover, this preference for the spectacle of the theater seems to lie in the idea that truth will be revealed in a real human physical embodiment of vice on the stage (as opposed to the prophetic embodiment of the Word) that is simply not available to the printed word; written text has become, in its battle over political signifiers ("the rights of Succession and Claims to the Crown"), a prelinguistic chaos of "snarling and grumbling" entirely divested of meaning and motivated primarily by the economic interest of the hawker/devil. Thus just as Dryden located the origins of Roman satire in the theatrical exorcism of sin, here the accurate enactment of vice, conspicuously outside of a market economy and thus apart from self-interest, will rid London of the "Epidemicall Disease" of false argument that, through the transformation of the devil from Puritan to balladmonger, in some sense replaces the complaint of earlier religious radicals and Dissenters. If the potential of the stage is somewhat undercut by the last stanza, and by the fact that this piece is itself a ballad, theater nevertheless remains the only hope for the restoration of order.

All this is not to say that the theater was somehow immune from the discourse of political propaganda, or that anyone at the time thought it was. In fact, it was one of the principal means of public dissemination of propaganda, both royalist and Whig. Precisely because of its public political engagement, however, this privileging of the stage as (quite literally) an apolitical theater of judgment is extremely important to an understanding of both *Mac Flecknoe* and the perceived need to regulate theatrical production, to subject it to a form of critical arbitration, which ultimately drives Dryden's poem. What both Rymer and the author of the *New Satyricall Ballad* suggest is that the actor replaces the prophet as the more accurate fulfillment of the law; the law itself is essentially Aristotelian, as in the case of Rymer's translation, or it is satiric, replicating the judicial strategies of the theater in its own insistence upon the right to judge. And so too *Mac Flecknoe*, while it is clearly not theater but poetry, at once comments upon the capacity of the theater to pass judgment and simultaneously authorizes its own judicial role by an appeal to the theatrical sign, the represented and representing body.

III

Like the idea of the metamorphosis of the word, a belief in the capacity of theater to affect real social structures was hardly new to Dryden. Davenant, for example, had argued for the effectiveness of heroic drama as a means of regulating social order in his "Preface to *Gondibert.*"[22] Yet *Mac Flecknoe* is perhaps the Restoration's most memorable and far-reaching statement of that theme, and it is certainly far more than an echo of earlier formulations. After all, Dryden's satire is not simply, as critics have so often claimed, "about" literary standards, and so about literature in its most general terms of wit, imagination, and dullness. Its terms are more widely applicable, but it is primarily concerned with theater as an arena for the arbitration of political and religious opposition. Early in the poem, the stage itself is equated with a Christian place of judgment. Describing "Barbican," the literal boundaries of Flecknoe's kingdom, Dryden writes:

> From its old Ruins Brothel-houses rise,
> Scenes of lewd loves, and of polluted joys;
> Where their vast Courts the Mother-Strumpets keep,
> And, undisturbed by Watch, in silence sleep.
> Near these a Nursery erects its head,
> Where Queens are form'd, and future Hero's bred;
> Where unfledg'd Actors learn to laugh and cry,
> Where infant Punks their tender Voices try,
> And little *Maximins* the Gods defy.
>
> (*MF*, 70–78)

Here the stage and the brothel are conflated, both by physical proximity (as Dryden maps out the geography of the kingdom he creates) and by the interweaving of metaphor in the passage: "Queens" and "Punks" are actresses, but also prostitutes, and both professions are linked by the political vocabulary that metaphorizes them and turns them into figures of speech. At the same time, in the midst of this spatial and metaphorical confusion, these lines echo Cowley's description of an underworld located

Beneath the Dens where *unfletcht Tempests* lye,
And Infant *Winds* their tender *Voices* try,

. . . . . . . . . . . . . . . .

Beneath th'eternal *Fountain* of all Waves,
Where their vast *Court* the *Mother-waters* keep,
And undisturb'd by *Moons* in Silence sleep.[23]

This allusion, in turn, identifies "Dens" with brothels and hence with theater, suggesting that "Hell" is located precisely where, of course, it was—beneath the Restoration stage. Thus for Dryden, the stage itself becomes a locus of accurate, objective, and efficacious judgment.

It is precisely this figurative association of theater and hell, moreover, which is realized at the end of the poem, as the stage itself becomes a poetic mechanism for separating the goats from the sheep, enacting a final satiric judgment against both Flecknoe and Shadwell.

For *Bruce* and *Longville* had a *Trap* prepar'd,
And down they sent the yet declaiming Bard.
Sinking he left his Drugget robe behind,
Born upwards by a subterranean wind.
The Mantle fell to the young Prophet's part,
With double portion of his Father's Art.

(*MF*, 212–17)

In this passage describing the final flatulent fall of the aging monarch, the reign and the prophecies of Flecknoe are theatrically arbitrated in two different senses. The last comment on the reign of that Zedekiah and false prophet is carried out through theatrical allusion, since the trap is the same as that prepared for Sir Formal in *The Virtuoso;* at the same time, the function of the throne/stage/privy/hell that forms the trap is to identify Flecknoe's worth (or lack of it) as king, prophet, and playwright. Moreover, as the trap is sprung upon the "yet declaiming" monarch, succession becomes confused with political revolution: the natural order, as always in *Mac Flecknoe*, gives way before the unnatural, and thus the event seems to offer an equally pertinent comment on Shadwell's status as a "young Prophet" and a "true-blue-protestant-poet."

At the same time as it represents this theatrical judgment, however, *Mac Flecknoe*, like the more general terms of the fight between Dryden and Shadwell, is very much concerned with the poet's own right and authority to arbitrate political opposition. *The Medal of John Bayes* (1682), presumed to be the immediate impetus for Dryden's official acknowledgment of his authorship of *Mac Flecknoe*, insisted on Shadwell's own prophetic status, trying to "avert those Plagues which we deserve," and attacks Dryden and the Tories on precisely the matter of the right to judge:

> 'Tis you who in your Factious Clubs vilifie the Government, by audaciously railing against *Parliaments*. . . . If anything could make the King lose the love and confidence of his people, it would be your unpunished boldness, who presume to call the *Freeholders* of England the Rabble, and their *Representative* a Crowd, and strike at the very Root of all their Liberty. . . . Who made ye Judges in Israel?[24]

It is this question which Dryden had earlier asked of the Whigs in his own poem *The Medall,* and this question which *Mac Flecknoe* implicitly answers through its primary metaphors. As the playwright takes on the part of king and prophet, and as Dryden uses the principal analogy of political rule and succession to describe the pretenses of both Shadwell and Flecknoe to literary greatness, the analogous realms of politics and prophecy become subject to the same forms of critical legislation as the drama itself.

Thus Flecknoe's opening speech, another kind of judgment as he rationalizes his choice of a successor, figures Shadwell's poetic ability in terms of both politics and prophecy.

> . . . Sh——'s genuine night admits no ray,
> His rising Fogs prevail upon the Day:
> Besides his goodly Fabrick fills the eye,
> And seems design'd for thoughtless Majesty;
> Thoughtless as Monarch Oakes, that shade the plain,
> And, spread in solemn state, supinely reign.
> *Heywood* and *Shirley* were but Types of thee,
> Thou last great Prophet of Tautology:
> Even I, a dunce of more renown than they,
> Was sent before but to prepare thy way.
>
> (*MF*, 23–32)

Here, of course, the mock-heroic comparisons of Shadwell to both monarch and prophet ridicule his literary abilities, but Dryden's particular use of the mock-heroic, we must also note, effectively corrupts the vehicle of his metaphor as well as its tenor. Shadwell's "Majesty"—as well as his poetry—is "thoughtless," the oaks that symbolize his rule are lethargic, if not fallen (over), and his prophesies are senseless repetition. Shadwell is a bad king and a false prophet precisely because he is a bad playwright: dull, tautological, and pedantic. And so Dryden suggests, implicitly at least, that the very act of critically regulating the drama authorizes his poem's claim to legislate both political and religious institutions, as it does so emphatically in its final lines.

As a myth of the formation of social structure, then, *Mac Flecknoe* insists that both religious and political order, represented by the roles of king and prophet, are functions of literary production. Arbitrated by the theater, which both literally and figuratively marks the boundaries of Flecknoe's society, they are formed through the mimetic process; as metaphors for theater, they are subject to the same legislation as the sign itself. This is not, however, for Dryden a cultural authority based upon a structure of rigid signifiers, the analogue to the essentially political force of the prophetic word and thus a source of exclusion, oppression, or damnation in a system organized by cultural hegemony. Baudrillard has said of parody that it "makes obedience and transgression equivalent" and thus "cancels out the difference upon which the law is based."[25] In fact, much the same might be said of Dryden's conception of satiric theater, in part because of the unusual relationship it offers between signifier and signified. The fact that the very actor who represents crime or vice also serves as a means of vitiating that crime means that theater is a medium in which the signs of transgression inevitably function as judgments upon themselves, not by association or analogy, but by a principle of identity inherent in the dual nature of the signifier. As such, the sign does not merely fulfill the law, replacing both the word of the prophet and the executive function of government, nor does it serve, like Ford's "grammar," as a means of replicating and ordering itself as sign. Rather, represented as literary product and literary icon, the signifier embodies the transgressive. It can create social order only as it serves as both crime and punishment, and thus only as it itself is inherently unstable. Paradoxically, the violation of the law becomes the sign of the authority of the signifier.

Thus while *Mac Flecknoe* itself is not theater, and so cannot present the embodiment of the visual icon in the same way as live performance, the iconographic structures of the poem do closely parallel the theater's investment in symbol as Dryden replicates, within his poem, the authoritative structure of the double signifier. Throughout the poem, acts of transgression produce material signs that, in their inadequacy to the heroic world with which they are compared, are themselves rendered instruments of justice. At Shadwell's coronation he is invested with the symbols of his office:

> In his sinister hand, instead of Ball,
> He plac'd a mighty Mug of potent Ale;
> *Love's Kingdom* to his right he did convey,
> At once his Sceptre and his rule of Sway;

. . . . . . . . . . . . . . . . .
His Temples last with Poppies were o'erspread,
That nodding seem'd to consecrate his head.
(*MF*, 120–27)

These are symbols of power in a mock-heroic universe, and they are suited to that world because they represent the sins rather than the valor of its hero. As mock-heroic, however, they execute judgment through the very comparisons that that form implies. Shadwell's implied gluttony, drunkenness, sloth, and opium addiction lead to the "goodly Fabrick," itself a sign of his transgression, which both condemns him as a prophet and ascetic and designs him for "thoughtless majesty" (*MF*, 26). Likewise, Flecknoe's supposed inadequacy as a dramatist produces *Love's Kingdom*, here the thoroughly useless scepter of anarchy, which implies, in its failure as a sign of the heroic, the punishment of decay and social disintegration.

More pervasively, the inferior poetry of Heywood, Shirley, Ogilby, and of course Shadwell himself produces the material of the kingdom over which that monarch will rule, ridiculing and punishing him both in the comparison of that kingdom to the Rome of Augustus Caesar and in the conflation, as we have already seen, of privy, brothel, and Hell. At Shadwell's coronation

No *Persian* Carpets spread th'Imperial way,
But scatter'd Limbs of mangled Poets lay:
From dusty shops neglected Authors come,
Martyrs of Pies, and Reliques of the Bum.
Much *Heywood*, *Shirly*, *Ogleby* there lay,
But loads of *Sh*—— almost choakt the way.
Bilk't *Stationers* for Yeomen stood prepar'd,
And *H*—— was Captain of the Guard.
The hoary Prince in Majesty appear'd,
High on a Throne of his own Labours rear'd.
(*MF*, 98–107)

Flecknoe's own productions form both the throne that is the symbol of his office and the scaffold that becomes the site of the final judgment of his reign, opening as we have seen into the hell of his eventual punishment. At the same time, the scatological humor of the passage, also realized in the material productions of Flecknoe's "Labours," effects the present judgment of Dryden's own satire, enacting "justice" on the writings of Shadwell and Flecknoe, as well as on their politics.

Thus the emphasis on the materiality of the symbol simultaneously enables and degrades it, much as the actor's embodiment of the character of vice both represents and condemns. Its presence as object allows it to serve both as a locus for (product of/sign of) sin, while its referential function as part of the larger mock-heroic text permits it to expose that very vice: Flecknoe's texts are both his greatest crime and his greatest curse. Much as the word of the prophet effected punishment, as it was both the Word of God and, when unheeded, the justification for God's wrath, the strength and efficacy of this judgment lie, ultimately, in its suggested inevitability, as sins create a system of signs, the signs of transgression that in turn precipitate, as Rymer had suggested, a certain inevitable dramatic succession of punishment.

On the one hand, this conception of the satiric signifier ultimately suggests that Dryden's investment in the exclusionary nature of critical law is perhaps not as great as it is usually made out to be. Like the theatrical sign that arbitrates social order by representing transgression, the law that regulates literary culture is itself based on a fundamental instability that Dryden readily accepts. Critics long endorsed the notion that Dryden, "[preferring] cerebral to physical humor,"[26] attacked Shadwell for his crudity in an attempt to establish a polite, balanced, and decorous English verse. More recently, Laura Brown has sought to reconcile that perceived reserve with the poem's scatological humor in her description of a schizophrenic Dryden whose "ideology can be seen to belie his own experience as well as the realities of his age."[27] But Dryden's use of gross materiality in *Mac Flecknoe*, the "scattered limbs of mangled poets" (*MF*, 99) and the "morning toast that floats along" (*MF*, 50), is in fact crucial as a means of embodying vice (poor writing) within the logic of the poem; without it the kind of arbitration that Dryden proposes would be impossible. Within his aesthetic sensibility the grotesque and the real, as we use those terms to describe Dryden's essentially symbolic use of the dross of material substance, have an important role, precisely because of their dual nature within the poem as physical detail and symbolic signifier. They are, as we have seen, both that which is defined by the logic of the poem as transgressive and (quite literally) the signs of transgression that ensure its detection and punishment.[28]

Nevertheless, *Mac Flecknoe* is not only concerned with the way in which text creates society but also with the way in which culture itself is structured, and if Dryden eagerly adopts strategies that he himself defines as crude and farcical, his attack on Shadwell for "selling bargains" does exhibit a determined appeal to the laws of literary criticism, laws set up very much against the market economy that produces the text of Flecknoe's kingdom and thus the kingdom itself and laws crucial to the maintenance of political stability in an age of party. The problem with theater in Flecknoe's kingdom, as we have seen in other passages, is that it has become a form of prostitution and a process of excretion that renders the product meaningless, except as an object for sale. Flecknoe's offhand criticism of Ben Jonson—"Where sold he Bargains, Whip-stitch, kiss my Arse / Promis'd a Play and dwindled to a Farce?" (*MF*, 180–81)—suggests the extent to which Dryden's critical attack on Shadwell is also a repudiation of an economic order that abandons literary greatness (represented throughout *Mac Flecknoe* by the figure of Jonson) and thus political order in favor of self-interest and monetary success. It might, of course, be argued that as a personal attack the aesthetic claims of the poem can be disregarded as so much personal and political propaganda. But if Dryden's attack was partly personal, he was also engaging a new and significant description of cultural division, according to which the term "scribbler" (much like the incendiary cry of "Papist") was used merely to denote an absolute, arbitrary, and exclusionary difference of opinion, at the same time as the widespread prevalence of plagiarism, imitation, unauthorized collections and editions, and the sordid curse of writing for hire made such distinctions virtually impossible. Shadwell refers to Dryden as a "Hired Libeller" and a plagiarist;[29] Dryden calls Shadwell a "kilderkin of wit" (*MF*, 196); and thus we find ourselves, rather like Ford, in search of a grammar to arbitrate this exchange in order to correctly interpret the signs of transgression that each proposes.

In fact we can, I think, see both *Mac Flecknoe*'s appeal to a critical structure that it itself fails to uphold, as well as his criticism of a literary marketplace of which he was a part, very much as a result of an ambivalence concerning both the economic production of the "material image" and a related unwillingness to forgo a desire for imposed hegemony in the face of political crisis. As royalists in the 1660s had fretted over the power of a commercialized polemical press, and as Ford worried about the possibility of counterfeit signs of transgression, Dryden himself was just as concerned with the possible miscarriage of production (with, that is, excretion) in an age in which materialism meant not only self-interest but Whiggishness and the opposition to traditional moral economies on which authority could be based, as we have seen in *A Dialogue Between Content And Complaint*. And thus *Mac Flecknoe* repeatedly reflects Dryden's own fear that the very image that links transgression and punishment in his poem will ultimately be left meaningless by the process that creates it. Over and over again, the link between crime and punishment proceeds through a logic of creation or emanation: Shadwell's gluttony, as we have seen, produces the bulk that is both the evidence of his transgression and the manner of his punishment, and his ignorance produces the play that is the symbol of his lack of efficacy or authority. But at the same time, the rendering of the sign as material (especially in the form of literary text) always threatens to leave it dismembered, alienated, and ultimately without signification in the world of Dryden's poem, a pile of "reliques," "scatter'd Limbs," and human waste. The problem with the real, the material, the grotesque—not identical but certainly linked as aesthetic terms in *Mac Flecknoe*—is, as so many critics have proven in their concern for the "indecorum" of the poem, that it always threatens to be merely the transgression that it embodies, rather than the locus of a symbolic logic of transgression and punishment. Describing the grotesque in graphic detail and using the terms of excrement and mutilation, as Dryden does throughout *Mac Flecknoe*, repeatedly draws the charge of crudity.

Thus if *Mac Flecknoe* is a poem that argues that symbol and text create both structure and order, it is not entirely comfortable with the relationship between the transgression of that order and the linguistic structures the poem proposes, as Dryden's text is perpetually threatened by the very chaos and decay that it describes and continually teeters on the verge of a collapse into the realm of expletive "snarling and grumbling." At times, the grotesque image seems to overwhelm the poem altogether:

With whate'er gall thou sett'st thy self to write,
Thy inoffensive Satyrs never bite.
In thy fellonious heart, though Venom lies,
It does but touch thy *Irish* pen, and dyes.

(*MF*, 199–102)

The final exhalation that marks the simultaneous conclusion of sentence, couplet, and image suggests that Shadwell's "*Irish* pen," more deadly than venom, destroys not only his own satire but the continuity of Dryden's poem as well. At other times, Shadwell's poetic faults materialize in Dryden's own verse, becoming the fabric of his poetry in a satiric imitation whose ability to compel judgment depends wholly on its status as recognizably bad prosody.

St. *Andre's* feet ne'er kept more equal time,
Not ev'n the feet of thy own *Psyche's* Rhime:
Though they in number as in sense excell;
So just, so like tautology they fell,
That, pale with envy *Singleton* forswore
The lute and Sword which he in Triumph bore.

(*MF*, 53–58)

Moreover, with a much broader sense of the dangers posed by the satiric symbol, Dryden also seems to understand that his use of the transgressive figure threatens the very stability of the metaphorical structures that hold his poem and his country together. If the dual nature of the symbol allows, even necessitates, a place for the grossly material, a depicted breakdown in the metaphorical structure of the poem ultimately suggests that the inability to distinguish signifier from signified threatens the symbolic (and political and cultural) order through the very process of exchange that renders Shadwell's kingdom a world of commodities, of lifeless material, and thus of remains and excrement. Ostensibly, of course, *Mac Flecknoe* uses the political (as well as the prophetic) as a means of both commenting upon the process of literary production and establishing an essentially political distinction between good king and bad king, good writing and hack scribbling. But just as politics itself could be analogized in terms of representation, the tenor and vehicle of Dryden's metaphor are easily reversible—this is as much a poem about politics as it is about theater; and by a somewhat perverse logic, this interchangeability suggests an explanation of what is really wrong with Shadwell's kingdom, as political, theatrical, and prophetic all are leveled (or razed) before the processes of production and consumption that commodify and reify everything they can in the name of self-interest. Here prostitutes are actresses, but they are also queens, and Shadwell rises from the brothels as the prince "by ancient Dekker prophesied long since" (*MF*, 87). This multiplicity, however, does not bind these realms in stable analogies, but rather threatens to destroy them all, for—as the logic of the poem constantly reminds us—the prostitute is neither good actress nor good queen, nor is a brothel the appropriate cradle for a great prince. A bad playwright is not a competent king, in part because he is swayed to produce garbage (or incendiary propaganda) in order to make a living, and thus it is that we see in *Mac Flecknoe* a desire to retreat back into the rhetorical structures of the political and the arbitrary—and into satire, the human assertion of the right to profess a thoroughly human judgment. The very exchange to which both bodies and texts are subject renders them gross and material, and hence potentially able to defy the very symbolic order that they create, escaping the analogies between political, cultural, and religious orders that, for Dryden, organize both the poem and the world. In the world of *Mac Flecknoe*, that is, the monarch can no longer afford to "join with self-interests," even as he must accept the potentially chaotic and ineradicable nature of their being.

Thus it is that Dryden insists upon a literary criticism structured as law, a system of regulation that effectively seeks to replace a diminished political authority, like that of Ford in that it proposes a mechanism for correctly interpreting the signs of transgression, unlike in that it insists upon its own ability to correctly arbitrate those signs. And thus too *Mac Flecknoe* can tell us much, not only about Dryden's own conceptualization of aesthetics but also about the place of the growing frequency and urgency of the depiction of the division between high and low culture in this politically precarious period. Dryden's poem is of course only one example of this emergent formulation, but as a response to a world in which he perceives even theater as subject to the same control of the devil/hawker that threatened to destroy all political and religious order in the face of unbridled self-interest, it does suggest the extent to which a critical legislation sought vainly to impose a largely inefficacious set of distinctions upon a rampant and uncontrollable economy of literary production—itself a sign of political opposition—in which all such distinctions were superfluous, or meaningless, or both. It also, I think, says something about the mechanisms of cultural hegemony in the late 1670s and early 1680s. If representation defined the dynamics of political and religious division (as in *A Lamentation*), a desire to impose some system of order in the face of political chaos, intrigue, and suspicion is certainly understandable, if ultimately untenable. Attempting to effectively transform the mechanisms and institutions of political and religious order into a cultural discourse that could more effectively regulate the process of polemical production—itself depicted as the origin of all social institution, order, and conflict—*Mac Flecknoe* ironically guaranteed both the survival and the institutionalization of the essentially political distinction between popular and polite while fostering a conception of the literary marketplace as part of a symbiotic system of literary productions and standards.

Yet while *Mac Flecknoe* may be said to have ultimately guaranteed an understanding of literary merit with long-term consequences for modern canon production, for the perceived function of literary criticism, and for the institutionalization of literary study itself, in the short run—and seemingly in his own estimation—that poem represents a battle that Dryden unequivocally lost. With the coming of the Glorious Revolution and the failed agenda of the Stuart loyalists, Dryden found himself displaced, disempowered, and constrained to write from the very position of political opposition he had once so detested, while the position of poet laureate descended to his own antihero, that vilified "Kilderkin of wit" who proved not Flecknoe's heir but his own. Dryden's later work often savors of quiet resistance, underlying but never quite controlling works such as *Amphitryon* and *The Fables*.[30] At the same time, the political battles of the Exclusion Crisis that Dryden so condemns in *Mac Flecknoe* proved to be only the beginning of party struggles that both the Revolution of 1688 and the political strategies of the final Stuart monarchs exacerbated and institutionalized until, by 1710, British politics seemed a litany of party slurs, Whig and Tory, faction and moderation. In this environment was born Dryden's worst nightmare, the Grub Street hack, willing to sell both pen and personal beliefs for supper and a garret room. And thence, too, emerged the early eighteenth century's greatest testimony to all that Dryden's Tory politics had stood against—the elevation of conflict, the commercialization of representation, and above all the glorification of self-interest—Bernard Mandeville's *Fable of the Bees*.

# 5

# Providence, Party, and Hegemony in Mandeville's *Fable of the Bees*

The Glorious Revolution of 1688–89 dashed all of Dryden's precarious hopes that a politics of culture might help to stabilize an ailing political state. If anything, the events of 1688-89 accelerated the formation of political parties, begun but hardly completed in the 1670s and 1680s. Parliamentary factions jostled for position in the wake of the Revolution, seeking influence with the newly established reign of William and Mary. Meanwhile, the increased importance of loyalty to alliances within the Commons in particular made notions of party allegiance ever more central to the practical workings of politics. The new prominence of the political machinery which developed in response to the unprecedented frequency of parliamentary elections in the period provided a forum for the definition of party interests and an opportunity for polemical print that helped to focus party identity.[1] And thus the bestial "snarling and grumbling" of *A Lamentation* matured into the distinct articulation of Whig and Tory politics.

For a conservative like Dryden, the party politics of the 1690s presaged an end to the notions of political hegemony so earnestly negotiated by writers and politicians of the earlier Restoration. Seeming to belie even the most carefully treasured optimism about the power of representation to balance order and opposition, the very institutionalization of Whig and Tory, while it did offer to contain political division in some ways, also suggested the possibility of a permanent cultural divide upon the English political and aristocratic landscape. Exacerbating the fear of such potentially splintering antagonisms was the highly vocal, almost at times hysterical, activity of a popular press that by the first decade of the eighteenth century was full of the rage of party, presenting embattled Whigs and Tories mired in vitriolic prose and unthinking hatred, each side seemingly certain that the other intended nothing less than the destruction of the nation. Depictions of the infamous Calves-Head Club, among others, focused political anxieties about the vehemence of party, while contributing to the sense that party alliance meant nothing less than open warfare.[2] Whigs accused Tories of harboring a secret affection for tyranny and oppression that could be realized only by the subjection of English nationhood to French Jacobites, while Tories taunted Whigs with the same accusations of religious fanaticism and anarchism that had shackled their Commonwealth forebears, claiming that their aims were nothing less than a second civil war.[3] And thus the perceived role of printed propaganda in the creation of political opposition is suggested by the preface to Jonathan Swift's *Tale of a Tub*, in which the author complains of the contentiousness of political writing, "the Danger hourly increasing, by new Levies of Wits all appointed (as there is reason to fear) with Pen, Ink, and Paper which may at an hours Warning be drawn out into Pamphlets, and other Offensive Weapons, ready for immediate Execution."[4] So too it is in this period—in Swift's own text, in fact, among others—that we see the emergence of the Grub Street hack, ready at a moment's notice to advocate any political position in exchange for an evening's meal, and egging on an internal strife in which he (or she) took at once all parts and none.

At the same time, the growing influence of Whiggish economic principles, once seemingly confined to the supposedly separate sphere of commerce but now impinging directly upon the political state, threatened to transform conceptualizations of power and political authority in ways that radically questioned the connections that earlier writers had drawn between economy and political negotiation. With the creation of national financial institutions and national financial interests any lingering pretense that power and money were not deeply interconnected seemed no longer tenable. Ironically, at the same time, as Colin Nicholson has argued in *Writing and the Rise of Finance,* such openly economic understandings of power meant, on the one hand, new relationships between citizens more beholden than ever to their own financial interests and, on the other, a government whose power seemed increasingly demystified.[5] The subsequent elevation of self-interest—guilt-ridden, often vilified, but nonetheless inevitable—threatened models of political authority centered around the primacy of national hegemony and demanded new theories of cultural unity, leaving some to feel that by the first decade of the eighteenth century English society had become irreversibly "fractured" into a myriad of competing and often self-contradictory political, economic, and philosophical voices.[6]

Despite such urgent complaints of imminent chaos, however, from at least one point of view the reality of party politics and the elevation of the economic principles of a new Whig ascendancy after 1689 were not so much a narrative of radical reform as they were a new version of political oligarchy. The postrevolutionary power of the Whigs—no longer confined to back rooms and opposition politics—was certainly restrained to some extent by William III's careful attempts to balance power between the parties, but it nevertheless rendered them no longer reformists but rather a part of the problem in the eyes of many of their traditional supporters. For many Whigs, institutionalization and political power led to the perception that they had become complacent and self-satisfied, harboring a self-serving interest in the maintenance of the status quo. And thus, despite Tory fears of the chaos that might result from the shift in the balance of power after 1688, by the first decade of the eighteenth century it was the Whigs themselves who were under attack as stodgy, oppressive, and indifferent to reformist causes. A 1701 *Letter to a Modern Dissenting Whig* complained that so-called Modern Whigs "have quitted their Cause and Principles only for private Ends, and are apostatized from their Ancient Faith." These new Whigs, the author claims, have been corrupted by their power, deserting their former brethren and quickly mutating into the shape and form of their earlier Tory opponents; having been rewarded by William for their part in the Revolution, "these sanctify'd Knaves fell to the old trade of buying and selling of Offices . . . these State-Ants laboriously carried the Wealth of the Nation to their own Heaps."[7] Attacking the "present Practices" of the Whig party leaders as corrupt and self-aggrandizing, the *Letter* suggests that their belief in the political power of finance and trade had not produced a hoped-for revolution in the nature of power itself, but rather merely contributed to the ossification of older dynamics of elitism and oppression, leaving the true reformists out in the cold once again. Other writings echoed such concerns on the part of "old" or more radical Whigs; one pamphlet even suggested that the new modern Whigs had learned everything they knew about corruption by studying the legendary licentiousness of the early Restoration court.[8]

All of which left the Whig party of the 1690s and early 1700s with a significant dilemma: how to consolidate the economic power and political influence they had gained without seeming to the eyes of both critics and supporters merely to reduplicate the strategies of a Stuart government that had itself already understood, as we have seen, the need for arbitration, compromise, and economic theories of the relation between text and society. It was a problem, moreover, whose import was magnified by the fact that it was not merely a Whig issue, but a concern for all who sought to reestablish power in the wake of the Glorious Revolution—a political, religious and cultural event, even arguably economic in its impact—that many historians have read as more genuinely revolutionary than the civil wars themselves.[9] Defined by institutionalized difference, the inextricability of power and finance, and a fear of tyranny associated with France and with Jacobitism, politics after 1689 demanded the redefinition of social order in ways that could accommodate the changed realities of practical politics and a deep suspicion of the rhetoric of negotiated hegemony that the conceptualization of politics in economic terms had itself engendered.

This chapter examines that process of redefinition through an exploration of Bernard Mandeville's much-maligned *Fable of the Bees*. The relevance of the *Fable* to early-eighteenth-century ideas about hegemony and authority, and to the practical working of early-eighteenth-century institutions, has often been underrated. Mandeville's contentious style, his deliberate representation of his own philosophical radicalism, and the vigorous attacks by critics upon the 1721 edition of the *Fable* have often seduced scholars into swallowing wholesale Mandeville's version of his own marginality. His relative silence on the subject of his personal political views—exaggerated by his often garrulous social commentary—has made him difficult to fit into the dynamics of party politics, and even those students of the period who try to place the *Fable*, often quite compellingly, in the context of early-eighteenth-century economic development tend to view him as a transitional figure, neither wholly capitalist nor fully conscious of the issues of class in a capitalist society, and thus somehow disappointingly incomplete.[10] Nevertheless, the *Fable* does serve to exemplify the crucial problems of representing and consolidating authority in a world in which the appeal to force was patently counterproductive and social structures themselves were understood to be bound and stabilized by essentially economic institutions: Mandeville's text agonizes, at the very least, over a complicated series of relationships among representation, self-interest, and the creation of a stable society in ways that echo the concerns facing both Williamite politicians in the 1690s and the supporters of Anne in the early years of the eighteenth century. In its persistent concern with the process by which human society is created and managed in spite of the fact that "no Species of Animals is . . . less capable of agreeing long together in Multitudes than that of Man." *The Fable of the Bees* returns repeatedly to the central question of how any authority can possibly hope to bind such recalcitrant and essentially self-interested creatures within orderly institutions.[11] The answer inevitably involves an examination of the manipulative and evaluative power of representation, as children and adults alike are duped by the distorted reflections of self presented to them by parents, friends, legislators, texts, and the amorphous but pervasive presence of culture itself.

As it does so, *The Fable* appears at first glance to leave behind the prophetic adaptations of earlier writers concerned with the nature of social order—seems even in fact to purposely discard them as destructive, absolutist, and impractically wedded to old notions of political hegemony. *The Grumbling Hive*, first published in 1705 and eventually the nucleus of the *Fable*, centers around a disastrous case of providence enacted. In the *Fable*, the transformations of providence are debilitating, leading not to a prosperous society but to a kind of primitivism according to which the bees, previously figured as human, become animals once again and reside in a kind of noble savagery reminiscent of European depictions of Native Americans—the inevitable losers in the imperialist economy that Mandeville describes. Throughout the *Fable*, in fact, Mandeville is wary of appeals to divine judgment, mitigating the force of the traditional prophetic voice by declaring that luxury, managed well, is not a crime and defying the voice of the grumbler by asserting that no nation ever "came to Ruin whose Destruction was not principally owing to bad Politicks, Neglects, or Mismanagements." Prophecy in fact destroys that which binds society together and renders it prosperous; it effaces the economic order that controls the first half of *The Grumbling Hive* and destroys quite literally the material fabric of culture.

And yet prophecy does play a significant role in the *Fable*. It may be destructive and absolutist—blatantly opposed to the economic prosperity that Mandeville embraced—but it is also unquestionably potent and efficacious: the society of bees is remade because of its own negative self-representations in a cataclysm as thorough as anything the most strenuous seventeenth-century prophet had envisioned. Thus *The Fable of the Bees*, with its own adaptation of the prophetic, its concern with the process of social and cultural formation, and its insistent relocation of political power into an economic value system consistently figured as represented and therefore as itself a product of culture, does not so much discard prophecy in favor of economy as it does set the two in parallel as alternative and (ultimately) equally absolute means of effecting social order. And as it does so, the *Fable* depicts the paradox of Williamite authority, as its attempts to avoid and discredit political absolutism themselves create a new form of cultural authority, openly relativist and yet ironically thoroughly absolutist. In the *Fable* those terms are not dialectic opposites but complementary states, and their coexistence is not the result of confusion or inconsistency, but a condition of postrevolutionary political and textual authority. In the *Fable*, as in other texts of the early eighteenth century, individuals are bound into a common state by an essentially economic order; within that system, one's social value, and thus, in a sense, one's authority, depends—much as it had for Hobbes—upon the ability to represent oneself as valuable according to a set of culturally constructed standards. Yet whereas for Hobbes power had been defined simply as the representation of power and of riches—terms essentially absolute and not deconstructable—for Mandeville culture itself is exposed through its relation to the prophetic as a system of powerful but constructed rules and regulations, oppressive, controlling, and essentially arbitrary. Thus Mandeville ultimately outlines an understanding of the paradox of cultural absolutism—realizing in part through his treatment of the prophetic voice the concerns so tentatively latent in *Mac Flecknoe* and elaborating a theory of culture itself that even those later writers horrified by Mandeville's much-vilified philosophies would have to negotiate.

I

Like earlier periods of political strain, the 1690s and 1700s saw the revitalization of prophetic discourse—now reinvigorated by dissenters and "old Whigs" unhappy with the relative moderation of Williamite and "new Whig" politicians, by the economic hardships induced by continental wars, and by a Jacobite opposition to court politics—rendering Mandeville's representation of a society transformed by prophetic text all too current and all too potentially real. The French Enthusiasts have long been the most visible of early-eighteenth-century prophetic manifestations, partly because they figured so largely in contemporary Francophobic attacks upon enthusiasm, and so it often seems that prophetic rhetoric was merely a foreign import alien to English soil by the start of the eighteenth century. Yet French prophetic writing thrived in part upon the renewed popularity of a native English prophecy that deliberately reenacted the titles and the rhetoric of the 1650s. A pamphlet entitled *England's Warning-Piece*, for example, was "[humbly] offered to the Consideration of the *Lords* Spiritual and Temporal, and *Commons*, in *Parliament* assembled," and predicted the dire providential consequences of English government corruption. Speaking in the hopes "that God would open [Parliament's] eyes"—and lead them to pass a bill denying members of Parliament the right to hold any other government office—the author reminds a hostile audience that the

> *Jews* were severely chastised for their great Hypocrisy, Cruelty and Oppression, and general Corruption of Manners, Mic.3. Jer.5. and the several warnings that God gave them by the Mouth of his Prophets, was spoken to us, and to all Nations . . . we have seen and felt visible. . . . Tokens of God's Displeasure, and must expect the severest of his Judgements, if the Yoke of Oppression be not removed.[12]

At the same time, radical prophecy became, however ironically, a common form among Jacobites alienated by the Glorious Revolution. The jeremiad, as we have seen, had been favored as an instrument of social control by both Tories and High Anglicans during the 1670s, and examining the aftermath of the Glorious Revolution, Paul Monod points to what he terms a Nonjuring jeremiad as a popular form for expressing resentment against Williamite government and extolling the cause of a pretender whom God himself would revenge.[13] Calling upon the language of radical religion to express their own political purpose, the authors of such pieces, whether radical dissenters or Jacobite sympathizers, insisted that God's judgments were not events of the past, rendered superfluous by the Protestant Succession, but rather ongoing, relentlessly delivering his prophets from harm and oppression by threatening once again to forcefully eradicate their opponents.

In *The Grumbling Hive* as well, providential history, as we have seen, plays a central role, generating both the symbolic action and the moral so crucial to the genre of fable itself. Like the radical prophecies of the seventeenth century, Mandeville's poem depicts the dissolution of a social structure based on greed and corruption, and the subsequent construction of a new order of virtue built around the survival of a pious few. At the beginning of that text, the busy hive is riddled with—even organized around—a vicious combination of deadly sins and social follies; moved by the complaints of unhappy bees, Jove (divine wisdom) passes judgment upon the hive, essentially ruining a hitherto prosperous society. By the end of the poem, the hive has been reduced by its distresses, but like the children of Israel they have also been glorified for their sufferings, triumphing, if "not without their Cost." Much as *Annus Mirabilis* predicts the birth of a blessed society emerging from the ashes of a ravaged London—a birth precipitated by the pleadings of the prophet king—and as *Mac Flecknoe* portrays the all too literal excretion of a kingdom by its prophet, *The Grumbling Hive* depicts a new social order effected by the represented complaints of its citizens.

Yet while the archetypal story of God's vengeance and the subsequent claims about the power of human text inherent to the genre both lend a skeletal framework to *The Grumbling Hive*, Mandeville's poem does not represent any simple or unequivocable transformation of national transgression into political hegemony through the power of representation. In fact, the text actually rejects many of the assumptions on which both prophecy and complaint had traditionally relied, refusing to easily accept either the socially destructive influence of vice or the oft-repeated belief that spiritual conformity leads inevitably (if only eventually) to national prosperity.

In Mandeville's poem, as in *Englands Great Happiness*, traditional "Complaints" "when rightly considered are some of our main temporal advantages," and the "Crimes" of Mandeville's hive have duly "conspir'd to make them Great" (*FB,* 2.24). At the same time, Mandeville portrays grumblers, those who complain about the "simple vices" of the merchant class (cheating, lying, and fraud), as themselves petty, hypocritical, corrupt, and destructive:

> . . . they, at every ill Success
> Like Creatures lost without Redress,
> Curs'd Politicians, Armies, Fleets;
> While every one cry'd, *Damn the Cheats*,
> And would, tho' conscious of his own,
> In others barb'rously bear none.
>
> (*FB*, 1.26)

The grumbler himself, for Mandeville, is a kind of criminal, guilty of violating the rules of both capitalist and charitable economies, while his complaining threatens the very political, military, and economic stability of the state. If the land "sinks," Mandeville goes on to suggest, it is the grumbler's fault for griping in the first place. And in fact complaints do lead directly to economic crisis—a genuine fear in the growing markets of the early eighteenth century—as the newfound honesty with which the bees are plagued catalyzes spiraling deflation, reduced spending, and large-scale unemployment. The bees' laments destroy a national infrastructure as surely as the Fire of London itself had done: building halts, and once-great halls are let and suffered to decay while

> . . . the once gay
> Well-seated Household Gods would be
> More pleas'd to expire in Flames, than see
> The mean Inscription on the Door
> Smile at the lofty ones they bore.
>
> (*FB*, 1.32–33)

International political and military power likewise fall prey, as anticomplaint tracts often suggested they would, to the social effects of internal dissatisfaction, reduced by the effects of their complaints to a meek and humble colony, far different from the noble and opulent society that Dryden had predicted at the end of *Annus Mirabilis*. Complaint may produce a virtuous and orderly society, but not without destroying the economic order that truly defines it—and not without its own manifestation of human vice.

In this attack on providential rhetoric, Mandeville's *Fable* reflects the vocally articulated concerns of many for whom affirmations of the continued possibility of providential vengeance seemed, much as they had in the earlier Restoration, inflammatory fictions designed to perpetuate conflicts and divisions that they themselves created. Some expressed fears that prophecy once again threatened a return to the conflicts of the 1640s, reenacting civil war by reviving its discourses and thus recasting current political struggles in terms of past divisions. An attack upon the popular work *The Judgment of Whole Kingdoms and Nations*, "that vile Pamphlet, the 8th Edition whereof is now published and spread abroad to promote Treason, and revile Kingly Government," for example, rejects the discourse of providential judgment as a last irritating and even potentially dangerous reminder of the evils of civil war. "It is not intended," the author admits,

> to examine and explore all the malicious Falsehood of this indigested Rhapsody of fanatical Nonsense, . . . we shall leave this Sink of Corruption, which has been gathering ever since the Foundation was laid for the bloody Rebellion in forty-one, being above 70 Years, to be purg'd by the no less powerful Element of Fire, to which it deserves to be committed.[14]

Just as the Great Fire of 1666 had been necessary to burn away the last architectural evidence of civil conflict, so the censoring fires that would destroy the contested claims to providential reading are necessary to rid the nation of the discursive remains of internal warfare and provide closure for a nation still seemingly troubled by the earlier debates of "the bloody Rebellion in forty-one." Likewise Daniel Defoe, in a 1710 ballad entitled *The Age of Wonders*, attacks the church for creating through prophetic discourse what he implies is a new civil war. Using the image of the "the world turn'd upside down"—an image that had originated in civil war balladry—he ironically renders the Anglican clergy the intellectual and political heirs of mid-seventeenth-century religious fanaticism:

> Nature's run mad, and madmen rule,
> The world's turn'd upside down.
>
> . . . . . . . . . . . . .
>
> The pulpit thunders death and war,
> To heal the bleeding Nation;
> And sends Dissenters to the Dev'l
> To keep the Toleration.[15]

For both these authors, providential rhetoric threatens the dissolution of social order precisely because it is a language that does not merely signify but rather transforms and inverts society itself, creating corruption and revolution.

Williamite politicians eager to remake Low Church Protestantism and effect closure on the religious and political struggles of the previous half-century equally disparaged radical prophetic discourse, in part as a means of erasing their own historical association with radical prophecy and thus recasting themselves as the new leaders of English commercial progress. At the time of the accession of William III in 1688–89, great care was taken to distance the "Protestant Reformed Religion" established by the Glorious Revolution from the seditious discourse of civil conflict that had been so often associated with Low Church Protestants over the previous fifty years. As the very symbol of sedition and radical dissent, prophecy itself had to be not merely rejected but also transcended in a vision of England united after long struggles by a monarchy capable of representing all reasonable interests with equal ease and effectiveness and so able to usher England into a new age of colonial power and financial growth.

Thus typical, for instance, of early Williamite propaganda is a 1688 engraving entitled "England's Memorial Of its Wonderfull deliverance from French tyrany and Popish oppression. Performed Through Almighty Gods infinite goodness and Mercy by His Highness William Henry of Nassau The High Mighty Prince of Orange." This piece allegorically portrays an England carefully and organically united. At the very center of the print stands an orange tree that represents both the new monarch and the British people—as well as British trading power in the Mediterranean—unifying both the nation and the engraving with its spreading, protective, and fruitful majesty. The English, sheltered by the tree of Orange (and by "the balme and blessing of God"), are gathered together in its shade—commons, nobles, and clergy sharing a common benevolence and prosperity.

As it creates such a picture of English unity, moreover, this print alludes directly to the traditional images of providential discourse, clearly still troubling reminders of a past history of civil discord. Notably, however, it depicts a very different image of God's providence than that which we have seen in earlier prophecies—an image based not on the portrayal of divine vengeance but upon the representation of God's merciful delivery of his chosen people out of the hands of their enemies. Taking up, in a sense, after the plot of radical prophecy is already over, relegating both the persecution of England and also the images of prophecy to the past, it objectifies the discourse of providential judgment itself—isolating its major tropes and turning them against themselves. The plate portrays scourge, internal social division, and the execution of divine justice, all traditional elements of the jeremiad, but repeatedly these tropes are understood as

*England's Memorial*, 1688. The British Museum.

precisely that—tropes—and in effect, as weapons, and so are turned away from England (the Royal Orange Tree) and toward France. They are directed outward against the enemies of England, but never proposed as a means of self-regulation. Here in fact, the pestilence is not sent from God as a warning to his people; rather it is displaced into a corruption proceeding from the council of "his most Christian Scourge of Europe," Louis XIV, in league with a host of devils and Catholic clergy. Because the "Royal Orange Tree" is unaffected by the French plague, protected by the breath of God that (in the upper-right corner) literally and figuratively opposes the sinister contagion of the devils, the pestilence redounds upon the French, vilifying them even further. Likewise the visitations of tyranny and civil strife are the sole provenance of France, as the plate depicts the French king "murthering his owne subjects." In perhaps the most telling detail of all, those Englishmen who are corrupted by the French taint are spatially removed from England. They are not identified, as are the others, by their place in English society; rather they are "the whole Heard of Papists and Jesuits," a group unto themselves—subhuman at that—and they are portrayed not as tares among the wheat but as cattle already outside of English fields, in the process of running away to France much as the king himself had done. In this print, then, the conventional tropes of radical prophecy are used not as a vehicle to self-revelation (or even self-investigation) but as a means of externalizing and historicizing the entire cycle of transgression and punishment, scapegoating French, Catholic, and Jacobite in order to portray the social cohesion of England as a nation under Protestant rule.

For Williamite supporters (particularly Whigs) who were eager to put the legacy of radical prophecy behind them, renewed threats of internal division and even civil war were not the only dangers of a lingering prophetic tradition. As the representation of the French in *Englands Memorial* might also suggest, however, prophecy did not merely raise the specters of half-crazed prophets roaming the streets of English villages without their clothes on—almost foolish perhaps from the historical distance of 1690—but also foregrounded the more pressing horrors of Jacobite uprising and ultimately tyranny itself. Whereas for royalists in the early Restoration disorder had meant radicalism, fanaticism, republicanism, and even, on occasion, anarchy, many Whigs and moderates after the Revolution of 1688 (not necessarily hearty supporters of a strong monarchy) saw the primary threat to English political order as overly centralized power, often associated with Jacobitism and French tyranny—the oppressive French government to which providential rhetoric has been relegated by *Englands Memorial*. Those invested in a Williamite monarchy as a viable alternative to Jacobite power feared not anarchy, but absolutism, and understood revolution not as the overthrow of monarchy, but as the suppression of Parliament and the subsequent denial of the native liberty of the subject.

For many writers, then, the prophetic voice offered not only the threat of irresolvable difference but also the devastating potential for absolute hegemony enacted in the wake of promised judgment. Antipathy directed against prophecy—and the so-called grumbling with which prophecy was inevitably associated—thus focused for these authors around anxieties concerning the possible effects of political faction upon the constitutional freedoms of the British people. A 1689 pamphlet against grumbling and the calling for divine judgments—a pamphlet entitled, in fact, *The Grumbletonian Crew Reprehended*—blasts the stirrers of civil discord on the grounds that they are unfit to live in a free society. "Certainly," the author opines,

> they are very fit for Slaves, who cannot find in their Hearts to be very thankful for their Liberty: which being the case of our present Grumbletonian Crew, it were Pitty, if they might not have leave, to transplant themselves into some *Catholic* Country; where they may have their ears bor'd through to the Door Post, in Token of an Everlasting Servitude; and may solace themselves with the full Fruition and Enjoyment of all the good Effects of Popery and Arbitrary Power; which now they have lost the Benefit of in England.[16]

This attack, with its wonderfully grotesque depiction of French punishment, is of course a slight upon both Charles II and James II and upon the pretensions to absolute rule associated with both Catholicism and loyalty to the Stuarts by those eager to find in William a willingness to be led by Parliament. At the same time, however, it also suggests that grumbling and the cry for providential visitation are fit only for those who seek either to oppress or to be oppressed. Complaint, accused from the 1650s on of being the production of those who look to enforce their own political and religious ideals at the expense of the beliefs and liberties of others, thus becomes associated here with both tyranny and—ironically—the very punishments enacted by the early Stuarts against religious radicals in the less tolerant atmosphere of the earlier seventeenth century.

Echoing such concerns about the tyrannical effects of prophecy and grumbling, the anonymous author of a later pamphlet entitled *Awake Sampson, The Philistines Are Upon Thee!*—seemingly a Dissenter who had gained some freedom under Williamite toleration—castigates those who adopted a prophetic rhetoric as a means of agitating for a Stuart government that would, he feared, renew the persecution of the sects, and he warns:

> [T]ake heed Oh Murmerers! Lest God deal with you as with the *Israelites* in *Samuel's* time, when that People had such Experiences of the Goodness of God by his many deliverances . . . but (too much like unto you) this was not satisfactory unto them, but they would choose a King. . . . And when they were to be gratified, *Samuel* was ordered by the Lord, to shew them the manner of their King (*viz.*) *This shall be the manner of the King that shall reign over you, he will take your Sons and Daughters for Himself, and he will take your Fields and your Vineyards . . . and the Lord will not hear you in that day* . . . and Methinks! the *Israelites* yoke under their King is easie to what we may expect. . . . Don't mistake, if ye by your Murmurings provoke the Lord to Anger, and your hatred of one another, break his commands, and bring the *French* among you.[17]

By attempting to interpret and represent evils that do not, this pamphlet claims, exist—in this case the lack of representative government—the people of England make their situation worse rather than better. England, as the author portrays it, has been showered by God's blessings, freed from judgments, plagues, and corruption; and complaining about such benevolence to a merciful but testy God can only precipitate judgment and lead to eventual oppression.

As the attitude of *Awake Sampson* toward the genre of complaint itself might suggest, moreover, the irony of that pamphlet is not only the political recognition that revolution can result in destructive hegemony, but the understanding that prophetic language itself destroys because it too inevitably unifies and tyrannizes, effacing and destroying fertile difference. The divine judgment represented in that pamphlet is not merely a punishment, but also a horrible mistake. It literally realizes, as prophetic language was supposed to do, the pronounced desires of the prophet/grumbler, yet ultimately destroys rather than empowers through the transformations it represents, not as in the case of *Mac Flecknoe* because of the failure of the prophetic speaker, but rather, inexorably, because of the nature of providential rhetoric itself. The grumblers—misguided as they may be—neither fail, nor (strictly speaking) achieve the results that they desire. Rather, their literal desires are made real (materialized) through the power of providential judgment. The grumblers in *Awake Sampson* are given the king they so badly want, but made substantial, all wishes and all predictions must be limited by the parameters of a fallen world, subjected to a single and imperfect shape and form—reified, made rigid and inflexible, and thus drained of the potential that had inhabited the desire. As a result, the king whom they receive is not exactly what the Israelites had had in mind, representing in his tyrannical nature not only the political repression of the desires of the subjects by the unbridled power of the human monarch but also the repression perpetrated by prophetic language itself, overdetermining meaning and restricting the liberty of the word—the potential of representation. In effecting that which it envisions, that is, the prophetic text became for many in the 1690s itself a form of tyranny.

For Mandeville as well, although he does not directly address the issue of tyranny or absolutism in *The Grumbling Hive*, the social revolution that follows from the grumbling of the bees manifests itself not as internal division, but rather as unwonted (and unwanted) unity, a mending of internal squabbles, antipathies, miscommunications, and deliberate misdirections. The effect of the absolute transforming power of the word is destruction, but it is also hegemony, imposed in a sense from without and leading to inevitable decay. Leaving behind an economy based upon the self-interested manipulation of others, an economy dependent upon the internal differences endemic to individualism, the transformed hive embraces a new economy of charity in which even the clergyman himself—symbol of self-interested corruption:

> . . . chas'd no Starv'ling from his Door,
> Nor pinch'd the Wages of the Poor;
> But at his House the Hungry's fed,
> The Hireling finds unmeasur'd Bread,
> The needy Trav'ler Board and Bed.
>
> (*FB*, 1.30)

Marking a return to social organicism unmarked by economic or political difference—an organicism that stresses the interdependence of social groups rather than the competition among them—the transformation of the hive destroys by conflating distinctions of class and party. The hollow tree into which the entire hive swarms at the end of the poem symbolizes the total abnegation of self and self-interest, the ultimate subordination of self to society—as all inhabit a mutually barren space undistinguished by the usual signs of wealth and privilege that distinguished private dwellings in the period.

Even the fable form that Mandeville adopts in *The Grumbling Hive* represented for the early eighteenth century an attempt to find a meaningful alternative to the seeming absolutism of prophetic rhetoric. Theories of the function of fable common during the Restoration and early eighteenth century often saw fable as a natural replacement for a prophetic form rendered impracticable by historical circumstance. Roger L'Estrange, in the introduction to his *Fables of Aesop And Other Eminent Mythologists*, opined that to "Tell the House of *Israel* of their Sins, and the House of *Jacob* of their Transgressions: was a Guide, Undoubtedly, like an *Old Almanack,* for the Year 'twas Writ in; but Change of *Times* and *Humours*, calls for *New Measures* and *Manners*; and what cannot be done by the Dint of *Authority*, or Perswasion, in the *Chappel*, or in the *Closet*, must be brought about by the *Side-Wind* of a Lecture from the Fields, and the forests."[18] Fables, like prophecy, were understood to have the ability to make men "lay aside their Prejudice, to change their ill Customs, and to bridle their unruly Passions," but they were understood to do so, as L'Estrange suggests, not by force or by the wholesale transformation of society, but rather by the gradual inculcation of moral principles conveyed through the creatures of "the Fields and the forests" and designed according to the much-worn Horatian formula to "at once both teach and delight Mankind."[19] At the same time, as Jayne Lewis has suggested in her treatment of early modern fable, fables were often perceived as capable, where prophecy so often was not, of accommodating the cynicism regarding the nature and efficacy of text that the civil wars had produced, permitting the indeterminacy of ambiguous meaning, resisting the attempt to overdetermine the reading process, and confessing, as Lewis suggests, their own multivalence and thus their inability either to offer an unproblematized vision of truth or to enact that truth in any simple or meaningful way.[20] The moral of Mandeville's *Grumbling Hive*, devilishly presenting as a simple matter of fact the caveat that "Fools only strive / To make a Great an Honest Hive," characteristically resists both a final determination of meaning and the rhetorical enactment of its social vision. Leaving the reader to negotiate between the alternatives of honesty and greatness, that fable rejects the tyranny of the text and infuriates those uncomfortable with irresolvable ambiguity (*FB,* 1.36).

Yet even while much of the challenge of writing text in a social context as Mandeville and others saw it was undeniably to find a way of organizing society through representation without insisting upon closure, hegemony, or the public and universal interpretation of law, those looking to redefine political and cultural authority after 1688 were unwilling to completely ignore the potential of textually created hegemony, especially given the need to consolidate power in the political arena that developed after the Glorious Revolution. Thus while many writers of the early eighteenth century sought the purposely duplicitous or unreadable signifier, seeking in the irreducibility of the sign some relief from the pressure of both public reading and the struggle for political power, they often did so in ways that sought to enable the continued creation of interpretive order. The goal for these writers was to redefine social and cultural order, and often they did so by turning to new constructions of both social cohesion and textual efficacy. Enabling, they hoped, the continued creation of interpretive hegemony, they redefined that hegemony in terms of social structures based on the strategies of exchange and negotiation—strategies that the Restoration had been at best able to embrace ambivalently. And thus it is to the particular relations they established among economy, representation, and interpretation that we now turn.

## II

The representational strategies adopted by those writers who sought to redefine or remake theories of social cohesion on a Whiggish economic model understood text not merely as a form of commercial product subject to the laws of the marketplace, but also as a creative force within a capitalist economy. For such authors, text did not create order by establishing the laws and boundaries of society, but rather by generating the conditions of the market itself, and thus of exchange, of negotiation, and of the complex series of social interchanges that those activities represented within a commercial order. As *The Grumbling Hive* would seem to suggest, moreover, a social order based not upon obedience but upon the network of exchanges that bind men together in the mutual gratification of individual self-interest relied for its preservation and success upon a theory of representation that regarded text not as an instrument of judgment and execution, transforming real space and real institutions through the enactment of punishment upon represented transgression, but rather as a means of preserving society by rendering the transgressive, the disobedient, and the grossly material valuable. Representation, that is, was designed not to purify or unify society by judging intrinsic merit, but rather (much as economic speculation encouraged investment not according any notion of essential value but rather according to market value and expected returns) it set the market price that becomes in a capitalist society the commonly accepted standard of reasonable exchange and at times makes even the most worthless of products profitable, valuable, and socially beneficial.

For Mandeville, writing in 1705, after the founding of the Bank of England and the creation of the powerful East India Company, the nature of social cohesion lay in trade, finance, and the series of economic exchanges that bind a city like London together. In his text, society does not merely benefit from economic prosperity, but is in fact held together by the circulation of capital. In *The Grumbling Hive* social order is not, as it had been for Dryden, ostensibly political, defined by laws and national borders, but rather economic, the result of internal bonds and exchanges as opposed to externally imposed limits. For Dryden the ultimate symbol of social order had been the walls of London itself, burned down in *Annus Mirabilis* as a reminder of ongoing hostility between court and city, and corrupted in *Mac Flecknoe* by both literal and figurative prostitution to commercial interests. Mandeville, on the other hand, defines social success almost exclusively as financial prosperity, and the ties that bind his "fair Augusta" are the daily exchanges of coin that literally betoken a flourishing city. Workers are tied to their patrons by the exchange of goods and services that are required by the "Lust and Vanity" of the upper classes; even "Sharpers, Parasites, Pimps, Players, / Pick-pockets, Coiners, Quacks, [and] South-sayers" are brought into an uneasy kind of social order, tied to their victims by the money that invariably passes from prey to predator (*FB*, 1.18, 19). The continual circulation of currency ensures full employment, defusing tendencies toward social unrest, and providing all members of society with a mutual interest in the exchanges that mark their daily lives far more effectively than abstract notions of honor or the threat of law; for Mandeville the worst criminal by far is the miser who hoards all up and thus may be productively, if not exactly justly, robbed. Making "Jarrings in the main agree" and "Parties directly opposite, / Assist each other, as 'twere for Spight," the ties created by economic exchange even succeed in mastering the political faction and party opposition that seemed so clearly to threaten early-eighteenth-century society (*FB*, 1.24, 25).

In *The Grumbling Hive*, moreover, society prospers because of the ability of its members to represent both themselves and their goods as more valuable than they are, and because of the willingness of the buyer to accept those representations as real. Hypocrisy, itself a form of duplicitous representation, is in many ways the principal "virtue" that makes the hive successful. Lawyers prosper by bringing suits that have no merit, generating financial gain out of nothing at all. Physicians, often those who have no skill and little training, add to the domestic economy by prescribing for patients whom they cannot heal and hypochondriacs who are not sick to begin with, while they benefit foreign trade by administering medicines unnecessarily imported from foreign lands. The economy that binds the hive together in a prosperous and orderly relationship, moreover, is driven by luxury, that which makes of the inherently worthless and unnecessary a valuable commodity. Immoderate "Diet, Furniture, and Dress," along with liveries, coaches, horses, and country houses, all useless except as symbols of pride and privilege, are given value and maintain a constant flow of money and credit that both increases the hive's prosperity and maintains it in a certain orderly working condition (*FB*, 1.25). Notably, the hive is punished for its grumbling first and foremost by the removal of fraud and hypocrisy, actions that precipitate its certain destruction. The resulting inability to recognize one's neighbors who "in borrow'd Looks well known, / Appear'd like Strangers in their own" all bring the bustling prosperity of the discontented hive to a grinding halt (*FB*, 1.28). Forcefully ridding the hive of the vicious and the transgressive, Jove's judgment effectively disables the complex system of necessarily hypocritical representations (negotiations) that have enabled both enemies and competitors to coexist within a stable society while simultaneously gratifying their own inevitable self-interests. As a result, the representation of value seems a viable alternative to the forcible transformation enacted by the prophetic voice, not only allowing but even encouraging the duplicity and ambiguous signification necessary for both economic growth and the freedom from tyranny (both political and hermeneutic) that British patriots cherished.

Mandeville was of course frequently condemned by his contemporaries for his claims that hypocrisy and luxury together had the power to render the English nation both coherent and strong—particularly after the 1721 publication of the *Fable*. Yet in many ways Mandeville's *Fable of the Bees* merely reproduces in baldly economic terms a theory of representation that was inherent in, even fundamental to, the most polite of early-eighteenth-century discourses. Contemporary theories concerning the social efficacy of genteel behavior, spawned in part by the Societies for the Reformation of Manners, relied upon an understanding of representation that assigned value to an individual—in veiled but distinctly protoeconomic terms—as that person was capable of representing himself or herself, not according to the accuracy of the representation but for its compliance with predetermined notions of desirability. The value of representation in a social context, that is, lay not in its mimetic qualities, but in its ability to transform the represented into the epitome of social interest. Thus an instructional pamphlet confidently entitled *The Rules of Civility; or, the Maxims of Genteel Behavior* pleasantly reminds its gentle reader that

> to compleat our selves in true *Politeness*, we need go no farther than the Rules of Civility; and that Civility being nothing but a certain Modesty and Courteous Disposition which is to accompany us in all our Actions, we could not more usefully discourse of any other Virtue, (suppose we were able) considering this directs us to the acquisition of a thing, that conciliates Applause, and the Affection of the whole World.[21]

Here civility, couched in terms of the acquisition of material goods, is defined by the author as "disposition," or rather the ability to represent oneself as civil through the nature of one's actions. It does not, and indeed cannot, refer to essence, for "that which is decent and commendable in one

Nation is ridiculous in another." Rather, it serves as an "ornament" to "Prudence and Learning" that is inherently hypocritical in some sense because it can only function at the level of representation. Yet ultimately it is that ornament which defines the cultural value of its owner, enabling the individual to be esteemed by others and thus increasing the value of his or her initial "acquisition."[22] Even in theories of gentility, supposedly the very antithesis of market interests, the language of investment and its social function are not deeply buried but rather lurk immediately below the surface, oddly echoing Mandeville's notions of the social value of hypocrisy.

In the political sphere, moreover, the notion that representation had the ability to create social value and thus to make that which is inherently worthless contribute to both personal and national prosperity offered a viable alternative to the seemingly destructive polemical battles that Swift had demonized in *Tale of a Tub*, in part by refiguring political interest in the terms of seemingly more flexible discourses of economy and behavior. Both the political fence-sitting characteristic of so-called trimmers and Occasional Conformity—each a kind of hypocrisy as Mandeville defines it—were lauded by supporters as the only means of avoiding the inevitably tyrannical results of entrenched opposition predicted by the author of *Awake Sampson.* Even though many opponents of these practices regarded Occasional Conformists and trimmers as purely self-interested and desirous only of increasing their own financial worth—one pamphlet of the period, for example, defined trimming as "preferring men of opposite parties and principles, and so keeping fair with both, for Private interest, without regard to the publick Safety"—others saw the deliberate misrepresentation of one's own beliefs for the purpose of increasing one's political and economic value as both necessary and productive to society as a whole, thereby serving the national interest.[23] Thus the author of one pamphlet insisted, "I must needs say, I know none but the poor Trimmer, that can plead not guilty to [the] Indictment [of causing civil chaos]; tho' he has been represented, as one of the worst of Sinners, and snarl'd at on every side, whilst he has been Industriously endeavouring the good of all."[24] Likewise, the author of *Moderation a Virtue* argued that Occasional Conformists should be given the government positions they were denied on the grounds that *"peacable Dissenters* . . . are the Governments best Friends," and "that the imploying of Protestant Dissenters is in the Interest of the Church of *England*, and greatly tends to the strengthening of it."[25] Arguing that the trimmer's and the Occasional Conformist's ability to publicly represent themselves as other than what they truly or essentially are renders them not only serviceable to the national interest but more valuable than those who confuse their personal interests with the common good, these pieces offer in the form of hypocritical representation an essentially economic solution to an ostensibly political crisis.

Such arguments for the benefits of a social cohesion based upon the representation of value and the appeal to both self-interest and national interest thus seemingly solved many of the problems that the new Whigs in particular, along with others equally suspicious of absolute oppositions and polemical representation, saw in the more traditional rhetoric of prophecy and party that Mandeville for one so clearly rejects. Unlike prophetic discourse, which insisted that private sins provided ample justification for public judgments, a rhetoric of represented value deliberately divorced the public representation of self from purely personal beliefs and actions, thus enabling the peaceful coexistence of private transgression (the refusal to align personal principles with the laws of religion, party, or polite society) and obedience (represented compliance with public order). For Mandeville and many of his contemporaries the preservation of disobedience was not only unavoidable but the very foundation of a society seeking to free itself from the perceived threat of French tyranny, which was represented as inherent in Jacobitism and thus associated with the Stuart monarchy of the early Restoration. By deliberately equating the transgressive and the disobedient with the private sphere and then just as self-consciously positing a distinction between private and public—albeit one that was at best highly artificial—these writers seemingly advocated, even guaranteed, a kind of personal freedom while retaining, if not social hegemony, then at least social coherence.

Thus by its supporters, the practice of moderation, for example, was supposed to transcend the rigid and ultimately destructive letter of the law invoked by prophecy, grumbling, and the strict maintenance of absolute oppositions between Whig and Tory, Conformist and Dissenter. The author of *Moderation a Virtue*, accusing the Church of England of the "Appearance of *Zeal*"—that identifying scar of seventeenth-century fanatics—and "enslaving Designs," asserts that

> *Occasional Conformity* is not a *late Invention of crafty Men to get into Places*, but the Effect of *Christian* and *Catholick Principles*, which the *Moderate Dissenters* professed long before the *Corporation and Test Acts were made*. The practise was *antecedent* to the Laws, and therefore could not be *an Artifice* which the *Iniquity of Men had found out to elude 'em.*[26]

Seemingly offering a viable alternative to the absolute and intolerant laws that defined political and religious opposition, so-called moderation became an viable strategy by which order could be preserved. The private political and religious beliefs of trimmers and Nonconformists could, at least in theory, be thoroughly disloyal; that disloyalty, in its turn, rendered their public conformity an even more valuable act to both individual and state in an age of political negotiation. No longer represented as a material product with an essential lack of worth that would eventually both betray and punish in an increasingly powerful market economy, the act of disobedience, duplicity, and even sin itself came to be valued instead, in a kind of pre-Keynesian economic theory of supply and demand, at the price that the buyer (society itself) was willing to pay—a price that was sustained and even inflated by a process of representation that was, and was understood to be, transgressive, misrepresentative, and purposely misleading.

Thus reconceiving society as a market system bound and ordered by represented values and economic exchange seemed in part to offer a viable means of effecting the reconsolidation of authority that Whig politicians so desired without insisting upon the absolute hegemony or overdetermination that they feared. And yet, somewhat ironically, Mandeville's *Fable* does not simply accept value as a means of escaping the rigid dialectic between obedience and opposition, order and transgression. For ultimately that text recognizes, quite explicitly in fact, that the marketplace is not free from its own form of law, and even its own manifestation of tyranny; nor does the productive coexistence of transgression and obedience necessarily render political, religious, cultural, or even rhetorical absolutism impossible.

Much they are in *Mac Flecknoe*, the transgressive, the vicious, the grotesquely material, and the marketplace—all interrelated in *The Fable of the Bees* by a series of interlocking metaphors—are ubiquitous in Mandeville's text. The very preface opens with an "Anatomy of dead Carcases" that is quickly metonymized into an analysis of social, cultural, and economic order. And while Mandeville, unlike Dryden, does not shy away from embracing the material at every turn, like Dryden his concern is with law and regulation—that which imposes order on material chaos. From the very beginning of the *Fable*, Mandeville's forensic interest in both literal and metaphoric bodies is not merely with the material that comprises them, but with the laws that govern circulation—the circulation of blood, the circulation of capital, and ultimately the movement and effects of power itself. The initial lines of the *Fable* assert that

> Laws and Government are to the Political Bodies of Civil Societies, what the Vital Spirits and Life itself are to the Natural Bodies of Animated Creatures; and as those that study the Anatomy of Dead Carcases may see, . . . the chief Organs and nicest Springs more immediately required to continue the Motion of our Machine, are not the hard Bones, strong Muscles

> and Nerves, nor the smooth white skin that so beautifully covers them, but small trifling Films and little Pipes that are either over-look't, or else seem inconsiderable to Vulgar Eyes. (*FB,* 1.3)

Here the private self, the transgressive, and the material signifier are quite literally the body itself: the bones, the organs, the muscles and nerves, and the "small trifling Films and little Pipes" that comprise for Mandeville the human anatomy. Physician that he is, he is only too aware of the extent to which material substance without law, like the body without life, becomes merely a dead carcass, worthless, meaningless, inanimate, and even, at its worst, corrupting and contagious, spreading disease and disorder. And thus although Mandeville understands that material is vitally necessary to meaning—neither life nor law being capable of functioning in the absence of the gross material that literally informs it—he is also continually conscious of the power of value judgments, as he begins to develop a theory of the way in which social values are imposed through a cultural economy.

Acknowledging that the transgressive, the disobedient, the immoral, and the material are not merely social but also aesthetic issues—spheres of discourse invariably intertwined in a society that understood hegemony to depend upon representation—*The Fable* repeatedly attempts to explain the process of representative valuation by which the dross of society is rendered both useful and valuable. In "The Origin of Moral Virtue," Mandeville explains that mankind is made tractable and encouraged to follow social regulations not out of any fear of force or bodily harm, but rather because lawgivers have carefully divided them into two sorts of people—namely, the right and the wrong, the good and the bad, the sheep and the goats. It "is impossible," he says, "by Force alone to make [man] tractable," and therefore the makers of society "began to instruct [mankind] in the Notions of Honour and Shame" through a process of what Mandeville calls "emulation."

> To introduce, moreover, an Emulation amongst Men, they divided the whole Species into two Classes, vastly differing from one another: The one consisted of abject, low-minded people, that always hunting after immediate enjoyment, were wholly incapable of Self-Denial, and without regard to the good of others, had no higher aim than their private Advantage. . . . These vile grov'ling Wretches, they said, were the Dross of their Kind, and having only the Shape of Men, differ'd from Brutes in nothing but their outward Figure. But the other Class was made up of lofty, high-spirited Creatures, that free from sordid Selfishness, esteem'd the Improvements of the Mind to be their fairest Possessions; and setting a true value upon themselves, took no delight but in embellishing that Part in which their

> Excellency consisted; such as despising whatever they had in common with irrational Creatures, opposed by the Help of Reason their most violent Inclinations; and making continual War with themselves to promote the Peace of others, aim'd at no less than the Publick Welfare and the Conquest of their own Passion. (*FB*, 1.43)

In this passage, the law that gives life and force to the body politic, making its subjects tractable, is not a division based on essential quality, nor does it seek to forcibly exclude mankind's worst qualities; rather it depicts an entirely relativist structure created by a process of representation that itself serves as the origin of quality or value and so creates a social order based upon that textual economy, while it depends, as Mandeville later suggests, upon the very worst of man's emotions—pride—for its effectiveness. According to this description, both order and hierarchy are established and maintained by essentially misleading depictions of human nature that establish difference and distinction where in essence there is none, fraudulently dividing the "vile, grov'ling Wretches" from the "lofty, high-spirited Creatures" who form the basis of an orderly society, and setting a higher value upon the latter in order to encourage all men to represent themselves as virtuous and public-minded. Thus locating the very basis of social order and stability in the creation of artificial differences and the represented manufacture of social value itself, Mandeville suggests that it is the power of representation to establish an economy of behavior that allows society to function on a daily basis.

And yet in many ways the relativism of these standards of behavior, even as they seemingly enable and encourage the duplicity that was central to Whiggish notions of social order, actually create an understanding of the interpretive process that closely recapitulates the relationship between text and social order established by the self-proclaimed radical prophecy of the mid-seventeenth century, that other form of judgment present in the *Fable*. Behavior itself becomes a literal representation of the very form of cultural dominance that Dryden had feared and fought in *Mac Flecknoe*—an absolutism born only of the values of the marketplace. Children—omnipresent in the *Fable*, representing both a state of malleable immaturity and the psychological naïveté that renders all humans from infant to adult manipulable and hence controllable—are continually represented undergoing a process of education that ironically duplicates, in many ways, the rhetorical strategies of the prophetic texts that *The Grumbling Hive* so emphatically shuns. Both education and art (by which he means the learned artifice that defines polite society) become for Mandeville forms of law and judgment, reiterating rather than abandoning the terms of prophecy. The reader—

in this case the individual undergoing the process of education (fulfillment of the law) that the previous passage describes—is offered, as in radical prophecy, a choice of action, behavior, and self-representation that potentially enables the creation of stable social bonds. Much as the seventeenth-century prophetic text had forced the choice between salvation and destruction, Mandeville's governors force the reader to identify with one of two possible social and behavioral fates, and because social value is defined as the product of representation and the values of various representations are not truly relative but rather predetermined by unwritten, but powerful and arbitrary cultural standards, the reader who chooses badly is as surely condemned to destruction in the eyes of society as any civil war recalcitrant. Indeed, according to Mandeville so powerful and so uncontrollable is the force of human emotions, particularly the pride to which this process appeals, that the reader may not have the ability to make the wrong choice, and thus text (as a process of social and cultural education) has, as it had for the prophets, an absolute efficacy—an unrestrained capacity to enact both the cultural standards and the social order that it depicts. In a society based essentially on commercial relations, the continued presence of the irreconcilably disruptive and destructive power of human emotion merely feeds a new form of tyranny based not on force but on the manipulation of human psychology. Relativism and arbitrary judgment are in fact intertwined in a society whose institutions are built upon commerce and the public determination of cultural value, and thus, as Mandeville himself maintains in the *Fable*, it is not force or military power, but "what men have learned from their infancy [that] enslaves them" (*FB*, 1.330).

For Mandeville, in fact, the rhetorical efficacy of text, as a form of representation, lies entirely in this ability to reconcile transgression and absolutism without conflating them. In his analysis of the writing of Richard Steele, presumably a reference to the *Tatler* and *Spectator* papers to which he himself was a frequent contributor, Mandeville analogizes the efficacy of Steele's work in terms of the very behavioral instruction effected by the separation of mankind into two classes—one heavily praised, the other brutally derided. "When the Incomparable Sir *Richard Steele*," he explains,

> in the usual Elegance of his easy Style, dwells on the Praises of his sublime Species, and with all the Embellishments of Rhetoric sets forth the Excellency of Human Nature, it is impossible not to be charm'd with his happy Turns of Thought, and the Politeness of his Expressions. But tho' I have been often moved by the Force of his Eloquence, and ready to swallow the ingenious Sophistry with Pleasure, yet I could never be so serious, but

> reflecting on his artful Encomiums I thought on the Tricks made use of by the Women that would teach Children to be mannerly. When an aukward Girl, before she can either Speak or Go, begins after many Intreaties to make the first rude Essays of Curt'sying, the Nurse falls in an ecstacy of Praise; *There's a delicate Curt'sy! O fine Miss! There's a pretty Lady! Mama! Miss can make a better Curt'sy than her Sister* Molly! . . . These extravagent Praises would by anyone, above the Capacity of an Infant, be call'd fulsome Flatteries, and, if you will, abominable Lies, yet Experience teaches us that by the help of such gross Encomiums, young Misses will be brought to make pretty Curt'sies, and behave themselves womanly much sooner, and with less trouble, than they would without them. (*FB*, 1.53–54)

Here Mandeville compares Steele's text to an artificial representation created by parents and nursemaids—a representation that, however false, will inevitably create the real world ("Miss") in its image because of the infallibly mechanical nature of a human pride that inevitably seeks to increase the individual's social value. Steele's ability to enact cultural change and create a polite English nation thus inheres in his capacity to represent relative cultural standards as locally absolute and socially valuable, a process that he encodes within the text itself as he rewards mankind with praise for virtues that, according to Mandeville, they do not possess. In the face of its own emotions, mankind is powerless to resist, and thus the text is ultimately able to produce the society that it envisions.

Even the textual strategies that Mandeville adopts within the *Fable* suggest his sense that in a world where representation fosters cohesion by creating value, both text and the set of cultural standards that it represents offer a new manifestation of absolute authority. Truth, or textual authority, operates for Mandeville in a way that suggests this new understanding of textual absolutism. Unlike the works of Butler and Dryden, who were preaching to the converted and assuming the complicity of their audience in the satiric vision of the world that they created, Mandeville's *Fable* is predicated on rhetorical opposition. It assumes from its opening lines a reader who will either "wilfully or ignorantly [mistake] the Design" or "think it Criminal to suppose a necessity of Vice in any case whatever," continually ventriloquizing the voice of dissension and going out of its way to create the appearance of a controversy that did not, in actuality, erupt until after the publication of the 1721 edition, which contained the "Essay on Charity, and Charity-schools." The *Fable* has a certain dialogic quality throughout, and the second volume, published in 1723, was formatted as an extended conversation.[27] Constantly recovering rather than banishing the gross material of both human body and human nature, which, as he suggests in his opening paragraph, are always closely allied, Mandeville consistently makes a place for the disruptive and the impolite.

And yet, ironically, it is the *Fable,* far more than *Hudibras* or *Mac Flecknoe,* that assumes for itself the status of truth, based upon a fiction of scientific observation and an appeal to the supposedly objective language of anatomy. Literalizing on the very first page the metaphor of the body politic, and thus assuming that its language is medical and empirical rather than philosophical or metaphysical, Mandeville's text ultimately refuses to concede that truth is open for negotiation. And thus the same grotesque realism that in Dryden's text seemed to represent the transgressive and destructive influence of the material word becomes for Mandeville a source of absolute authority. His famous image of a sow devouring an infant is neither disruptive of his argument nor contrary to his professed aesthetic principles, nor is it dangerously duplicitous, as it would undoubtedly have been for Dryden. Rather, the incontrovertible nature of both the image and the horror it evokes offer for Mandeville a form of objective or scientific proof that gives value to his argument. Both image and emotion are real, as Mandeville defines them, and thus incontrovertibly linked by a psychology guaranteed effective because it has been reduced to an infallible mechanical process.

Likewise, the process of interpretation and the building of interpretive communities that the *Fable* in its entirety represents accentuate the sense of textual authoritarianism as they replicate the very process of education, of teaching value, that forms its subject. Because it assumes, perhaps more than any other text of its day, both the reality and the utility of the material image, Mandeville's text forces its reader through the very same process of indoctrination that it describes, not only thereby producing—at least in theory—the coherent society that it seeks to explain but also determining or setting its own value as a philosophical treatise in the process. As the sow's "filthy Snout [digs] in the yet living Entrails" of the infant and "[sucks] up the smoking Blood," Mandeville assumes in the reader the same set of emotional responses that he locates in the observer of this horror, thus creating a kind of affective community, albeit one based not on altruistic and disinterested love of others, but rather on a pity born of personal discomfort and self-interest; the reader's own uneasiness, in turn, becomes a proof of the very philosophical argument for the self-interestedness of pity that Mandeville seeks to make. The grotesque material image thus becomes both the means by which we are intended to evaluate Mandeville's text—that is to say, the means by which Mandeville asserts and creates the authority of his text—and subsequently valuable in its own right.

In fact, by repeatedly explicating his own explications, simultaneously performing as it were the functions of author, commentator, and critic, Mandeville—always conscious of his complicity and his place in an economically organized society—offers a kind of valuation of his own philosophical pronouncements analogous to the developing practice of literary commentary that was itself becoming a marketable if much abused occupation during the period. *The Fable of the Bees*, in its 1714 and 1721 editions, was a complicated series of texts spawned by the original poem in the sense that each offered in its own way a form of commentary upon the understanding of social formation and social hegemony inherent in *The Grumbling Hive;* it is not itself a fable but rather is about the original fable that forms the nucleus of the work, repeatedly reenacting the moment of social and artistic creation and thus reestablishing the very sense of interpretive community that fable and the rejection of the prophetic mode had seemed to decry. If the moral of *The Grumbling Hive* leaves the reader with a choice between pastoral honesty and vicious prosperity, frequent assertions to the effect that "the laziest and most inactive, the profligate and most mischievous are all forc'd to do something for the common good" (*FB,* 1.86) implicitly define (and thus in a sense create) the common good as financial prosperity and social order as those interactions that contribute to it, insidiously insisting upon an overdetermined interpretation of the original fable. Likewise, both "The Origin of Moral Virtue" and "A Search into the Nature of Society" recreate the moment at which man is made sociable and thus capable of entering into orderly social relations. The emphasis of both upon vice and "Evil both Natural and Moral" as the primary ingredient in "a Populous, Rich and Flourishing Nation" (*FB,* 1.325) offer commentary upon *The Grumbling Hive* by recreating through the process of interpretation the powerful community that the bees themselves had lost because of their inability to reach consensus on the nature of national interest.

Yet in the end, to point to Mandeville's vision of a society in which transgression and disobedience coexist with absolutist orders of conduct is not to suggest that he was in any sense duplicitous or hypocritical. For Timothy Dykstal the double vision implicit in Mandeville's ability to balance transgression with arbitrary authority, relativism with absolutism, or, as he puts it, "the interested motives behind the conversations that drive the emerging capitalist order" with "an Enlightenment ideal of disinterestedness," represents a kind of fatal inconsistency and a blindness to his own personal complicity in an invariably self-interested society.[28] Yet for Mandeville these seeming dialectics were hardly inconsistent, but rather necessary contradictions for a political society that increasingly defined itself in economic terms, the inevitable price of simultaneously elevating freedom and order. Mandeville himself seems relatively untroubled by the notion of economic absolutism; both his "Essay on Charity and Charity-Schools" and his *Modest Defense of Public Stews*—parts of which are echoed in "Remark H" of the *Fable*—represent a fairly frank recognition that defining culture in economic terms merely creates new systems of hierarchies and exclusions. Yet his open recognition that the laws of the marketplace were in many ways as tyrannical as the political systems they sought to replace was one that writers who followed him could simply not ignore. And thus it was Alexander Pope, some ten years later, who depicted in its full horror the nightmare vision of cultural economy and cultural empire implicit in Mandeville's vision.

# 6

# A Taste for Spectacle: The Ambivalence of Satiric Judgment in Pope's *Dunciad*

By the late 1720s, that commercialization of English political and aesthetic culture that Dryden had feared and Mandeville had viewed simply as an incontrovertible reality was in imminent danger of being taken for granted. England had survived the South Sea Bubble, and although that disaster precipitated negative commentary and some changes in the most extravagant of speculative practices, in the long run it also proved that the nation was capable of withstanding the tribulations of capitalist investment while continuing to grow inexorably into a colonial power.[1] The ascendancy of Whig government under thc leadership of Robert Walpole, associated by his contemporaries with (often the grossest and most corrupt of) trading interests, refigured British politics in contemporary texts as a semilegitimate business venture—a metaphor that culminated in the 1730s with Gay's *Beggar's Opera*. At the same time, the emergence of men like Edmund Curll, Bernard Lintot, and John Rich not only as successful businessmen but also as powerful influences on the process and nature of artistic production ensured that aesthetic principles and commercial interests grew inextricably intertwined. Complaints about luxury continued in the form of concerns about effeminacy, emasculation, and the sapping of British strength, but they did so against the backdrop of a society that, if anything, increasing fetishized the material of culture and relished—both in print and action—the accessibility of an essentially middle-class cultural aesthetic whose defining characteristic was the fact that it was available for sale in print shops, from booksellers, and most publicly at the theater. The powerful theatrical and political spectacle once represented by the coronation of Charles II, with all of its implications for the nature of power and the role of representation in the maintenance of government, was now for sale, as all but the poorest were aware.

Among the writers most deeply implicated in the concerns and choices faced by the writers of the 1720s was Alexander Pope. In many ways, Pope's writings reveal a history of contradictory stances in his relations with English commercial culture, for while he frequently denigrated the work of those he regarded as hacks, he also turned a commercial press to his own advantage with his editions of Homer and Shakespeare; and while he repeatedly attacked conspicuous consumption as a sign of gauche taste and cultural illegitimacy, he perhaps did more than any other writer of the eighteenth century to sanctify the material possessions made possible by a nascent British imperialism.[2] Pope, one might argue, both embraced and feared the changes being wrought in English culture, and thus his life and work offer interesting commentary on the fate of the commercialized cultural hegemony that Mandeville and others had envisioned.

Pope's *Dunciad*, in particular, has often been read as the culmination of an eighteenth-century satiric tradition—the epitome of a literary mode that values above all else the preservation of such neoclassical virtues as decorum, moderation, and judgment against those often explicitly commercial forces that threaten to overwhelm them. As a result, the poem has become a focal point not only for explorations of Augustan satire but also for studies of eighteenth-century attitudes toward the grotesque, the human body, and the Grub Street world that literally crams Pope's poem to overflowing, oozing its way into prologues, footnotes, and appendices.[3] Significantly, most critics treat not the three-book *Variorum*, which appeared in 1729 and stood as the text of *The Dunciad* for over a decade, but *The New Dunciad* printed in 1742, a date that for many conveniently marks the end of both Pope's own career and the Augustan age.[4]

Yet in many ways, the exemplary status that Pope's epic satire has achieved often tends to obscure the poem as much as it illuminates it, in part because of the insistence that *The Dunciad* be "typical" of the period both in its concern with Grub Street chaos and in the satiric stance that it assumes. Perhaps most at fault are the studies that, identifying Pope's frequent references to Dryden's *Mac Flecknoe*, treat *The Dunciad* as if it were a final revision of the fears about commercial print culture that had been expressed in the earlier poem.[5] But just as misleading may be those which tend to see *The Dunciad* as the highest expression of an early eighteenth-century fear of cultural anarchy. A number of recent critics have valued Pope's poem as representative of eighteenth-century confrontations over cultural space that aimed to set cultural standards and enforce cultural hegemony.[6] Too often, the effect of both these approaches is to render *The*

*Dunciad* an index of the critical judgments of the period without sensitivity to the genuinely ambivalent attitude towards commercial and material culture that the poem ultimately represents.

By any estimation, of course, *The Dunciad* (like *Mac Flecknoe* before it) is about writing, about the challenge of distinguishing good efforts from bad, and about the chaos—cultural, social, and even political—that can result from the failure to properly legislate the commercial production of text. The world of Pope's poem is a world turned upside down by the relentless propagation of the written word, infested by greedy booksellers and disreputable patrons, set at odds by the conflicts in and out of the theaters, and ultimately brought to (or at least prepared for) destruction by the very king/critic/playwright it elects as the earthly representative of dulness. And so too *The Dunciad* is a poem about both the ability and the right to pass judgment—to impose order on a world (not unlike early-eighteenth-century London) rendered anarchic by print culture. Concerned not only with the separation of literary goats from sheep, but also with the very process of criticism by which that distinction is established, Pope's satire repeatedly depicts moments at which errors in judgment contribute to the relentless erosion of order: the crowning of Theobald (Cibber), the public competitions of the second book, and the final benediction of the great goddess herself in the four book *Variorum* all enact public recognition of (the lack of) literary merit, and all effectively help to spread the influence of Dulness around the land.[7]

Yet whereas for Dryden the ability of human text to effect judgment and to organize social structures had lain in large part in the allusions to the prophetic voice that underlie and give form to that poem, *The Dunciad* ultimately rejects the vatic as a viable mechanism for translating human judgment into real social or cultural order. In *The Dunciad*, Settle is the prophet who attempts to call down judgment on a reprobate people;[8] he is in fact writer, king, and prophet, potential symbol of the authority to define the bounds of political and cultural hegemony and the predictor of the (grotesque) glories of empire to come. But unlike the Old Testament prophets, he can only predict, without any hope of being able to realize the nation he foresees. He is not a living monarch but a dead king, and as such is quite impotent to bring that empire to fruition. Describing future glories that he himself cannot achieve, he explains to his successor Theobald (Cibber in *The New Dunciad*) that "These, Fate reserv'd to grace thy reign divine, / Forseen by me, but ah! with-held from mine."[9] Expression of the law through the prophetic voice, in *The Dunciad* at least, is no longer sufficient to establish the necessary order (or disorder) of empire—that, it seems, has become for Pope the province of the succeeding playwright/critic—while even the law itself, in the person of Dulness, is revealed as corrupt and chaotic.

And thus it would be a mistake, I think, to speak of *The Dunciad* in the context of either Dryden's mock-epic or a more general early-eighteenth-century instinct for cultural preservation without acknowledging the reluctance—even inability—of Pope's poem to enforce the civil and cultural laws (or boundaries) that will contain chaos, either in the represented kingdom of Dulness or in the structural apparatus of its own text. In *Mac Flecknoe*, the preservation of social and cultural order, however precarious, had rested upon the public legislative efforts of the good poet/prophet/critic, capable of codifying the standards of good writing as well as punishing those who fail the letter of the law, thus implying the power of the poetic legislator to generate a strong nation in opposition to the filth and decay that emanates from the bad poet/ruler. Whereas *Mac Flecknoe*, however, seems always concerned with establishing and preserving the boundaries that shape cultural order and national prosperity, *The Dunciad* is more often occupied with representing the dissolution of even the most basic conceptual divides. Not only is the kingdom of Dulness a place where generous and talented writers are often seduced along with the mediocre and the inept, it is also a cultural chaos that defies the distinction between legislator and transgressor. When the scribbler can be judged only out of his own mouth, and the satiric act becomes, as Pope himself declares, an act of mercy ensuring both bread and fame to the Grub Street hack, the line between satiric text and depicted confusion begins to fade, and is eventually overrun by an ever-expanding textual apparatus that is at once a product of both Pope and dunce. The ultimate triumph of Dulness is, after all, the final judgment that paradoxically elides all boundaries, covering everything equally in its eternal obfuscatory fog.

It is with this annihilation in mind, I believe, that we need to reevaluate our assumptions, not perhaps about Pope's genuine desire both to assert standards of good writing and good criticism and to punish those who transgress, but about the connection he perceived between the satiric/prophetic act and cultural (or social) hegemony. In depicting the dissolution of culture in terms of both kingship and empire—even in alluding to the epic form itself—Pope was certainly conscious of the long literary association between maintaining standards of culture and building a strong, well-ordered nation. But in his willingness to forgo "the walls which fair Augusta bind," Pope, unlike his predecessor Dryden, seems able—perhaps from choice, perhaps out of necessity—to conceive of standards without order, and to judge (and even to punish) without expecting either to purge or to homogenize (*MF* 64). In particular, the doubts *The Dunciad* raises concerning the ability of any written word to define "the law," in conjunction with the poem's treatment of the difficulties of enforcing that law through public representations of judgment when representation itself has become a kind of negotiable commodity, suggests that Pope ultimately accepts, even as he laments, the real failure of the satiric act of judgment in the public sphere. In the first book of *The Dunciad*, after all, "Poetic Justice" lives with Dulness, discarding morals in favor of money in part because, as Mandeville had earlier claimed, law had come to be understood as a product of a commercialized order, not antithetical to it. And in the end, it is that tolerance for inefficacy in the context of early-eighteenth-century thought about the social, cultural, and political functions of judgment itself that ultimately leads *The Dunciad* to question both the capacity of the satirist to create a universally conceived order and the very desirability of maintaining a cultural empire.

I

Pope himself was no stranger to the language of prophecy, nor was he unwilling to assume the voice of the prophet at need. In a 1704 pamphlet entitled *God's Revenge Against Punning*, he had called for divine vengeance against false wit, while a later letter addressed to Edward Blount declared that "I really wish myself a prophet."[10] By 1720, however, such seeming presumptions were less in favor than ever, as many disturbed by prophetic claims to the ability to know or even to properly interpret the will of providence saw the proclaimed judgments of would-be prophets as impotent, and often as destructive of the very social and political order that such foretellings ostensibly sought to preserve. The incendiary activities of early-eighteenth-century Enthusiasts who claimed divine inspiration as justification for socially divisive rhetoric had helped in particular to foster a reaction against avowals of prophetic insight; even the least volatile assertions of an understanding of providence were viewed with skepticism and sometimes fear, and such debates continued well into the 1720s. Thus in *The Grounds and Rule both of Interpreting and of Trying the Interpretations of Extraordinary Events*, sometime fellow of Merton College Richard Meadowcourt acknowledges to his God that "Thy *Mercies* and Thy *Judgements* transcend the limits of our imperfect *Knowledge*." "No *Interpretations*," he argues, "by which *Particular Events* are declar'd to be *Mercies* or *Judgements*, can with *absolute Certainty* be depended on as true," and

> the Misery and Ruin of a whole *Nation* and *People*, has sometimes been owing to a *misinterpreted* Token of *divine Wrath* and a *mistaken* Apprehension and Sense of Judgements.
>
> Thus has the *Appearance* of a Comet prov'd *fatal* to *Kingdoms*; and *Armies* have been *routed* by an Eclypse of the Sun. Thus have *Seditions* been kindled by the *Flame* of an Exhalation; and the *Peace* of a *Government* has been *shock'd* by the *Explosion* of a Meteor. And *thus* in every Age and Country have the *rash Interpretations* of *particular Events* been attended with the most sinful and mischievous Effects.[11]

Other writings of the period—Henry Hetsell's defense of Bernard Mandeville's *Fable of the Bees* and Daniel Defoe's *Journal of the Plague Year* among them—proved equally leery of attempts to guarantee the effective execution of the Word (law) by reading providence, likewise citing the political and social chaos that could arise from interpretive dissent.[12]

Unwilling, however, to renounce entirely the power of the human judge to create order within the boundaries he defines (either by divine fiat or by the accurate reproduction of the divine will), other early-eighteenth-century writers generated alternatives to the model of translation offered by prophetic speech. One frequent solution was to reconceive the process of judging itself not as the act of interpretation that Meadowcourt decries (linking signs of divine displeasure with the appropriate transgressive act) but as the valuation with which Mandeville had played, albeit in a rather different form—assigning proper worth to human actions through commonly recognized representations in order to enable fair and honest exchange in the complex nexus of human interactions that comprise both culture and society. In a sermon preached before the Kingston Assizes in 1724, Nicholas Brady, a prominent Low Church minister, argued that virtue is inherently valuable while sin is "barren," "unfruitful," and "unprofitable," "since it only produces such things, as are either of no Use at all, or else of a pernicious and destructive Nature."[13] Faced with the representation of worthlessness in the spectacle of criminal trial and execution, moreover, the conscience of any spectator/transgressor will present his

> sins to him in their natural Deformity, and thereby fill him with Shame and Confusion of Face. . . . [He] will be convinced, how far he has descended from the Dignity of his Nature, how little he has answered the Ends of his Creation, how wofully he has impaired the divine image that was imprinted upon him.[14]

Revealing, and thus representing, the sins of known transgressors in civil trial will ultimately uncover the debasement of others and, at least by Brady's logic, effect their reformation. Thus, implicitly comparing the self-representation (itself conceived of as an artistic reproduction) generated by an individual's actions to a form of divine coining—bad actions deface and devalue man's natural social currency—Brady suggests that the purpose of human judgment is specifically to ensure the profitability of a nation's citizens by exposing the devaluation that their transgressions have metaphorically perpetrated upon them, while the act of judging itself becomes a matter of assigning value by enabling an accurate perception of the representation of transgression. In the absence of a belief in the ability of the prophet to transform divine law into social order, a faith in man's unremitting desire to maximize his profits ensures the maintenance of a stable and virtuous society.

While *The Dunciad*, on the other hand, seems generally uninterested in the language of civil trial—for all of the depicted acts of judgment in *The Dunciad* there are no criminal executions—it is also true that Pope rests his assessment of the public function of critical (literary) judgment precisely upon the metaphor of the courts. "Whoever publishes," he asserts in the "Letter to the Publisher" that precedes both *The Dunciad* and *The New Dunciad*, "puts himself on his tryal by his country" (*Dunciad*, 1729, p. 13). And for many in the early eighteenth century, explanations of the efficacy of critical judgment looked much like Brady's analysis of civil justice insofar as writers tended to see the ability of proper aesthetic judgment to order the world as a matter of exposing precisely the inherent worth of which Brady had spoken.[15] One 1725 pamphlet entitled *A Letter to my Lord ***** On The Present Diversions of the Town* argued, for example, that taste created social hierarchies through a process of valuation, much as Brady's public trial had done. "A Taste," the anonymous author claims

> is as sure a Distinction of a Gentleman, as his *Behavior*, and a much happier one than his Quality: This creates him Respect only among the lowest of Mankind, That commands it even from the highest. It is a proof of the Greatness of a Man's Wit, as well as his Soul, since it requires a Capacity to judge, and Generosity to judge with Candor: It scorns the low Entertainments of Narrow Minds, who are delighted with any thing that glitters; it enquires into the real merit of every thing, and values nothing without it.[16]

Here taste, compared explicitly to the behavior (human action) that for Brady had been both a kind of coinage and a form of capital, becomes the fundamental ordering principle of both nature and society. It gives meaning to the world at large, organizing the material (which in *The Dunciad* seems always to be getting in the way) by providing "things" with an appropriate and defining worth. In the process, it determines the value (social status) of the one who judges; he is ranked according to his ability to perceive properly. It separates the gentleman from "the lowest of Mankind" with a greater efficiency than the mere accident of birth, and also makes meaningful the finer distinctions among men of quality. At the same time, accurate judgment ensures not only social but spiritual stability, testifying to the worth of a man's soul as well as of his mind, and exercising an economy of charity in its inherent "generosity"—a generosity that both marks social distinctions and maintains healthy relations between groups and factions. Potentially divisive interpretations of providential law become unnecessary risks in a world that achieves order not by enforcing it, but merely, it seems, by perceiving it.

In *The Dunciad*, as well, the critical act repeatedly becomes a matter of perceiving and representing value (however erroneously), as booksellers vie for the products of authors fabricated by Dulness, and theaters thrive on the patronage of a misled nation. Yet for Pope, doggedly committed to a notion of intrinsic value that Mandeville had openly rejected, one of the greatest threats posed by Dulness is precisely her ability to falsify literary value. Dulness, in her very presence, is both obfuscatory and, at the same time, visually deceiving—masking, as had Brady's devil, the underlying deformities of hack productions. The kingdom of Dulness, the birthplace of bad writing and bad taste, is cloaked in mists as dark as the universal night that marks the end of the arts and the end of the poem. At the same time, the transgressions of Pope's Grub Street hacks are not merely blinding but actively deceptive, as Dulness herself, "the cloud-compelling Queen," transforms the grotesque population of her kingdom into something superficially more valuable. Surveying her realm,

> She, tinsel'd o'er in robes of varying hues,
> . . . . . . . . . . . . . . . . .
> Sees momentary monsters rise and fall,
> And with her own fool's colours gilds tham all.
>
> (*Dunciad*, 1729, bk. 1, ll. 79–82)

Not once but twice in the second book her obfuscatory influence takes the form of transforming hack writers into valuable authors sought by greedy, grasping booksellers anxious to make a profit. Moreover, much as the efficacy of judgment for both Brady and the author of *A Letter* lies in its status as an epistemologically privileged event—"[laying] open the cheats of that grand Deceiver [Satan]" that have "dress'd and set off [sin], with seeming Pleasure, Reputation, or Advantage"—in *The Dunciad*, as well, the satirist's (implicitly sound) critical judgment often proceeds by a logic of publicly exposing a transgression that conceals intrinsic value.[17] As Theobald burns his own volumes in book 1, the purifying and illuminating fire causes each work to betray its inherent flaws:

> The opening clouds disclose each work by turns,
> Now flames old Memnon, now Roderigo burns,
> In one quick flash see Proserpine expire,
> And last, his own cold Aeschylus took fire.
> (*Dunciad*, 1729, bk 1, ll. 207–10)

Likewise, Pope suggests the real value of the author created in order to inspire Curll and Lintot to race through a process of dissection, exposing to public view the gross and worthless materials of his interior: "[a] brain of feathers, and a heart of lead" (*Dunciad*, 1729, bk 2, l. 40). In much the same way, the diving competition of the second book metaphorically turns the competitors inside out, perpetrating their inner state upon their bodies, at the same time as the waste that covers them suggests the worthless, even destructive, nature of the polemic they produce.

And yet, as the cases of both the divers and Curll somewhat paradoxically suggest, *The Dunciad* seems also to display an ambivalence toward the representation of the grotesque as a revelation of the transgressive and the vicious that was the essence, as we have seen, of eighteenth-century conceptions of the translation of judgment into social and cultural boundaries. One of the perceived problems that *The Dunciad* represents, after all, is the emergence of the literary marketplace as a site that potentially confuses standards of value. The frequent Dulness-inspired misjudgments of patrons and booksellers, for instance, never allow the reader to forget that the effect of critical misjudgments born of self-interest and stupidity is a chaotic disjunction of the commercial value of the written product from its intrinsic worth. When in the second book Dulness creates her author out of air, encouraging the booksellers to race for the marketable prize, the joke, as it were, cuts two ways. In creating the figure, Dulness has implied that nothing (air) is worth something, while the blind eagerness of the booksellers leads them to appraise a little as a lot. The inevitable result is bemirement and confusion, as Curll is beshitten and the destructive reign of Theobald (Cibber) is legitimated.

At the same time, however, Pope does not represent such a confusion of values with the sole intent of attacking the commercialization of literature. Such attacks were routine and cliché by the 1720s, while Pope himself had few qualms about his own marketability; besides, it is just such an understanding of the poem that has frequently led us (often unfruitfully and sometimes unfairly) to employ it as an index rather than a rhetorically conscious text. Rather, problems of the perception of value in *The Dunciad* seem to raise even more fundamental questions about the nature of both the public representation of judgment and its audience—concepts crucial, as we have seen, to early-eighteenth-century theories of social order. Left—in the absence of the arbitrary authority that prophet and king potentially represent—to the whims of the public and the self-interest of critics, the spectacle of corruption (worthlessness) is all too often embraced within *The Dunciad* as a sign of divine blessing. The diving competition, after all, does not enact the judgment of the poet/king, but rather serves (like the epic games to which it alludes) to legitimate his rule. And in fact, the eighteenth-century political concerns with "pretence" to which Pope so often alludes both in *The Dunciad*'s apparatus and in his portrayal of the ambiguities of political succession suggest that many writers of the period appear equally anxious about the human capacity to determine intrinsic worth—to separate the judgment of transgression from the propagation of its image—in the absence of a defining reading of providential law. Nowhere, perhaps, were these anxieties about the public function of spectacle so energetically discussed as in literature about the theater—particularly the spectacle theater and harlequinade that figure so prominently in Pope's poem. For him, as for others, innovations in the early-eighteenth-century theater epitomized the problems of publicly "producing" or even properly representing inherent worth (thereby creating an ordered society) in the presence of an audience capable of judging more efficiently with their wallets than their eyes. And thus it is to the eighteenth-century theater that we now must turn.

## II

Much has been written about the use of the spectacle of judgment as a means of enforcing social hegemonies in early modern Europe since Michel Foucault famously argued that the public exhibition of execution helped to maintain order in eighteenth-century France. Carol Flynn, for one, has suggested that the satiric texts of Pope and Swift punish by rendering the bodies of their victims a kind of visual spectacle; they concretize the attacked, she claims, absorbing "hair and nail, spittle and blood" into the text, transforming them into a rhetorical enactment of physical punishment. At the same time, the theater, in particular, has become a focal point for those concerned with the role played by public representations in formulating both ideology and cultural identity in early modern England, as discussions of the staged representation of power have often suggested that those images served to reinforce existing political and social institutions.[18]

It is certainly true that the theater had served, and continued to serve, as an important locus for the public enactment of judgment in the seventeenth and early eighteenth centuries. For one thing, the theater was itself a recognized location for the realization/staging/enactment of social and providential order to the extent that it was a place capable of depicting both idealized societies and the legally and morally appropriate execution of judgment upon carefully staged villains. Thus, as we have seen, Thomas Rymer had argued the moral superiority of drama over history on the grounds that poetic justice is potentially more perfect and more instructive than the seeming vagaries of providence. Likewise, deliberately appealing to Rymer in his 1712 letter "To the *Spectator*, on Poetical Justice," John Dennis asserted that the

> Doctrine of Poetical Justice is not only founded in Reason and Nature, but is itself the Foundation of all the Rules, and ev'n of Tragedy itself. For what Tragedy can there be without a Fable? or what Fable without a Moral? or what Moral without poetical Justice? What Moral, where the Good and Bad are confounded by Destiny, and perish alike promiscuously?[19]

For Dennis, moreover, it is that concept of "poetical justice" which forms the very basis of social stability. Criticizing Addison's *Cato* on the grounds that it does not mete out an appropriate justice in its resolution, he complains that he

> cannot discern what knowledge Moral or Intellectual can be drawn from [the death of Cato]. The dire effects of Civil discord were known to all Mankind, long before *Cato* was writ; . . . As the Action of this Play is the Death of Cato, no Instruction but one of these Three can be possibly drawn from it. That a man of consummate Virtue, must expect to end unfortunately: Or that if a Man of an accomplish'd virtue, happens to be unfortunate, 'tis his duty to put an end to his Misfortunes by a Dose or a Dagger, or that if such a one presumes to resist the Invaders of his Country's Liberties he must expect to fall in the Attempt.[20]

For Dennis, as for Rymer before him, the only proper action of the stage is that which teaches moral behavior and thus ensures a strong and stable nation by representing the lessons of an idealized providence.

It is also clear from other sources that by the mid-1720s theater had become a forum for the public exercise of judgment not only upon the stage but also by the audience, and was perceived to effect social hierarchies merely by gauging the particular taste of the individual. Thus the same pamphlet that saw judgment as a means of exposing the true value of both judge and judged asserted that the ability to judge theatrical merit was perhaps the most important of all tastes:

> [S]ince one of the best Proofs a Man can give of his *Politeness*, is his Taste of these various Drawings of *Nature*, I am fearful lest we should, by our Neglect of them, degenerate into Ignorance and *Stupidity:* Besides, I have been long of your *Lordship's* opinion, that an *Elegance* in Thinking is one of the best Preservative's against the Corruption of our *Morals*.[21]

The proper (and popular) critical judgment of the theater had come to seem as much a means of maintaining social, cultural, and moral order as did the theatrical spectacle of the execution of judgment itself.

Yet somewhat paradoxically, it was in part this transference of the power of the theater to judge to the audience and to their ability to perceive theatrical merit that made the stage a particularly controversial example of the ambiguities of public judgment. By the 1720s many perceived that the status of the theater as a locus for the maintenance of social and cultural order had been severely compromised. Spectacle theater in particular, with its elaborate costuming, its special effects, and its rejection of moral in favor of visual display, seemed the darling of a corrupt public taste that was driven both by the natural banality of "the people" and the greed of theaters eager to lure such insipid audiences—at the expense of the theater's ability to represent the "poetical justice" that was so important to Rymer and Dennis. As early as the end of the seventeenth century, Dryden had argued that spectacle without moral (without, that is, either providential plan or instructive fable) was at best a form of idolatry:

> Thunder and Lightning now for Wit are play'd,
> And shortly Scenes in *Lapland* will be laid:
> Art Magic is for Poetry profess'd,
> And Cats and Dogs, and each obscener Beast
> To which *Aegyptian* Dotards once did bow,
> Upon our *English* Stage are worshipped now.[22]

The stage, which in *Mac Flecknoe* had been so crucial as a locus of judgment, when given over to spectacle becomes for Dryden an expression of heresy. "Wit" (the wit of spectacle theater), he claims, has become "the only Drug in all the Nation"; it numbs the judgment of the spectators even as it creates its own market by a logic of addiction. The enactment of judgment becomes an occasion for wonder, not at the terrible effects of divine retribution, but instead at the remarkable advances in special effects on the British stage: fires, explosions, contortionists, and celebratory dances in which gods and devils join in a kind of unintentional parody of universal harmony.

Thus as theatrical innovations proliferated in the early eighteenth century, so did attacks upon the theater's neglect of its perceived social and moral function. In 1724, for example, a pamphlet entitled *The British Stage: A Farce* parodied one of the most famous harlequinades of early-eighteenth-century London, Thurmond's *Harlequin Dr. Faustus*. The anonymous author, satirizing the spectacle of the day, presents a cast of unlikely characters for his own rewriting of the Faustus story:

> Here you've a Dragon, Windmill, and a Devil,
> A Doctor, Conjuror, all wond'rous civil;
> A Harlequin, and Puppets, Ghosts, and Fiends,
> And Raree-show to gain some actors ends.[23]

For this author, the entertainment (and commercial) value of the show has overwhelmed its moral obligations. Traditional categories and hierarchies are overturned as the devil, in *Dr. Faustus* the agent of divine retribution, is thrown in with dragons and windmills, and is remarked on not for his capacity to inspire terror, but for his civility, his ability to provide a "polite" entertainment.

Attacks upon the theater for moral degeneracy were of course no newer to the eighteenth-century than its perceived status as a place of public judgment. Parliament had closed the theaters during the English civil wars on ostensibly moral grounds, and complaints concerning the debauchery of the Restoration theater (and in particular Restoration actresses) had abounded at the end of the seventeenth century, not least in Jeremy Collier's *Short View of the English Stage*. Nor was the potential inefficacy of public spectacle confined to the stage; recent examinations of public execution in England have suggested that the commercial and popular concerns associated with such events made them less an exhortation to order and piety than an occasion for petty crime, public unrest, and the commercial exploitation of the body of the condemned—both before and after death.[24] Yet the theater (spectacle theater in particular, along with the harlequinades, pantomimes, and masquerades with which it was closely associated) did seem perhaps the most poignant example of the extent to which notions of judgment based on an economy of taste not only threatened the ability of the stage to establish social (even heroic) order, but also marked a new divergence between the representation of justice (as executed by the spectacle of judgment) and the ability of that spectacle to enact real social, political, or cultural order. For it was on the stage that the representation of transgression (as well as the transgressive representation) became most clearly a commodity, threatening the social efficacy of the very act of judgment that had quite literally produced it. If for Brady and the author of *A Letter* the act of judgment had been valuable for its ability to expose—and thus publicly represent—the inherent deformity and debasement of transgression, spectacle theater was itself a popular part of a market economy, setting value on the deformed and the grotesque at the whims of a viewing public willing to pay for contortionists and grotesqueries. Valuing the image as image, that is, rather than as the public disclosure of vice, the theater could actively undermine the very notion of the intrinsic worthlessness of sin that was so crucial to explanations of the efficacy of the public spectacle of judgment.

It is this fear that the public appetite for the vicious and grotesque would ultimately render the representations of public judgment meaningless that lies at the heart of *The British Stage*. In its very dramatis personae, the pamphlet suggests a certain perversion of "poetical justice." Among the masquerading actors are an owl (representing the stage) and an ass (the embodiment, the pamphlet tells us, of the taste of the town). Yet this satiric debasement is undercut as the pamphlet informs its reader that it is these characters that the audience wishes to see, not for the morals they offer, but for the novelty of the costumes. Moreover, in the course of the pamphlet/play, the devil gives Harlequin a wand that both endows him with the power to transform people and objects at will, much as Marlowe's Mephistopheles had granted Faustus the power of the occult, and makes him, the pamphlet suggests, a producer of harlequinades. Endowed with this new power, Harlequin changes the ass (that is, the town) into "a modish citizen, with Horns exalted on your Forehead"; to the owl he says, "be you no longer a Bird of Prey, but assume the fine gentleman," thus confusing and disguising (if only by half) the corrupted nature of these characters.[25] Reenacting a kind of pantomime and costuming that allowed the stage to represent "Puppets who were Men, and Men who were puppets" (Rich in particular was known for his ability to "turn himself into 'a wild Beast, a Bird, or a Serpent with a long Tail, and what not'"), Harlequin breaks down the distinctions between man and beast, honorable and corrupt, all the while suggesting that it is these obfuscating transformations which draw paying customers and best suit the public taste.[26]

Ultimately then, the suggestion of *The British Stage* is that the transformations that Harlequin irresponsibly renders, themselves his cardinal sins, create a spectacle theater akin to that of Thurmond and Rich, a spectacle that itself erodes the capacity of the theater to enforce natural and moral distinctions as it corrupts the ability of the audience to judge correctly. The original Faustus story, of course, does include a notion of poetic justice as both Faustus's bargain and his subsequent follies are punished in his eventual damnation, the fulfillment of his contract. In this pamphlet, however, that lesson too is lost. Taken by the sight of Harlequin's damnation, the ass (town judgment) merely adds to the confusion, conflating heaven and hell on stage: "Ha—ha—Entertainment upon Entertainment! How well the Gods and Devils agree!"[27] When the devil comes to take Harlequin, the ass (and by implication the audience) still does not fully grasp the moral of the story, throwing it off lightly in comparison to the "wonders" of the stage: "[T]his is a tragical ending—Sorrow we find is the Event of Mirth, and Punishment the Reward of unbounded Passions—But we are oblig'd to *Harlequin for the representation.*"[28] Even at the pamphlet's end, a satiric epilogue continues to hinder the sorting out of judgments, both on stage and in the audience, furthering the confusion caused by the play itself. It tells its reader,

> This play, tho' void of all the Comick Rules,
> The Men of Sense can please, as well as Fools;
> Applause hath found beyond all Drama's past,
> So true's our judgement, and so good our Taste.[29]

Here *The British Stage* ostensibly separates "the Men of Sense" from the "Fools" who seem to comprise most of the audience (readers) according to the same hierarchies defined by taste in *A Letter to My Lord* *******. But unlike *A Letter*, this pamphlet ultimately recombines them, undermining any faith that its own staging of the transgressive image might help to determine either social hierarchy or cultural order. According to this author, in the absence of a higher providence (a representable law), the stage can at best render potential anarchy among its viewing public.

Thus it was that the theaters themselves came to be associated even with explicitly economic and political division. In *The Touch-stone*, James Ralph describes well-publicized fights between the prima donnas of the British stage as "Civil Wars" fought because of "Thirst of Royal Sway" and "natural Love of Empire."[30] At the same time, Ralph uses the harlequinade as a metaphor for political deception. "The nimble *Arlequin*," he says:

> (who has his nose at every Man's Ear, and a Slap at every Man's Rump; who, like the *Camelion*, can change to any Colour, and with *Proteus* assumes all

> Shapes) by the dextrous Management of a simple wooden Stick, would readily point out to us a first M[iniste]r.[31]

The wand of Harlequin, so important in *The British Stage* as a sign of the theater's power to confuse transgression and judgment, becomes a symbol of both the moral and the sexual ambiguity seemingly necessary to political success. The result, it implies, is a political arena that favors, in the figures of Proteus and the color-changing chameleon, image over essence, and leads inevitably to deception and disorder. Even Heidegger, who had himself been accused of "[cooking] up an Entertainment call'd a Masquerade, where even the most refin'd Politics of the infernal Cabinet are reduc'd to practice," suggested that it might be best

> Like brave *Don Quixot*, to engage
> The darling *Windmill* of the Stage;
> Teach the *Beau Monde* to be less civil
> To their old Enemy the *Devil*.[32]

It is this attitude toward the potentially confusing, even divisive effects of spectacle upon social order, I would claim, that ultimately lies at the heart of Pope's *Dunciad*, informing that poem's understanding of both its own rhetorical strategies and culture itself.

## III

*The Dunciad*, admittedly, is not controlled by the metaphor of theater in the way that Dryden's *Mac Flecknoe* had been. In the earlier poem the London landscape is almost literally contained by the confines of the theater, while theater in *The Dunciad* is merely a part (albeit a crucial one) of a much larger panorama. Nevertheless, Pope's poem does point to the decay of poetic justice and audience judgment as a symbol of the failure of the spectacle of judgment in a world controlled by the commercial production of culture. In *The Dunciad* the perceived anarchy of the theater, as well as the resulting doubt about the theater's ability to serve as a stable locus for the execution of proper social or cultural judgment, exemplifies Pope's representation of the spectacle of transgression as a dangerously imprecise and shifting mode of signification—with serious implications for his understanding of the effects of satire upon both culture and society.

Under the sway of its playwright/critic/king, theater in *The Dunciad* serves as a represented site of public judgment. When Settle calls in a moment of lucidity for divine judgment upon the dunces, "one wide conflagration swallows all" in the pyrotechnic display that characterized eighteenth-century spectacle theater (*Dunciad*, 1729, bk. 3, l. 236). It is theater, too, that serves to expose. Rapt by the grotesque predictions of Settle, Theobald (Cibber) is assured that "each monster meets his likeness in thy mind" (*Dunciad*, 1729, bk. 3, l. 248); the playwright cannot help but stage the corruption of his own thought in his productions, thus holding it up to public view. And yet, in *The Dunciad*, it is theater that also invariably leads to chaos. When Settle calls for judgment, judgment immediately follows:

> All sudden, Gorgons hiss, and Dragons glare,
> And ten-horn'd fiends and Giants rush to war.
> Hell rises, Heav'n descends, and dance on Earth,
> Gods, imps, and monsters, music, rage, and mirth,
> A fire, a jig, a battle, and a ball,
> Till one wide Conflagration swallows all.
> (*Dunciad*, 1729, bk. 3, ll. 231–36)

Divine vengeance is presented as spectacle theater, relying, in the vision of apocalypse that it presents, upon the technical innovations of the eighteenth-century stage for its effect—the dancing, music, and pyrotechnics of this "wide conflagration"; judgment is (as in *The British Stage*) quite literally performed as a rewriting (or rehearsal) of the Harlequin Dr. Faustus. But like the spectacle of judgment in *The British Stage*, theatrical judgment in *The Dunciad* abandons the laws of providence in favor of the perversion of nature—both, it would seem, because this dead prophet lacks consistent vision and because the law (Dulness) is itself corrupt. And thus the new Jerusalem is just as hideous, if not more so, than the old:

> Thence a new world to Nature's laws unknown,
> Breaks out refulgent, with a heav'n its own:
> Another Cynthia her new journey runs,
> And other planets circle other suns:
> The forests dance, the rivers upward rise,
> Whales sport in woods, and dolphins in the skies,
> And last, to give the whole creation grace,
> Lo! one vast Egg produces human race.
> (*Dunciad*, 1729, bk. 3, ll. 237–44)

This new world, created (like the human race that inhabits it) in a birth so monstrous as to be ridiculous, defies the laws of physics and the laws of "Nature." Rivers run backwards, and trees are not only ambulatory but also well-trained in modern dance. The elements themselves are confused as whales and dolphins, creatures of the water, take to the earth and to the air. Thus Settle's theatrical moment of inspired judgment leads not to reformation but to greater confusion.

At the same time, it is theater that at once creates and destroys a culture/empire of Dulness in the Grub Street world. Responding to Theobald's delight at the horrors promised to his poetic reign, Settle portrays a theater that will literally "produce" imperial prosperity as it exposes the flaws of the bad playwright/king to public appraisal, building an empire whose strength relies on the commercial success of its stage domain:

> Son! what thou seek'st is in thee. Look and find
> Each monster meets his likeness in thy mind.
> Yet would'st thou more? In yonder cloud behold!
> Whose sarcenet skirts are edged with flamy gold,
> A matchless youth: His nod these worlds controuls,
> Wings the red Lightning, and the thunder rolls.
> Angel of Dulness, sent to scatter round
> Her magic charms o'er all unclassic ground:
> Yon Stars, yon suns, he rears at pleasure higher,
> Illumes their light, and sets their flames on fire.
> Immortal Rich! how calm he sits at ease
> Mid snows of paper, and fierce hail of pease;
> And proud his mistress' orders to perform,
> Rides in the whirlwind, and directs the storm.
> But lo! to dark encounter in mid air
> New wizards rise: here Booth, and Cibber there:
> Booth in his cloudy tabernacle shrin'd,
> On grinning dragons Cibber mounts the wind:
> Dire is the conflict, dismal is the din,
> Here shouts all Drury, there all Lincoln's-Inn;
> Contending Theaters our empire raise,
> Alike their labours and alike their praise.
>
> (*Dunciad*, 1729, bk 3, ll. 246–68)

Like the judgment of Settle, this myth of creation reveals the potential for the wizard/manager to quite literally bring a new world into being on the stage; unlike the vision of the earlier poet/prophet, the monsters of the playwright's mind seem to really be able to bring this to pass, as they eventually do in *The New Dunciad.* Yet here the theater over which Theobald will reign is marked not only by the chaotic effects of spectacle, perverting nature and portraying disorder upon the stage, but by the contention between the theaters for the all-important approval of the audience. As such, it is an empire founded on commercial warfare and the radical disjunction between popular and (what Pope suggests to be) intrinsic value—a realm defined not by order but by civil wars and factional division, not to mention a mess of paper and pease. As commercial product, theater cannot restrain disorder, but builds a divided society based upon both the illusory nature of the staged image and real political and economic strife.

In *The Dunciad*, moreover, it is precisely the theater's figurative appropriation of the ability to create not merely cultural but also political and economic (dis)orders—fulfilling the role of the impotent prophet that it effectively replaces—that ultimately seems to define for Pope the very real dangers of public spectacle. The theater is not, of course, as we have seen, the only ritualized spectacle of judgment in the poem: the coronation at the end of the first book, the public competitions of the second, and even the ritual procession that brings "the Smithfield Muses to the ear of Kings" all serve as essentially staged "popular" affirmations of public authority. But as a form of spectacle that openly recognizes its own status as representation, theater in *The Dunciad* does realize the latent potential of other forms of spectacle to become merely illusion and commodity as the judgment of the spectator may dictate—particularly when divine law itself is corrupt and inefficacious. Theobald is a bad king (because he is a bad poet) but he is nevertheless endorsed by a croaking nation blinded by the false display of monarchy perpetrated by the Goddess Dulness, while hopes of profit lead both the competitors and the spectators of the second book to misinterpret disgrace as a validation of skill and judgment. At the same time, in assuming for itself the ability to stage (and thereby to destroy) not only culture but empire and the marketplace as well, theater becomes a place where all other errors in public judgment can be realized, and thus is promised to Theobald as the ultimate extent of his empire.

Representations of public judgment staged as spectacle rather than based in divine law or absolute prophetic authority tend to lead within *The Dunciad*, then, to a divided or anarchic society. *The Dunciad* does not, however, merely represent spectacles of judgment, moments at which sin and vice are put on public display to be rejected or endorsed at the will of an audience. Pope rather makes it clear that he conceives of his own poem as a form of public execution. "A Letter to the Publisher" justifies *The Dunciad* as an attempt to expose hidden vices untouched by law to public judgment; the obscurity of some of those attacked, Pope argues, "renders them more dangerous, as less thought of: Law can pass judgment only on open Facts, Morality alone can pass censure on Intentions of mischeif; so that for secret calumny, or the arrow flying in the dark, there is no publick punishment left but what a good writer inflicts" (*Dunciad*, 1729, p. 14). Thus he claims "it was an act of justice to detect the Authors . . . whose prostituted papers (for one or other Party, in the unhappy Divisions of their Country) have insulted the Fallen, the Friendless, the Exil'd, and the Dead" (*Dunciad*, 1729, p. 13). For him, the job of the satirist is to bring to justice those who have, under the cover of obscurity or anonymity, threatened to generate social and political chaos from their writings. And thus, much as the epic was understood to affect (and perhaps effect) both public judgment and social stability by authorizing (authoring) the power of both a ruler and his nation, dunciad is portrayed as "the greatest service [the poet] was capable (without much hurt or being slain) to render his dear country" because it will "dissuade the dull and punish the malicious" (*Dunciad*, 1729, p. 50). As a form of "publick punishment," it works to reject those things which threaten the people and institutions of the nation, and Theobald is thus, it seems, not the only one capable of staging empire.

Yet in conceiving of satire itself as a form of public judgment proceeding in the absence of any authoritative law—for "Law can pass judgement only on open Facts"—Pope ultimately suggests that satire, while it does punish, may of necessity ultimately contribute to social conflict rather than asserting some hegemonic national order. Somewhat ironically, given the claims that it makes for dunciad as a genre, *The Dunciad* takes as its motto a parody of Luke's account of the parable of the pounds ("Out of thine own mouth will I judge thee, wicked servant") with various implications. On the one hand, the allusion to the New Testament context suggests that the basis on which the transgressor will be judged is not the word of God or of his prophet, but of the sinner himself, condemned for his overly harsh judgment of others and exposed to justice by his own (however unintentional) representation of himself. The hacks of *The Dunciad*, then, are to be judged not according to absolute critical law, but by their own pronouncements, and hence, implicitly, their unwitting public exposure of their own transgressions. At the same time, in using that quotation Pope alludes to a well-known Jacobite pamphlet of 1719, *Ex Ore Te Teo Judico*, a piece that had been the cause of much public confusion and controversy because its satiric strategy of parodying Whig rhetoric had made it difficult to tell to which party the pamphlet belonged—an ambiguity that Pope himself adopts in the Scriblerian apparatus of the variorum editions of *The Dunciad*.[33] Even as the conflation of political and literary discourses within the poem suggests the public confusion to be wrought by the literary impostor (particularly in the second book), Pope himself deliberately ventriloquizes, allowing the dunce to speak the words that will condemn him but also suggesting that any act of public judgment may be the root of dissension and division, engaged as it is in the very partisanship that it decries. In the end, Pope himself laments the irony by which the only fame the hacks he attacks may ever really know will probably arise exclusively from their inclusion in *The Dunciad*.

It is with this in mind, I think, that we need to reexamine the claims of many critics for Pope as a kind of quintessential poet/aesthete of the eighteenth century—inevitably confining that which seeks to break the bounds of decorum within the confines of a polished couplet and rendering the grotesque transgressions of the Grub Street hacks "into the beauty of the line."[34] For just as *The Dunciad* seems invariably to recognize the essentially factious nature of satire, it also acknowledges the functional ambiguity of the satiric image, and ultimately admits the inability of that image to transcend the social chaos that, as Pope continually reminds us, has given it birth. Without the presence of law to give it meaning, the image of transgression in *The Dunciad*—that effect of which Brady was so confident—is always at the mercy of misguided public valuation and thus continually perverted from its rhetorical ends. *The Dunciad* repeatedly enacts moments when judgment is passed through the transformation of sin into object: in the contests of the second book, in particular, all participants are awarded prizes that in some ways epitomize their sins (for instance, the "Weekly Journals" of the mudslingers and the "China-Jordan" that Chetwood takes home). In some cases people themselves are turned in a sense into objects and made representative spectacles of transgression: Eliza Heywood and the tickled patron whose exposed genitals eventually decide the flattering contest both serve this function. And yet the wonder of *The Dunciad*—that element which makes it dunciad as Pope defines it in opposition to both the heroic and the tragic—is that these objects *are* prizes and not punishments, symbolically enacting the legitimation of the new king in their ritualized representation of approval. Likewise the hoarse croaking of the Grub Street nation becomes not a public exposure of their implicitly amphibian nature, but another step toward the establishment of the reign of Dulness. Subject to evaluation by the very public they are meant to satirize, the images of transgression become the culture that fuels the endless propagation that itself becomes a manifestation of the grotesque within the poem.

In that same vein, *The Dunciad* also, I think, suggests that as modern scholars we might want to examine very carefully the way the early eighteenth century understood the possibility or even desirability of building a rhetorical structure that would circumscribe and preserve the purity of culture or contain faction within a comfortable if monolithic social order. For Pope, at least, the punishment that the satirist inflicts is never represented as a process of assimilation; the great colonizer in the poem, after all, is Dulness herself with her "Universal Darkness," while rules have become as much a disease as the bad writing they seek to control. Nor is it a process of purging, for that Pope tells us is impossible. The propagation of text with the aid of both printing press and marketplace is too fast and too certain to be anything but an accepted fact, much like the other forms of social and political disorder that the poem also celebrates. In fact, if anything, *The Dunciad* consistently represents the need to maintain separation from the whole. Positioning itself not as an agent of culture but as its victim, Pope's text presents the final horror as the ultimate uniformity, as chaos and hegemony are conflated in the poem's final vision of apocalypse.

Such an analysis is not, I think, to infer that Pope in any way desired to validate the anonymous scribbling masses that he saw as the instruments of Dulness, or that he was unconscious of the effectiveness of self-representation. But it does, I think, suggest that by the 1720s culture itself could be perceived as an invasive anarchy of conflicting rules and standards that concealed the basic absence of any controlling law, and that in exposing what he perceived as the arbitrary nature of eighteenth-century taste, Pope thus ultimately rejects any notion of "culture" as it is conceived of in terms of power or institution. Perhaps in part because of his own social position, barriers in Pope's later poetry tend to be private—the doors of Twickenham rather than the walls of London—and they oftentimes unexpectedly divorce the act of writing from more social projects and institutions. Even *The Dunciad*'s claim to do its country service rests principally in its openly avowed role as a partisan response to personal attacks themselves spawned from private interest; although the dunces have "for several years past, . . . made free with the greatest Names in Church and State," *The Dunciad* is conceived only as a result of attacks upon the private bastion of Pope's "moral character" (*Dunciad*, 1729, p. 13). The most pressing danger, in fact, seems to be the private grudge surreptitiously raised to a universal principle, and in exposing that malicious elevation both in his attacks upon the dunces and in his explanation of his own motivations, Pope seeks not to create culture but to destroy the machinery that so relentlessly propagates it.

In 1729, the potential of that machine was but a vision for Pope, a potential future to be forestalled if not entirely exorcised. At the end of the *Dunciad Variorum* such nightmares fly away, banished for the moment by the blessed impotence of the outdated prophet. Yet perhaps the most poignant reminder of the inefficacy of satiric judgment as Pope understood it lies in the fact that by 1742 all the arts and sciences of the kingdom he creates together could not withstand the imperial and hegemonizing force of culture. The *New Dunciad*, in its final vision of everlasting chaos, evinces a fully matured skepticism about the power of both judgment and hegemony in the absence of the visible evidence of a more purely providential law. And while it is undoubtedly unfair to seize upon Pope as the exemplar of his age—to do so, in fact, would be merely to reduplicate the efforts of those who wish to enshrine him as the guardian of culture; and Mandeville, after all, was largely unaffected by the economic hegemony that so agitates Pope—it is difficult not to read into the progress of *The Dunciad* a disenchantment with the virtue of hegemony and a desire finally to leave behind the agonizing over printed polemic and public order that the civil wars had precipitated nearly a century before.

**Tailpiece: *The Bathos* by William Hogarth, 1764. The University of Chicago Library.**

# Tail-Piece: The Fate of Prophetic Hegemony

In 1764—more than twenty years after Pope finished *The New Dunciad*—William Hogarth completed his last work: *Tail-Piece: The Bathos*. In that engraving, Hogarth represents the death of Time. At the center of the piece a tortured, almost Blakean Chronos expires against a backdrop of ruined images; a broken hourglass and scythe lie by his side, and a withered tree partially blocks the dead sun god Apollo, whose chariot, linked to dead and dying horses, careens out of control across the sky. As the title of the print might suggest, moreover, the *Tail-Piece* does not simply indulge itself in the apocalyptic vision it represents. Inscribed "to the Dealers in Dark Pictures"—purveyors of a continental protogothicism—it also parodies the worn-out images of "The World's End," reducing them to symbols that are ultimately as material and as bathetic as the broken liquor bottle and brush that fill the picture's lower-right corner. "The World's End" has quite literally been reduced to a decayed sign through a visual pun that depicts a globe on fire painted on a tavern sign; meanwhile, the Fates serve as witnesses to the last legal testament of Time himself. Satirizing cultural atrocities to the last, Hogarth attacks the overeasy clichés of the continental painters with his own dark humor.

Yet if Hogarth attacks the use of imagery of apocalypse (or "the last judgment") by other painters, he also, it would seem, questions his own prior judgments upon others. Near the outstretched foot of the expiring Time burns one of his own engravings, entitled (with yet another visual pun) *The Times*. And it is here, perhaps, in this ambivalent self-parody that we can see Hogarth working out the anxiety about judgment, hegemony, and prophetic literature that so plagued Pope in the *Dunciad*. *The Times* (1762) is a plate whose aggressive satire is directed against the detractors of George III. Depicting (what else?) a fire, the picture represents factional attempts to fan flames that the king desperately seeks to suppress. Angry, in a sense, about its own inability to be another *Annus Mirabilis*, it threatens the complete destruction of the state by the fire (faction) that engulfs England and her allies; it has, in effect, become a radical prophetic statement. The fact that it is this very plate that is on fire in the *Tail-Piece* thus suggests a certain represented ambivalence toward Hogarth's own satiric project in the artist's final engraving as *Tail-Piece* depicts the prototypical—almost stereotypical—death of a genre. The prophetic rhetoric that played such a crucial part in the political polemic of the Restoration and early eighteenth century has finally, Hogarth suggests, outlived its usefulness.

To point to a mid-eighteenth-century loss of faith in both cataclysmic prophecy and, perhaps, hegemony—as both Pope and Hogarth seem to do—is not, of course, to imply the final failure of either, or to suggest that the link between the two was somehow limited to the brief historic moment that was Augustan England. The history of prophecy as a form of social commentary carries through the eighteenth century into the nineteenth and twentieth. Smart, Blake, Carlyle, and Byron, all anxious about the progress of their own societies, explore the range of prophecy as a genre and a discourse; and connections between the social ends of satiric rhetoric and the ambiguous nature of prophetic power inform the work of twentieth-century American and British satirists, Orwell and Huxley, West and Toole, among them. With a bill to declare a national day of fasting and prayer recently rejected in the United States Congress, the contemporary potency of the jeremiad impulse in particular provides a convenient reminder of the remarkable historical tenacity of a genre so often dismissed in academic circles as marginal and unworthy of serious attention.

And yet, as Hogarth's *Tail-Piece* accurately reminds us, the literary manifestation of the prophetic after 1750 was not the same as it had been during the Restoration and the first half of the eighteenth century. The cultural moment had changed, and with it the prophetic voice itself. Generic change is, after all, essentially a form of protean evolution—a shape shifting that responds to external pressures (political, ideological, and economic)—sometimes resulting in slow, almost imperceptibly incremental change, at other times leading to the seemingly radical disjunction that results from heightened environmental stress, and always interspersed with moments when particular cultural or discursive problems seem to come more clearly into focus than others around them before yielding once again to the pressure for change. Such was the fortune of prophetic rhetoric between 1650 and 1750. It was the trauma of the Restoration and the early eighteenth century, the vivid cultural memory of civil bloodshed, that provided the rather different pressure that distinguished the works of Butler, Dryden, Mandeville, and Pope from both earlier and later manifestations of the vatic. It set the prophetic mode apart during that period and made of it both a poignant symbol of political and cultural authoritarianism and a convenient locus for the expression of anxieties about social—cultural, religious, political, and economic—power. The particular mode of reading and writing that defined seventeenth-century radical prophecy, a mode of reading and understanding representation that inherently involved the related concerns of hegemony and authority, was in many ways unique, in its centrality if not in its essence, to the late seventeenth and early eighteenth centuries. So too, in many ways, was the authorial concern with writing culture—and with the creation of fictions about writing culture—enabled by both the structures and the failures of radical prophecy.

Yet ultimately, what is so remarkable about the prophetic adaptations of the Restoration and early eighteenth century—*Hudibras*, *Annus Mirabilis*, *Mac Flecknoe*, *The Fable of the Bees*, and *The Dunciad*—is not that they used prophecy to explore and discuss strategies for reconstructing authority in the wake of the civil wars, but that they did so in a way that made of culture a separate and potent sphere, no longer merely augmenting political power by presenting the signs of authority but rather positing itself as an alternative source of social institutions and social order. In their concern for articulating new theories of power (both political and authorial), Restoration royalists may have been driven by self-interest, may even in many ways have been disingenuous, open to claims that they sought to mask traditional power relations behind a discourse of negotiation and exchange. But if they did so, they did so partly in response to the unmistakable changes in the structure of power that the civil wars had wrought, and as they did so, they suggested in effect that all forms of order and hegemony are negotiated fictions. From the rusty sword of justice in *Hudibras* to the sinful authority of a penitent Charles II to the fatal ascendancy of Theobald, authority is false spectacle, a fiction of the opposition of order and transgression that ultimately relies upon its own insufficiency and the necessary willingness of an audience—inevitably itself a marketplace—to credit the represented economies that spectacle creates. And thus they themselves helped to reinforce the very changes they perceived. If, as Hobbes declared, the reputation of power is power itself, the representations of Restoration writers clearly fostered the very theories of power to which they saw themselves reacting.

In fact, ironically, for the period itself it was the emerging popularity of the fictional and essentially metaphoric nature of the economic representation of power that for many eventually left that fiction untenable, laid bare, useless, and even destructive. Forced to choose between, on the one hand, the absolute authority of an economy of culture that they themselves had created as a viable alternative to absolutist politics and, on the other, the necessary dissolution of the equation between hegemony and order, writers of the period were forced away from an increasingly useless model of prophetic efficacy and left to develop new strategies fitted to a world in which some feared the totalitarianism of culture as much as they did the divisive potential of civil conflict. Left to choose between the apocalyptic visions of Pope and Hogarth, on the one hand, and, on the other hand, the confining but comforting possibility of keeping one's own house in order (represented in part by the walls of Pope's own Twickenham), many opted to stay inside, recovering the Calvinist interiority always latent in the prophetic form but discarding the prophetic voice, at least temporarily, as a viable mechanism for ordering the outside world.

# Notes

## Introduction

1. Recent general studies of the literary impact of the civil wars on Restoration and early-eighteenth-century England include the collection of essays entitled *Literature and the English Civil War,* ed. Thomas Healy and Jonathan Sawday (Cambridge: Cambridge University Press, 1990); Nigel Smith, *Literature and Revolution in England, 1640–1660* (New Haven: Yale University Press, 1994); Steven Zwicker, *Lines of Authority: Politics and English Literary Culture, 1649–1689* (Ithaca, N.Y.: Cornell University Press, 1993); Richard Kroll, *The Material Word: Literate Culture in the Restoration and Early Eighteenth Century* (Baltimore: Johns Hopkins University Press, 1991); and Thomas Corns, *Uncloistered Virtue: English Political Literature, 1640–1660* (Oxford: Oxford University Press, 1992).

2. Barbara Lewalski, *Protestant Poetics and the Seventeenth-Century Religious Lyric* (Princeton: Princeton University Press, 1979), 4.

3. James Grantham Turner, *One Flesh: Paradisal Marriage and Sexual Relations in the Age of Milton* (Oxford: Clarendon Press, 1987), 81–95.

4. James Holstun, "Ranting at the New Historicism," *English Literary Renaissance* 19 (1989): 189–224; and idem, "Ehud's Dagger: Patronage, Tyrannicide, and *Killing No Murder,*" *Cultural Critique* 22 (1992): 99–142.

5. Phyllis Mack, *Visionary Women: Ecstatic Prophecy in Seventeenth-Century England* (Berkeley: University of California Press, 1992), 4, 94.

6. Clement Hawes, *Mania and Literary Style: The Rhetoric of Enthusiasm from the Ranters to Christopher Smart*, Cambridge Studies in Eighteenth-Century English Literature and Thought 29 (Cambridge: Cambridge University Press, 1996).

7. Hawes, *Mania and Literary Style,* 2.

8. James Holstun, *Ehud's Dagger: Class Struggle in the English Revolution* (New York: Verso Press, 2000), 12.

9. Christopher Hill, *The Experience of Defeat* (London: Faber and Faber, 1984).

10. Hawes, *Mania and Literary Style*, 129–229; Shaun Irlam, *Elations: The Poetics of Enthusiasm in Eighteenth-Century Britain* (Stanford, Calif.: Stanford University Press, 1999), 113–200.

11. Hawes, *Mania and Literary Style*, 102.

12. Hillel Schwartz, *The French Prophets: The History of a Millenarian Group in Eighteenth-Century England* (Berkeley: University of California Press, 1980).

13. *The Art of Lying and Rebelling, Taught by the Whigs* (London, 1713), 4.

14. This episode is described in J. Milton French, "George Wither in Prison," *PMLA* 45 (1930): 965.

15. N. H. Keeble, *The Literary Culture of Nonconformity in Later-Seventeenth-Century England* (Athens: University of Georgia Press, 1987), 22; Margaret Doody, *The Daring Muse: Augustan Poetry Reconsidered* (New York: Cambridge University Press, 1985), 30–56.

16. Lawrence Klein and Anthony La Vopa, introduction to *Enthusiasm and Enlightenment in Europe, 1650–1850*, ed. Lawrence Klein and Anthony La Vopa (San Marino, Calif.: Huntington Library, 1998), 5.

17. John Stachniewski, *The Persecutory Imagination: English Puritanism and the Literature of Religious Despair* (Oxford: Clarendon Press, 1991), 7.

18. Lawrence Stone refers to the English civil wars as "a major earthquake which brought crashing to the ground most of the key buildings of the old regime" ("The Results of the English Revolutions of the Seventeenth Century," in *Three British Revolutions: 1641, 1688, 1776*, ed. J. G. A. Pocock [Princeton: Princeton University Press, 1980], 24). Christopher Hill asserts that the wars resulted in a "new order" far more conducive to capitalism than that which had come before it ("A Bourgeois Revolution?" in Pocock, *Three British Revolutions*, 111).

19. See for example chapter 5, "The Monarchy and Parliament," in J. C. D. Clark, *Revolution and Rebellion: State and Society in England in the Seventeenth and Eighteenth Centuries* (Cambridge: Cambridge University Press, 1986), 68–91.

20. Peter Lake, of course, describes Elizabethan religious debate in *Anglicans and Puritans?: Presbyterian and English Conformist Thought from Whitgift to Hooker* (Boston: Unwin Hyman, 1988); he addressed the issue of religious polemic in the 1620s and 1630s at a 1996 NEH Institute seminar in Claremont, California. Samuel Pepys, *The Diary of Samuel Pepys*, ed. Robert Latham and William Matthews (Berkeley and Los Angeles: University of California Press, 1970), 1:38.

21. Sharon Achinstein, *Milton and the Revolutionary Reader* (Princeton: Princeton University Press, 1994), 9; Paula McDowell, *The Women of Grub Street: Press, Politics, and Gender in the London Literary Marketplace, 1678–1730* (Oxford: Clarendon Press, 1998), 9; David Norbrook, *Writing the English Republic: Poetry, Rhetoric, and Politics, 1627–1660* (Cambridge: Cambridge University Press, 1999), 13.

22. Achinstein, *Milton and the Revolutionary Reader*, 3, 12.

23. Michael Wilding, *Dragons Teeth: Literature in the English Revolution* (Oxford: Clarendon Press, 1987); Smith, *Literature and Revolution in England*, 1–19.

24. Norbrook, *Writing the English Republic*, 17–18.

25. Michael McKeon, *Politics and Poetry in Restoration England* (Cambridge: Harvard University Press, 1975), 47–78.

26. See part 3, "The Rhetoric of Resolution, 1659–1660," in Elizabeth Skerpan, *The Rhetoric of Politics in the English Revolution, 1642–1660* (Columbia: University of Missouri Press, 1992), 157–236.

27. Laura Knoppers, *Constructing Cromwell: Ceremony, Portrait, and Print, 1645–1661* (Cambridge: Cambridge University Press, 2000).

28. George Bishop, *The Last Trump. Or, One Warning more yet to the People of these Nations* (London, 1662), 12.

29. William Simpson, *From One who was Moved of the Lord God to go a Sign among the Priests and Professors of the Prophets* (London, 1659), 6.

30. Patrick Collinson, *The Religion of Protestants: The Church in English Society, 1559–1625* (Oxford: Clarendon Press, 1982), 268, 273; John Bossy, *The English Catholic Community* (New York: Oxford University Press, 1976), 108, 124.

31. Christopher Taylor, *The Whirlwind of the Lord Gone Forth* (1655), 11.

32. Martha Simmonds, *A Lamentation for the Lost Sheep of the House of Israel* (London, 1656), 2.

33. Works that I would consider particularly important and influential in that vein would be: Terry Castle, *Masquerade and Civilization: The Carnivalesque in Eighteenth-Century Culture and Fiction* (Stanford, Calif.: Stanford University Press, 1986); Carol Houlihan Flynn, *The Body in Swift and Defoe* (New York: Cambridge University Press, 1986); Ronald Paulson, *Breaking and Remaking: Aesthetic Practice in England, 1700–1820* (New Brunswick, N.J.; Rutgers University Press, 1989); and the first chapter of Paula Backscheider's *Spectacular Politics: Theatrical Power and Mass Culture in Early Modern England* (Baltimore: Johns Hopkins University Press, 1993).

34. Michel Foucault, *Discipline and Punish*, trans. Alan Sheridan (New York: Vintage Books, 1979).

35. *The Doleful Lamentation of Cheap-side Crosse* (1641), 1.

36. [Simon Ford], *Discourse Concerning God's Judgements* (1678); Nicholas Brady, *Sin Display'd in its Natural Deformity* (London, 1724).

37. Patrick Curry, in *Prophecy and Power: Astrology in Early Modern England* (Cambridge: Polity Press, 1989), has described the decline in astrological prophecy between 1660 and 1710 as part of a larger rejection of enthusiasm based upon political suspicions of radical religion and the increasing influence of natural philosophy institutionalized in the Royal Society; Margaret Jacob has likewise pointed to the "triumph" of the new science that replaced mechanical philosophy and the science of mid-century radicalism at the end of the seventeenth century (*The Newtonians and the English Revolution, 1689-1720* [Hassocks, U.K.: Harvester Press, 1976], 17). Iain Pears' *The Discovery of Painting* (New Haven: Yale University Press, 1988) suggests that the emergence of the concept of taste followed directly from a decline in the belief in providential logic and a desire for other forms of judgment.

38. Colin Nicholson, *Writing and the Rise of Finance: Capital Studies of the Early Eighteenth Century*, Cambridge Studies in Eighteenth-Century English Literature and Thought 21 (Cambridge: Cambridge University Press, 1994).

## Chapter 1. Polemic, Culture, and Conflict

1. Edward Burrough, *A Standard Lifted Up, and an Engine Held Forth, to all Nations* (London, 1657), 31–32.

2. Ibid., 14.

3. David Leverenz, *The Language of Puritan Feeling: An Exploration in Literature, Psychology, and Social History* (New Brunswick, N.J.: Rutgers University Press, 1980), 7.

4. McDowell, *Women of Grub Street*, 196.

5. Christopher Love, *England's Distemper, Having Division and Errour*, (London, 1651), 26.

6. John Phillips, *A Satyr Against Hypocrites*, (1655), 6–7.

7. Edmund Skipp, *The Worlds Wonder, Or the Quakers Blazing Starr* (London, 1655), title page.

8. Holstun, "Ehud's Dagger," 213.

9. Klein and La Vopa, introduction, 4.

10. See Keith Thomas, *Religion and the Decline of Magic* (London: Weidenfeld and Nicholson, 1971); Rupert Taylor, *The Political Prophecy in England* (New York: Columbia University Press, 1911); and Howard Dobin, *Merlin's Disciples: Prophecy, Poetry, and Power in Renaissance England* (Stanford, Calif.: Stanford University Press, 1990).

11. John Peter, *Complaint and Satire in Early English Literature* (Oxford: Clarendon Press, 1956).

12. Perry Miller, *The New England Mind: From Colony to Province* (Cambridge: Harvard University Press, 1953), 27–39; Sacvan Bercovitch, *The American Jeremiad* (Madison: University of Wisconsin Press, 1978). Donald Weber also discusses the jeremiad in America and its role in the rhetoric of the American Revolution in *Rhetoric and History in Revolutionary New England* (New York: Oxford University Press, 1988).

13. George Joye, *Jeremy the Prophet* ([Antwerp], 1534).

14. Ibid., A4r–v.

15. Henry Brinklow, *The Lamentacion of a Christian Against the Citie of London, made by R. Mors* (1542).

16. *Ieremiah Revived* (1648), 3.

17. Ibid., 3–4.

18. *The Doleful Lamentation of Cheap-side Crosse,* 2–3.

19. Ambrose Rigge, *The Good Old Way* ([London], 1669), 6.

20. William Simpson, *A Discovery of the Priests and Professors* (1660), 4.

21. A *Voyce Out of the Wildernes Crying* (London, 1651), A2r.

22. Perhaps the most sympathetic treatment of radical prophecy is R. A. Knox's *Enthusiasm: A Chapter in the History of Religion* (Oxford: Clarendon Press, 1950), which refers to the quaking and shaking and speaking in tongues associated with radical religion as puzzling abnormal phenomena (4). Jerome Friedman has less tolerantly called the Ranters of the mid-seventeenth century "class-conscious anarchists" (*Blasphemy, Immorality, and Anarchy: The Ranters and the English Revolution* [Athens: Ohio University Press, 1987], xi). Others have opted for theories of insanity; John Sena traces early accounts of the "madness" of radical Puritans in his essay "Melancholic Madness and the Puritans," *Harvard Theological Review* 66 (1973): 293–309.

23. Hawes, *Mania and Literary Style*, 82–83.

24. *An Alarme to England; or, A Warning Piece to the Inhabitants of Great Britain* (1657), 8.

25. *A Fannaticks Alarm, Given to the Mayor in his Quarters, By one of the Sons of Zion, become Boanerges, To Thunder out the Judgements of God against Oppression and Oppressors* (London, 1661), 4.

26. Nathanial Hardy, *A Sad Prognostick of Approaching Judgment* (London, 1658), 22–24.

27. Priscilla Cotton and Mary Cole, *To the Priests and People of England* (London, 1655), 2.

28. *Alarme to England*, 8.

29. Hester Biddle, *The Trumpet of the Lord Sounded forth unto these Three Nations* (London, 1662), 3.

30. Ambrose Rigge, *A Premonition to the Bishops and Priests* [London, 1676], 8.

31. Love, *England's Distemper*, 14, 28.

32. Edward Burrough, *A Trumpet of the Lord Sounded Out of Zion* (London, 1656), 2.

33. William Bayly, *A Warning from the Spirit of Truth* (1658), A2r–v.

34. McDowell, *Women of Grub Street*, 145.

35. Richard Bauman, *Let Your Words Be Few* (Cambridge: Cambridge University Press, 1983), 10.

36. Hawes, *Mania and Literary Style*, 90–93.

37. Simpson, *From One who was Moved,* title page.

38. Daniel Baker, *Yet One Warning More, To Thee O England* (1660), 1.

39. Ibid., 32.

40. Simpson, *From One who was Moved,* title page.

41. Ibid., 7.

42. Ibid., 3.

43. Ibid., 6.

44. Ambrose Rigge, *A Lamentation over England* (London, 1665), 1.

45. Ibid., 4.

46. Corns, *Uncloistered Virtue*, 190–93.

47. Abiezer Coppe, *A Fiery Flying Roll,* in *Selected Writings,* ed. Andrew Hopton (London: Aporia Press, 1987), 26.

48. Norbrook, *Writing the English Republic*, 13–14; James Holstun, *A Rational Millennium: Puritan Utopias of Seventeenth-Century England and America* (New York: Oxford University Press, 1987), 35–37.

49. *The Ranters Monster Being a True Relation of one Mary Adams, Living at Tillingham in Essex* (London, 1652), title page.

50. *The Joviall Crew, or The Devil Turnd Ranter: Being a Character of The Roaring Ranters of these Times* (London, 1651), 2.

51. William Prynne, *The Quakers Unmasked, and Clearly Detected,* 2d ed. (1655), 19.

52. Holstun, "Ehud's Dagger," 212. Turner has addressed some of the realities of radical religious libertinism in *One Flesh*, 81–87, while Leverenz has more generally noted in *The Language of Puritan Feeling*, 156, that erotic language was a long-standing and easily identifiable characteristic of radical Protestantism. The persistence of an erotic component in English radical Protestant thought and practice—and in attacks on radical religion—is apparent from Henry Abelard's study of the mid-eighteenth-century rise of Methodism, *Evangelist of Desire: John Wesley and the Methodists* (Stanford, Calif.: Stanford University Press, 1990).

53. Dennis Todd, *Imagining Monsters: Miscreations of the Self in Eighteenth-Century England* (Chicago: University of Chicago Press, 1995), 67–69.

54. Lois Potter, *Secret Rites and Secret Writing: Royalist Literature, 1641–1660* (New York: Cambridge University Press, 1989), 24.

55. Zwicker, *Lines of Authority,* 7.

56. John Steadman, *Milton and the Renaissance Hero* (Oxford: Clarendon Press, 1967).

57. Michael McKeon, *Origins of the English Novel, 1640–1740* (Baltimore: Johns Hopkins University Press, 1987), 48.

58. George Wither, *Vox Pacifica* (1645), 48.

59. David Johnston, *The Rhetoric of Leviathan* (Princeton: Princeton University Press, 1986).

60. Thomas Hobbes, *Leviathan,* ed. Michael Oakeshott (Oxford: Basil Blackwell, 1947), 56.

61. Ibid.

62. Phillips, *A Satyr Against Hypocrites,* 6–7.

63. Ibid., 21.

64. *The Ranters Monster,* 4.
65. Joseph Caryl, *Peters Patern* (1659), 6–7.
66. Doody, *Daring Muse*, 35.

## Chapter 2. Joining with Self-Interests

1. George Wasserman, "Carnival in *Hudibras,*" *ELH* 55 (1988): 79–87.
2. Samuel Butler, *Hudibras*, ed. John Wilders (Oxford: Clarendon Press, 1967), pt. 1, canto 1, ll. 245–50. All references to the poem will be to this edition, and will be cited in the text by part, canto, and line numbers.
3. John Wilders, introduction to ibid., xxxv.
4. Wasserman, "Carnival in *Hudibras,*" 82.
5. *The Lamentation of a Bad Market* (1660), title page
6. Ibid., 4–5.
7. *Bradshaw's Ghost*, 3d ed. (1659), 18.
8. *Lamentation of a Bad Market,* 7.
9. Frank Arthur Mumby, *Publishing and Bookselling: A History from the Earliest Times to the Present Day* (New York: R. R. Bowker Co., 1949), 105–6.
10. Samuel Butler, *Characters* (Cleveland, Ohio: The Press of Case Western Reserve University, 1970), 156.
11. *Bradshaw's Ghost,* 18.
12. Webster's articles on prophetic parody include "Swift's *Tale of a Tub* Compared with Earlier Satires of the Puritans," *PMLA* 47 (1932): 171–78; "Swift and Some Earlier Satirists of Puritan Enthusiasm," *PMLA* 48 (1933): 1141–53; and "The Satiric Background of the Attack on Puritans in Swift's *Tale of a Tub,*" *PMLA* 50 (1935): 210–23. More recently John Sena has continued this work in "Melancholic Madness and the Puritans."
13. *The Lamentable Complaints of Nick Froth the Tapster and Rulefrost the Cook* (London, 1641), 6.
14. *A Lamentation of the Ruling Lay-Elders* (1647), title page.
15. Ibid., 1–2.
16. Boris Thomashevsky, "Thematics," in *Russian Formalist Criticism: Four Essays*, ed. and trans. Lee T. Lemon and Marion J. Reis, Regents Critics Series (Lincoln: University of Nebraska Press, 1965), 95.
17. Ibid., 94.
18. *The Lamentation of a Sinner* (1659), 4.
19. Butler, *Characters,* 91.
20. Ben Jonson, *Every Man in His Humour*, ed. J. W. Lever, Regents Renaissance Drama Series (Lincoln: University of Nebraska Press, 1988), V.i.221–22.
21. John Dryden, "A Discourse Concerning the Original and Progress of Satire," in *Essays of John Dryden*, ed. W. P. Ker (New York: Russell and Russell, 1961), 2:52.
22. *Bradshaw's Ghost,* 4.

## Chapter 3. Interpreting Providence

1. David Ogg, *England in the Reign of Charles II* (Oxford: Clarendon Press, 1966), 199, 203–4.
2. Unfavorable accounts of the immorality of the Restoration court abounded, of course, from the early 1660s; Ronald Hutton describes some of the events leading to a

popular disgust with court behavior in *The Restoration: A Political and Religious History of England and Wales, 1658–1667* (Oxford: Clarendon Press, 1985), 185–90.

3. Edward Hyde, first earl of Clarendon, *The History of the Rebellion*, in *Clarendon: Selections from the History of the Rebellion and The Life by Himself*, ed. G. Huehns (New York: Oxford University Press, 1978), 424.

4. Michael McKeon's classic treatment of *Annus Mirabilis* suggests the importance of such emotive bonds in its treatment of paternal and familial metaphors in Dryden's poem (*Politics and Poetry in Restoration England,* particularly 47–78); Skerpan, *Rhetoric of Politics,* 171.

5. Cynthia Wall, *The Literary and Cultural Spaces of Restoration London* (Cambridge: Cambridge University Press, 1998), ix–x.

6. Readings of *Annus Mirabilis* are generally willing to view the poem as a fairly straightforward example of proroyalist propaganda; recent examples include James Winn, *John Dryden and his World* (New Haven: Yale University Press, 1987), 168–78; and Timothy Morton, "Trade Winds," *Essays and Studies* 49 (1996): 19–41. One notable recent exception is Paul Hammond's *John Dryden: A Literary Life* (New York: St. Martin's Press, 1991), 31–43.

7. Edward Waterhouse, *A Short Narrative of the Late Dreadful Fire* (1667), 2; John Allison, *Upon the Late Lamentable Fire in London* (1667), 3.

8. Richard Crane, *A Lamentation over thee, O London* (1665), 1.

9. Rigge, *A Lamentation Over England.*

10. J.G., *The Dreadful Burning of London* (London, 1667), 2.

11. Ibid., 3.

12. John Dryden, *Annus Mirabilis*, in vol. 1 of *The Works of John Dryden*, ed. H. T. Swedenberg et al. (Berkeley and Los Angeles: University of California Press, 1956), 98–99 (ll. 849, 860, 947–48). All further references to the poem will be to this edition and citations will be included in the text.

13. John Crouch, *Londonenses Lachrymae* (1666), 9.

14. *The Conflagration of London* (London, 1667), 32.

15. William Bayly, *The Dreadful and Terrible Day of the Lord God* (1665), 1.

16. *London's Remains* (London, 1667), 9.

17. Nathanial Hardy, *Lamentation, Mourning, and Woe* (London, 1666), 27.

18. *Conflagration of London,* 28–29.

19. Wiseman, *A Short and Serious Narrative of Londons Fatal Fire . . . A Poem. As Also Londons Lamentation to her Regardless Passengers* (London, 1667), 2.

20. This is an understanding of the theater that Dryden himself would promote two years later in his 1668 "Essay of Dramatic Poesy," though it is one that is perhaps most fully articulated slightly later in the 1677 publication of Thomas Rymer's "Tragedies of the Last Age"—particularly in Rymer's discussion of the relative merits of history and the stage.

21. Hardy, *Lamentation, Mourning, and Woe,* 2.

22. Wiseman, "London's Lamentation," in *A Short and Serious Narrative of Londons Fatal Fire,* 12.

23. Crouch, *Londonenses Lachrymae,* 3, 9.

24. *Conflagration of London,* 32.

25. Hardy, *Lamentation, Mourning, and Woe,* 28.

26. *Observations Both Historical and Moral Upon the Burning of London* (1667), 5–7.

27. Wiseman, *A Short and Serious Narrative,* 10.

28. Ibid., 10–11.
29. McKeon, *Politics and Poetry,* 47, 48.

## Chapter 4. "High on a Throne of his own Labours rear'd"

1. The most comprehensive biography of Shaftesbury is K. H. D. Haley's *The First Earl of Shaftesbury* (Oxford: Clarendon Press, 1968). In *The First Whigs: The Politics of the Exclusion Crisis* (London: Oxford University Press, 1970), J. R. Jones has traced Shaftesbury's role in the development of the Whig party.

2. Ogg, *England in the Reign of Charles II,* 610; *The Lamentation* (1679), broadside.

3. John Dryden, *Mac Flecknoe*, in vol. 2 of *Works of John Dryden*, ed. H. T. Swedenberg et al. (Berkeley and Los Angeles: University of California Press, 1972), 54–60 (l. 87). All further references to the poem will be to this edition with line references given in the text.

4. John Dryden, "A Discourse Concerning the Original and Progress of Satire," in *Essays of John Dryden*, ed. Ker, 57.

5. Doody, *Daring Muse,* 16; Michael Seidel, *Satiric Inheritance: Rabelais to Sterne* (Princeton: Princeton University Press, 1979), 148–49.

6. George McFadden, *Dryden: The Public Writer, 1660–1685* (Princeton: Princeton University Press, 1978), 19, 217–18.

7. Nigel Smith, *Perfection Proclaimed: Language and Literature in English Radical Religion, 1640–1660* (Oxford: Clarendon Press, 1989), 65.

8. [John Houghton], *Englands Great Happiness* (1677), A2r.

9. Ibid., 18; Bercovitch, *American Jeremiad,* xv, 11.

10. [Houghton], *Englands Great Happiness,* 3.

11. Laura Lunger Knoppers, "Milton's *The Readie and Easie Way* and the English Jeremiad," in *Politics, Poetics, and Hermeneutics in Milton's Prose*, ed. David Lewenstein and James Grantham Turner (New York: Cambridge University Press, 1990), 214.

12. John Spurr, "'Virtue, Religion, and Government': The Anglican Uses of Providence," in *The Politics of Religion in Restoration England*, ed. Tim Harris, Paul Seaward, and Mark Goldie (Oxford: Basil Blackwell, 1990), 29.

13. *Poems on Affairs of State* (London, 1716), 46.

14. See "Upon the Prorouging of Parliament" (48–49) and "The D. of B's Litany" (82) in ibid.

15. Robert Twisse, *England's Breath Stopp'd* (1665), 2.

16. Jean Baudrillard, *Simulations*, trans. Paul Foss, Paul Patton, and Philip Beitchman (New York: Semiotext(e), 1983).

17. [Robert Herrick], *Poor Robins Vision* (1667), 4.

18. Charles Blount, "The Epistle Dedicatory of *Religio Laici. Written in a letter to John Dryden,*" in *Dryden: The Critical Heritage*, ed. James Kinsley and Helen Kinsley (New York: Barnes & Noble, 1971), 161.

19. [Ford], *A Discourse Concerning God's Judgements*, 22.

20. Ibid., 36.

21. Thomas Rymer, "Tragedies of the Last Age," in *The Critical Works of Thomas Rymer*, ed. Curt A. Zimansky (New Haven: Yale University Press, 1956), 22.

22. William Davenant, "A Preface to Gondibert," in *Sir William Davenant's* Gondibert, ed. David F. Gladish (Oxford: Clarendon Press, 1971), 13, 30, 37–44.

23. Abraham Cowley, *Davideis*, in *The English Writings of Abraham Cowley*, ed. A. R. Waller (Cambridge: Cambridge University Press, 1905), ll. 75–80.

24. Thomas Shadwell, *The Medal of John Bayes* (1682), A2v–A3r

25. Baudrillard, *Simulations,* 40.

26. *The Works of John Dryden*, ed. Swedenberg et al., 2:308.

27. Laura Brown, "The Ideology of Restoration Poetic Form," *PMLA* 97 (1982): 405.

28. On a more practical note, I find it hard to see how anyone could fit Dryden's description of Shaftesbury as a "vermin wriggling in th'usurpers ear" (*The Medall*, l. 31) into the model of a cerebrally disposed poet.

29. Shadwell, *Medal of John Bayes,* A2v.

30. Cedric Reverend has described what he calls the subversive mode of Dryden's late poetry, attributing it to the poet's political circumstances after the Glorious Revolution (*Dryden's Final Poetic Mode: The Fables* [Philadelphia: University of Pennsylvania Press, 1988], 5).

## Chapter 5. Providence, Party, and Hegemony

1. For an overview of discussions about the formation of party politics in England, see B. W. Hill, *The Growth of Parliamentary Parties, 1689–1742* (Hamden, Conn.: Archon Books, 1976); and Geoffrey Holmes, *British Politics in the Age of Anne* (New York: St. Martin's Press, 1967).

2. Sir John Denham, *The Secret History of the Calves-Head Club, Complt. Or, The Republican Unmask'd* (London, 1705). The authenticity of the Calves-Head Club has, of course, been a matter of some dispute, but such evidence as there is for its existence is presented by Robert J. Allen in *The Clubs of Augustan London*, Harvard Studies in English 7 (Cambridge: Harvard University Press, 1933).

3. See for example G.B., *The Whigs Medley*, 1711 (engraving); and Gilbert Burnet, *A Sermon Preach'd at St. Bridget's Church* (London, 1714).

4. Jonathan Swift, *A Tale of a Tub with Other Early Works, 1696–1707*, ed. Herbert Davis (Oxford: Basil Blackwell, 1965), 24.

5. Nicholson, *Writing and the Rise of Finance,* 1–26.

6. Gary DeKrey, *A Fractured Society: The Politics of London in the First Age of Party, 1688–1715* (Oxford: Clarendon Press, 1985).

7. *A Letter to a Modern Dissenting Whig Concerning the Present Junction of Affairs* (London, 1701), 3, 10.

8. Benjamin Overton, *Good Advice to the Whigs, By an Old Dying Whig: Or, Mr.* Overton*'s Last Letter to his Friends With an Account of his Sickness and Death* (London, 1712), 10.

9. J. H. Plumb, *The Growth of Political Stability in England, 1675–1725* (New York: Macmillan, 1967); J. R. Jones, *The Revolution of 1688 in England* (London: Weidenfeld and Nicolson, 1972).

10. Jonathan Brody Kramnick's "'Unwilling to Be Short or Plain in Any Thing Concerning Gain': Bernard Mandeville and the Dialectic of Charity," *Eighteenth-Century* 33 (1992): 149–75, is a particularly good example of this kind of reading.

11. Bernard Mandeville, *The Fable of the Bees*, ed. F. B. Kaye (Oxford: Clarendon Press, 1924), 1:41. All references to the *Fable* will be taken from this edition and will be included in the text with volume and page numbers.

12. Robert Crossfield, *England's Warning-Piece* (London, 1704), 6–8.

13. Paul Kleber Monod, *Jacobitism and the English People, 1688–1788* (New York: Cambridge University Press, 1989), 26, 50.

14. *The Art of Lying and Rebelling, Taught by the Whigs* (London, 1713), 4–5.

15. Daniel Defoe, *The Age of Wonders* (London, 1710).

16. *The Grumbletonian Crew Reprehended* (London, 1689), 1.

17. *Awake Sampson, The Philistines are upon Thee!* (1696), 16–17.

18. Roger L'Estrange, *Fables of Aesop and Other Eminent Mythologists: With Morals and Reflections* (1692), B1r.

19. Pieter de la Court, *Fables Moral and Political. Translated from the Dutch.* (London, 1703), A5v–A6r, a1r.

20. Jayne Lewis, *The English Fable: Aesop and Literary Culture, 1651–1740*, Cambridge Studies in Eighteenth-Century Literature and Thought 28 (Cambridge: Cambridge University Press, 1996), 1–13.

21. Antoine de Courtin, *The Rules of Civility; or, the Maxims of Genteel Behavior* (London, 1703), 3.

22. Ibid., 4, A4v.

23. *A Dialogue Between a Member of Parliament, a Divine, a Lawyer, a Freeholder, a Shop-Keeper, and a Country Farmer; Or Remarks On the Badness of the Market* (London, 1703), 30.

24. Ibid., 7.

25. James Owen, *Moderation a Virtue: Or, The Occasional Conformity Justify'd* (London, 1703), 47.

26. Ibid., 14.

27. See, for example, Timothy Dykstal, "Commerce, Conversation, and Contradiction in Mandeville's *Fable*," *Studies in Eighteenth-Century Culture* 23 (1994): 93–110.

28. Ibid., 106.

## Chapter 6. A Taste for Spectacle

1. Dianne Dugaw, "'High Change in 'Change Alley': Popular Ballads and Emergent Capitalism in the Eighteenth Century," *ECL* 22, no. 2 (1998): 43–58.

2. Such at least is the claim of Laura Brown's controversial study *Alexander Pope* (Oxford: Basil Blackwell, 1985)

3. Pat Rogers's *Literature and Popular Culture in Eighteenth Century England* (Totowa, N.J.: Barnes & Noble, 1985) makes extensive use of the *Dunciad* in its analysis of popular culture in Georgian England, as does Brean Hammond's "'Guard the sure Barrier': Pope and the Partitioning of Culture," in *Pope: New Contexts*, ed. David Fairer (New York: Harvester Press, 1990), 225–40. Studies concerned more with eighteenth-century grotesque and the body include Rebecca Ferguson's "'Intestine Wars': Body and Text in *An Epistle to Dr. Arbuthnot* and *The Dunciad*," in Fairer, *Pope: New Contexts*, 137–52 and Helen Deutsch, "'The Truest Copies and the Mean Original': Pope, Deformity, and the Poetics of Self-Exposure," *ECS* 27 (1993): 1–27.

4. This is probably less true of Aubrey Williams's *Pope's Dunciad* (London: Methuen, 1955) than of others who followed him. Maynard Mack, on the other hand, is quite explicit in thinking of *The New Dunciad* as the poem's final version (*The Garden and the City* [Buffalo: University of Toronto Press, 1969]). Partly because it seems to me important to get some idea of the coherence of the original three-book *Dunciad* before later revisions and Pope's quarrels with Cibber produced what is in many ways a very different poem, and partly because of its interest in the cultural context of the poem's initial composition, this

chapter will take as its principal text the 1729 *Variorum*. The four-book *New Dunciad* will be alluded to only as it differs from or supplements the 1729 edition.

5. This is particularly true of texts that attempt to trace a satiric lineage through the late seventeenth and early eighteenth centuries. Both Ronald Paulson in *Breaking and Remaking* and Martin Price in *To the Palace of Wisdom: Studies in Order and Energy from Dryden to Blake* (Carbondale: Southern Illinois University Press, 1970), among others, tend to see *The Dunciad* as the poem that Dryden would have written if only he hadn't been so rushed—or if he had only lived to see the culmination of the "Augustanism" that he had begun.

6. Brean Hammond's "'Guard the sure Barrier': Pope and the Partitioning of Culture" provides the most recent example of such an approach to Pope's satire, though the assumptions that inform it can be seen even in Williams's insistence upon the basic "morality" of Pope's poem *(Pope's Dunciad).*

7. R. H. Griffith's "The Dunciad" (*Philological Quarterly* 24 [1945]: 155–57) still offers one of the best discussions of Pope's indictment of the role of the critic in the literary marketplace.

8. For a good discussion of Pope's connections to the prophets, see Robert Griffin's "Pope, the Prophets, and *The Dunciad*," *SEL* 23(1983): 435–46, which extensively documents Pope's debt to prophetic literature.

9. Pope, *The Dunciad* (1729), in vol. 5 of *The Twickenham Edition of the Poems of Alexander Pope*, ed. James Sutherland (New Haven: Yale University Press, 1953), bk. 3, ll. 273–74. All further references to the poem and its apparatus will be taken from this edition and will be included in the text with a date to indicate the 1729 *Variorum* and line or page numbers as appropriate.

10. Alexander Pope in a letter to Edward Blount, 3 October 1721, in *The Correspondence of Alexander Pope*, ed. George Sherburn (New York: Oxford University Press, 1956), 2:86.

11. Richard Meadowcourt, *The Grounds and Rule both of Interpreting and of Trying the Interpretations of Extraordinary Events* (London, 1723), 2–3, 10, 18.

12. See Henry Hetsell, *Remarks Upon Two Late Presentments of the Grand-Jury of the County of Middlesex* (London, 1729), 13–28; and Daniel Defoe, *A Journal of the Plague Year* (New York: Oxford University Press, 1969), 26–27.

13. Brady, *Sin Display'd in its Natural Deformity*, 4.

14. Ibid., 7–8.

15. In *The Discovery of Painting*, Pears has in fact argued that taste, like civil trial, came to replace providence as a fundamental organizing force in the period.

16. *A Letter to my Lord ******* On the Present Diversions of the Town* (London, 1725), 17.

17. Brady, *Sin Display'd,* 2.

18. Foucault, *Discipline and Punish;* Flynn, *Body in Swift and Defoe,* 196-97; Backscheider, in the first chapter of *Spectacular Politics,* has explored the Restoration conjunction of politics and theater in the service of ideology. Laura Knoppers, on the other hand, has recently—and quite suggestively—proposed the subversive potential of Restoration spectacle in *Historicizing Milton.*

19. John Dennis, "To the *Spectator*, on Poetical Justice," in *Critical Works of John Dennis*, ed. Edward Miles Hooker (Baltimore: Johns Hopkins University Press, 1939), 2:19.

20. Dennis, "Remarks upon *Cato*, a Tragedy," in *Critical Works of John Dennis,* ed. Hooker, 2:45.

21. *A Letter to My Lord ********, 17.

22. John Dryden, epilogue to *The Silent Woman*, in *The Works of John Dryden*, ed. George Saintsbury (Cambridge: Cambridge University Press, [1884]), 9:382–83.

23. *The British Stage: A Farce* (London, 1724), title page.

24. Frank McLynn gives a detailed account of this less-idealized reading of the spectacle of punishment in his *Crime and Punishment in Eighteenth-Century England* (New York: Oxford University Press, 1991), 257–76.

25. *British Stage,* 12.

26. Ibid., 3; Rogers, *Literature and Popular Culture,* 16.

27. *British Stage,* 22.

28. Ibid., 24.

29. Ibid.

30. James Ralph, *The Touch-stone* (London, 1728), 29.

31. Ibid., 178.

32. W.P., *A Seasonable Apology for Mr. Heidegger Proving the Usefulness and Antiquity of Masquerading from Scripture and Prophane History* (London, 1724), 4; John Heidegger, *Heydegger's Letter to the Bishop of London* (London, 1724), 6.

33. Monod, *Jacobitism and the English People,* 39–40.

34. Paulson, *Breaking and Remaking,* 76.

# Selected Bibliography

## Primary Sources


Abercromby, David. *A Moral Discourse of the Power of Interest*. London, 1690.

Addison, Joseph, and Sir Richard Steele. *Addison and Steele: Selections from* The Tatler *and* The Spectator. Edited by Robert J. Allen. San Francisco: Holt, Rinehart, and Winston, 1970.

*An Alarme to England: Or, A Warning-Piece to The Inhabitants of Great Britain.* 1657

Allison, John. *Upon the Late Lamentable Fire in London*. 1667.

*The Art of Lying and Rebelling, Taught by the Whigs*. London, 1713.

Aubrey, John. *John Aubrey's Brief Lives*. Ed. Andrew Clark. Oxford, 1898.

*Awake Sampon, The Philistines are upon Thee!* 1696.

Baker, Daniel. *Yet One Warning More, To Thee O England*. 1660.

Bayly, William. *The Dreadful and Terrible Day of the Lord God*. [1665?]

———. *A Warning from the Spirit of Truth Unto all Persecutors and Enemies of the Dear Children of God*. 1658.

Biddle, Hester. *The Trumpet of the Lord Sounded forth unto these Three Nations*. London, 1662.

Bingely, William. *A Lamentation over England*. 1682.

Bishop, George. *The Last Trump. Or, One Warning More Yet to the People of these Nations*. London, 1662

*The Book of Common Prayer*. 1608.

*The Book of Common Prayer*. 1633.

*Bradshaw's Ghost: being a dialogue*. [London], 1659.

*Bradshaw's Ultimum Vale*. Oxon, 1660.

Brady, Nicholas. *Sin Display'd in its Natural Deformity*. London, 1724.

Brinkelow, Henry. *The Lamentacion of a Christian Against the Citie of London, made by R. Mors*. 1542.

*The British Stage. A Farce*. London, 1724.

Broughton, Hugh. *The Lamentationes of Jeremy, tr. with great care of his Hebrew*. [Amsterdam], 1606.

Burrough, Edward. *A Standard Lifted Up, and An Ensign Held Forth, to all Nations*. London, 1657.

———. *A Trumpet of the Lord Sounded Out of Zion*. London, 1656.

Butler, Samuel. *Characters*. Ed. Charles W. Daves. Cleveland, Ohio: The Press of Case Western Reserve University, 1970.

———. *Hudibras*. Ed. John Wilders. Oxford: Clarendon Press. 1967.

Calvin, John. *The Institutes of the Christian Religion*. Trans. Henry Beveridge. Grand Rapids, Mich.: Wm. B. Eerdmans, 1957.

Caryl, Joseph. *Peters Patern*. 1659.

Coale, Josiah. *England's Sad Estate Lamented*. 1666.

*The Coffin Opened: Or, Self-Interest Discovered*. 1661.

Collins, Edward. *The Obligation of Human Laws, Asserted and Vindicated*. London, 1723.

*The Conflagration of London*. London, 1667.

Cooper, Anthony Ashley, third earl of Shaftesbury. *A Letter Concerning Enthusiasm*. London, 1708.

———. *The Moralists*. London, 1709.

Coppe, Abiezer. *Selected Writings*. Ed. Andrew Hopton. London: Aporia Press, 1987.

Cotton, Priscilla, and Mary Cole. *To the Priests and People of England*. London, 1655.

Court, Pieter de la. *Fables Moral and Political. Translated from the Dutch*. London, 1703.

Courtin, Antoine de. *The Rules of Civility: or, the Maxims of Genteel Behavior, As they are Practis'd and Observ'd by Persons of Quality*. London, 1703.

Cowley, Abraham. *The English Writings of Abraham Cowley*. Ed. A. R. Waller. Cambridge: Cambridge University Press, 1905.

Crane, Richard. *A Lamentation Over Thee, O London*. 1665.

Crossfield, Robert. *England's Warning-Piece*. London, 1704.

Crouch, John. *Londinenses Lacrymae*. 1666.

Davenant, William. *Sir William Davenant's* Gondibert. Ed. David F. Gladish. Oxford: Clarendon Press, 1971.

Defoe, Daniel. *The Age of Wonders*. 1710.

———. *A Journal of the Plague Year*. New York: Oxford University Press, 1969.

Denham, Sir John. *The Secret History of the Calves-Head Club, Complt. Or, The Republican Unmask'd*. London, 1705.

Dennis, John. *Critical Works of John Dennis*. Ed. Edward Miles Hooker. 2 vols. Baltimore: Johns Hopkins University Press, 1939.

*A Dialogue Between a Member of Parliament, a Divine, a Lawyer, a Freeholder, a Shop-Keeper, and a Country Farmer; Or, Remarks On the Badness of the Market*. London, 1703.

*The Doleful Lamentation of Cheap-side Crosse*. 1641.

*The Doubtfull Almanack. Or, A Very Suspicious Presage of Great Calamities Yet to Ensue*. London, 1647.

Dryden, John. "A Discourse Concerning the Original and Progress of Satire." In vol. 2 of *Essays of John Dryden*, ed. W. P. Ker. 2 vols. New York: Russell & Russell, 1961.

———. *The Works of John Dryden*. Ed. George Saintsbury. 18 vols. Cambridge: Cambridge Univesity Press, 1882–93.

———. *The Works of John Dryden*. Ed. H. T Swedenberg et al. 13 vols. Berkeley and Los Angeles: University of California Press, 1956–94.

Elborough, Robert. *Londons Calamity by Fire Bewailed and Improved*. 1666.

*Englands Remembrancer*. 1645 [1646].

*Englands Remembrancer: or, a Warning*. 1644.

*Englands Remembrancer: or, a Word in Season*. London, 1656.

Evans, Arise. *The Bloudy Vision of John Farly*. [London], 1653.

———. *A Voice from Heaven to the Commonwealth of England*. [London], 1652.

———. *The Voice of Michael the Archangel to his Highness the Lord Protector*. [London], 1653.

*A Fannaticks Alarm, Given to the Mayor in his Quarters, By one of the Sons of Zion, become Boanerges, To Thunder out the Judgements of God against Oppression and Oppressors*. London, 1661.

[Ford, Simon]. *Conflagratio Londinenses Poetice Depicta, or The Conflagration of London*. 1667.

———. *A Discourse Concerning God's Judgements*. 1678.

Foxe, John. *Acts and Monuments*. 8th ed. London, 1641.

G., J. *The Dreadful Burning of London*. London, 1667.

*Geneva Bible*. Madison: University of Wisconsin Press, 1969.

*The Grumbletonian Crew Reprehended*. London, 1689.

Hardy, Nathanial. *Lamentation, Mourning & Woe*. 1666.

———. *A Sad Prognostick of Approaching Judgment*. London, 1658.

Heidegger, John. *Heydegger's Letter to the Bishop of London*. London, 1724.

[Herrick, Robert]. *Poor Robin's Visions*. 1667.

Hetsell, Henry. *Remarks upon Two Late Presentments of the Grand-Jury of the County of Middlesex*. London, 1729.

Hobbes, Thomas. *Behemoth*. Chicago: University of Chicago Press, 1990.

———. *Leviathan*. Oxford: Basil Blackwell, 1947.

Hogarth, William. *Engravings by William Hogarth*. Ed. Sean Shesgreen. New York: Dover, 1973.

[Houghton, John]. *England's Great Happiness*. 1677.

Hutchinson, Lucy. *Memoirs of the Life of Colonel Hutchinson*. New York: Scribner & Welford, 1885.

Hyde, Edward, first earl of Clarendon. *Clarendon: Selections from The History of the Rebellion and The Life by Himself*. New York: Oxford University Press, 1978.

*Ieremiah Revived*. 1648.

Johnson, Samuel. *Lives of the English Poets*. Ed. George Birkbeck Hill. Oxford: Clarendon Press, 1905.

Jonson, Ben. *Every Man in His Humour*. Ed. J. W. Lever. Regents Renaissance Drama Series. Lincoln: University of Nebraska Press, 1971.

*The Joviall Crew, or The Devil Turnd Ranter: Being a Character of The Roaring Ranters of these Times*. London, 1651.

Joye, George. *Jeremy the Prophet*. [Antwerp], 1534.

*The Lamentable Complaints of Nick Froth the Tapster and Rulefrost the Cook*. London, 1641.

*The Lamentation of a Bad Market*. 1660.

*Lamentation of a Bad Market*. London, 1667.

*The Lamentation of a New Married Man*. [1628–29].

*The Lamentation of a Sinner, or Bradshavv's Horrid Farewell*. 1659.

*The Lamentation of Mary Butcher, now . . . in Worcester city-gaol*. [1700?].

*A Lamentation of the Ruling Lay-Elders*. 1647.

*The Lamentations of Jeremiah in Meeter*. 1652.

*The Lamentations of the Prophet Jeremiah, Paraphras'd*. 1647.

*Last Will of George Fox*. Date unknown.

L'Estrange, Roger. *Fables of Aesop and Other Eminent Mythologists: With Morals and Reflections*. London, 1692.

*A Letter to a Modern Dissenting Whig Concerning the Present Junction of Affairs*. London, 1701.

*A Letter to My Lord ******* On the Present Diversions of the Town*. London, 1725.

*London's Remains*. London, 1667.

Luther, Martin. *Luther: Early Theological Works*. Ed. and trans. James Atkinson. The Library of Christian Classics, no. 16. London: SCM Press, 1962.

Mandeville, Bernard. *The Fable of the Bees*. Ed. F. B. Kaye. 2 vols. Oxford: Clarendon Press, 1924.

Marvell, Andrew. *The Poems and Letters of Andrew Marvell*. Ed. H. M. Margoliouth. Oxford: Clarendon Press, 1927.

———. *The Rehearsal Transpros'd: Part One. Andrew Marvell*. Ed. Frank Kermode and Keith Walker. Oxford: Oxford University Press, 1990.

Meadowcourt, Richard. *The Grounds and Rule both of Interpreting and of Trying the Interpretations of Extraordinary Events*. London, 1723.

Milton, John. *Paradise Lost*. Ed. Merritt Hughes. Indianapolis, Ind.: Odyssey Press, 1962.

[Montague, Walter]. *Jeremias Redivivas*. 1649.

Morison, Sir Richard. *A Lamentation in whiche is Showed what Ruyne Cometh of Seditious Rebellyon*. 1536.

Naylor, James. *A Lamentacion (by one of Englands Prophets) Over the Ruines of this Oppressed Nation*. 1653 [1654].

———. *The Power and Glory of the Lord, Shining out of the North*. London, 1658.

*Observations Both Historical and Moral upon the Burning of London*. 1667.

Overton, Benjamin. *Good Advice to the Whigs, By an Old Dying Whig: Or, Mr. Overton's Last Letter to his Friends With an Account of his Sickness and Death*. London, 1712.

Owen, James. *Moderation a Virtue:, Or, the Occasional Conformity Justify'd*. London, 1703.

P., W. *A Seaonable Apology for Mr. Heidegger Proving the Usefulness and Antiquity of Masquerading from Scripture and Prophane History*. London, 1724.

Parry, Robert. *Lamentation of a Male-Content.* 1597.

Pepys, Samuel. *The Diary of Samuel Pepys.* Ed. Robert Latham and William Matthews. 2 vols. Berkeley and Los Angeles: University of California Press, 1970.

Phillips, John. *A Satyr Against Hypocrites.* 1655.

Phillips, Thomas. *The Booke of Lamentations: or, A Treatise of Hell.* London, 1639.

*Poems on Affairs of State.* London, 1716.

[Pope, Alexander]. *God's Revenge Against Punning.* London, 1704.

Pope, Alexander. *The Poems of Alexander Pope.* Ed. James Sutherland. Vol. 5. New Haven: Yale University Press, 1953.

———. *Pope: Poetical Works.* ed. Herbert Davis. New York: Oxford University Press, 1983.

*The Protestant Flayl.* 1682.

Prynne, William. *The Quakers Unmasked, and Clearly Detected.* 2d ed. 1655.

Ralph, James. *The Touch-stone.* London, 1728.

*The Ranters Monster: Being a True Relation of one Mary Adams, Living at Tillingham in Essex.* London, 1652.

Rigge, Ambrose. *The Banner of Gods Love.* 1657.

———. *A Lamentation over England because of the Judgements that is now Appearing against her for her Manifold Transgressions.* London, 1665.

———. *A Premonition to the Bishops and Priests.* [London, 1676.]

———. *To All who Imprison and Persecute the Saints.* [London], 1659.

Rolle, Samuel. *Hythuhls: or, the Burning of London in the Year 1666.* London, 1667.

Rollins, Hyder, ed. *Cavalier and Puritan.* New York: New York University Press, 1923.

Rymer, Thomas. *The Critical Works of Thomas Rymer.* Ed. Curt A. Zimansky. New Haven: Yale University Press, 1956.

Scarron, Paul. *Scarronnides: or, Virgile Travestie.* London, 1665.

Shadwell, Thomas. *The Medal of John Bayes.* London, 1682.

———. *The Virtuoso.* Ed. Marjorie Hope Nicholson and David Stuart Rodes. Regents Restoration Drama Series. Lincoln: University of Nebraska Press, 1966.

Simmonds, Martha. *A Lamentation for the Lost Sheep of the House of Israel.* London, 1656.

Simpson, William. *A Declaration Unto All Both Priests and People.* 1655.

———. *From One who was Moved of the Lord God to go a Sign among the Priests and Professors of the Prophets.* London, 1659.

———. *Going Naked a Signe.* 1660.

Stocker, T. *The Lamentations and Holy Mournings of the Prophet Jeremiah.* 1587.

Swift, Jonathan. *A Tale of a Tub with Other Early Works.* Ed. Herbert Davis. Oxford: Basil Blackwell, 1965.

T., U. *A Lamentable Representation of the Effects of the Present Toleration.* 1656.

Taylor, Christopher. *The Whirlwind of the Lord gone forth as a Fiery Flying Rolle.* 1655.

Taylor, John. *Aqua-Musae.* 1644.

Tossanus, Daniel. *The Lamentations and Holy Mourninges of the prophet Ieremiah, with a Paraphrase.* [1587?]

*A True and Exact Relation of the Most Dreadful and Remarkable Fires.* 1666.

Twisse, Robert. *England's Breath Stopp'd.* 1665.

Udall, John. *A Commentarie upon the Lamentations of Jeremy.* 1595.

Underhill, Cave. *Vox Lachrymae.* 1681.

*A Voyce Out of the Wildernes Crying.* London, 1651.

Waterhouse, Edward. *A Short Narrative of the Late Dreadful Fire.* 1667.

Whitelock, Bulstrode. *Memorial of the English Affairs.* 1682.

Wiseman, Samuel. *A Short and Serious Narrative of Londons Fatal Fire.* 1667.

Wither, George. *Britains Remembrancer.* Spenser Society Publications, nos. 28–29. Manchester, U.K.: Charles E. Simms, 1880.

———. *Carmen Expostulatorium.* 1647.

———. *The Dark Lantern.* 1653.

———. *Epistolium-Vagum-Prosa-Metricum.* 1659.

———. *Furor-Poeticus (i.e.) Propheticus.* 1660.

———. *A Proclamation in the Name of the King of Kings.* 1662.

———. *Salt upon Salt.* 1659.

———. *Sigh for the Pitchers.* 1666.

———. *Vox Pacifica.* 1645.

———. *What Peace to the Wicked?* 1646.

## Secondary Sources

Abelove, Henry. *Evangelist of Desire: John Wesley and the Methodists.* Stanford, Calif.: Stanford University Press, 1990.

Achinstein, Sharon. *Milton and the Revolutionary Reader.* Princeton: Princeton University Press, 1994.

Agnew, Jean-Christophe. *Worlds Apart: The Market and the Theater in Anglo-American Thought, 1550–1750.* New York: Cambridge University Press, 1986.

Alden, Raymond. *The Rise of Formal Satire in England.* University of Pennsylvania Series in Philology, Literature and Archaeology, no. 7. Philadelphia: University of Pennsylvania Press, 1889.

Allen, Robert J. *The Clubs of Augustan London.* Harvard Studies in English, no. 7. Cambridge: Harvard University Press, 1933.

Anselment, Raymond A. *"Betwixt Jest and Earnest": Marprelate, Milton, Marvell, Swift, and the Decorum of Religious Ridicule.* Toronto: University of Toronto Press, 1979.

Backscheider, Paula. *Spectacular Politics: Theatrical Power and Mass Culture in Early Modern England.* Baltimore: Johns Hopkins University Press, 1993.

Bakhtin, Mikhail. *Rabelais and His World.* Trans. Helene Iswolsky. Bloomington: Indiana University Press, 1984.

Baudrillard, Jean. *Simulations.* Trans. Paul Foss, Paul Patton, and Philip Beitchman. New York: Semiotext(e), 1983.

Bauman, Richard. *Let Your Words Be Few*. Cambridge: Cambridge University Press, 1983.

Bercovitch, Sacvan. *The American Jeremiad*. Madison: University of Wisconsin Press, 1978.

Berg, Christina, and Phillippa Berry. "'Spiritual Whoredom': An Essay on Female Prophets in the Seventeenth Century." In *Literature and Power in the Seventeenth Century*. Proceedings of the Essex Conference on the Sociology of Literature, July 1980. Colchester, U.K.: Department of Literature, University of Essex, 1981.

Bossy, John. *The English Catholic Community*. New York: Oxford University Press, 1975.

Brewer, John. *The Sinews of Power*. Cambridge: Harvard University Press, 1988.

Brown, Laura. *Alexander Pope*. Rereading Literature, no. 1. Oxford: Basil Blackwell, 1985.

———. "The Ideology of Restoration Poetic Form." *PMLA* 97 (1982): 395–407.

Bywaters, David. *Dryden in Revolutionary England*. Berkeley: University of California Press, 1991.

Castle, Terry. *Masquerade and Civilization: The Carnivalesque in Eighteenth-Century English Culture and Fiction*. Stanford, Calif.: Stanford University Press, 1986.

Clark, J. C. D. *Revolution and Rebellion: State and Society in England in the Seventeenth and Eighteenth Centuries*. Cambridge: Cambridge University Press, 1986.

Collinson, Patrick. *The Religion of Protestants: The Church in English Society, 1559–1625*. Oxford: Clarendon Press, 1982.

Corns, Thomas. *Uncloistered Virtue: English Political Literature, 1640–1660*. Oxford: Oxford University Press, 1992.

Coward, Barry. *The Stuart Age*. New York: Longman Group, 1980.

Curry, Patrick. *Prophecy and Power: Astrology in Early Modern England*. Cambridge: Polity Press, 1989.

Dane, Joseph. *Parody: Critical Concepts Versus Literary Practices: Aristophanes to Sterne*. Norman: University of Oklahoma Press, 1988.

De Krey, Gary Stuart. *A Fractured Society: The Politics of London in the First Age of Party, 1688–1715*. Oxford: Clarendon Press, 1985.

Deutsch, Helen. "'The Truest Copies' and the 'Mean Original': Pope, Deformity and the Poetics of Self-Exposure." *Eighteenth-Century Studies* 27 (1993): 1–27.

Dobin, Howard. *Merlin's Disciples: Prophecy, Poetry, and Power in Renaissance England*. Stanford, Calif.: Stanford University Press, 1990.

Doody, Margaret. *The Daring Muse: Augustan Poetry Reconsidered*. Cambridge: Cambridge University Press, 1985.

Dugaw, Dianne. "'High Change in 'Change Alley': Popular Ballads and Emergent Capitalism in the Eighteenth Century." *Eighteenth-Century Life* 22, no. 2 (1998): 43–58.

Dykstal, Timothy. "Commerce, Conversation, and Contradiction in Mandeville's *Fable*." *Studies in Eighteenth-Century Culture* 23 (1994): 93–110.

Edwards, Thomas R., Jr. "Heroic Folly: Pope's Satiric Identity." In *In Defense of Reading*. ed. Reuben Brower and Richard Poirer, 191–205. New York: E. P. Dutton, 1962.

———. "Light and Nature: A Reading of the *Dunciad*." *Philological Quarterly* 39 (1960): 437–63.

Elliot, Robert C. *The Power of Satire: Magic, Ritual, Art*. Princeton: Princeton University Press, 1960.

Ferguson, Rebecca. "'Intestine Wars': Body and Text in *An Epistle to Dr. Arbuthnot* and *The Dunciad*." In *Pope: New Contexts*, ed. David Fairer, 137–52. New York: Harvester Press, 1990.

Flynn, Carol Houlihan. *The Body in Swift and Defoe*. New York: Cambridge University Press, 1986.

Foucault, Michel. *Discipline and Punish*. Trans. Alan Sheridan. New York: Vintage Books, 1979.

French, J. Milton. "George Wither in Prison." *PMLA* 45 (1930): 959–66.

Friedman, Jerome. *Blasphemy, Immorality, and Anarchy: The Ranters and the English Revolution*. Athens: Ohio University Press, 1987.

Griffin, Robert. "Pope, the Prophets, and *The Dunciad*." *Studies in English Literature* 23 (1983): 435–46.

Griffith, R. H. *"The Dunciad." Philological Quarterly* 24 (1945): 155–57.

Gunn, J. A. W. "Mandeville and Wither: Individualism and the Workings of Providence." In *Mandeville Studies, 1670–1733,* ed. Irwin Primer, 98–118. The Hague: Martinus Nijhoff, 1975.

Habermas, Juergen. *The Structural Transformation of the Public Sphere*. Trans. Thomas Burger and Frederick Lawrence. London: Polity Press. 1989.

Haley, K. H. D. *The First Earl of Shaftesbury*. Oxford: Clarendon Press, 1968.

Hammond, Brean. "'Guard the sure Barrier': Pope and the Partitioning of Culture." In *Pope: New Contexts,* ed. David Fairer, 225–40. New York: Harvester Press, 1990.

Hammond, Paul. *John Dryden: A Literary Life*. New York: St. Martin's Press, 1991.

Hawes, Clement. *Mania and Literary Style: The Rhetoric of Enthusiasm from the Ranters to Christopher Smart*. Cambridge Studies in Eighteenth-Century English Literature and Thought, no. 29. Cambridge: Cambridge University Press, 1996.

Hayes, Tom. *The Birth of Popular Culture*. Pittsburgh, Pa.: Duquesne University Press, 1992.

Hill, B. W. *The Growth of Parliamentary Parties, 1689–1742*. Hamden, Conn.: Archon Books, 1976.

Hill, Christopher. "A Bourgeois Revolution?" In *Three British Revolutions: 1641, 1688, 1776,* ed. J. G. A. Pocock, 109–39. Princeton: Princeton University Press, 1980.

———. *The Century of Revolution, 1603–1714*. New York: W. W. Norton, 1961.

———. *The Experience of Defeat*. London: Faber and Faber, 1984.

———. *The World Turned Upside Down*. London: Maurice Temple Smith, 1972.

Hirst, Derek. *Authority and Conflict: England, 1603–1658*. Cambridge: Harvard University Press, 1986.

Holmes, Geoffrey. *British Politics in the Age of Anne*. New York: St. Martin's Press, 1967.

Holstun, James. *Ehud's Dagger: Class Struggle in the English Revolution*. New York: Verso Books, 2000.

———. "Ehud's Dagger: Patronage, Tyrannicide, and *Killing No Murder*." *Cultural Critique* 22 (1992): 99–142.

———. "Ranting at the New Historicism." *English Literary Renaissance* 19 (1989): 189–225.

———. *A Rational Millennium: Puritan Utopias of Seventeenth-Century England and America*. New York: Oxford University Press, 1987.

———, ed. *Pamphlet Wars: Prose in the English Revolution.* Portland, Ore.: Frank Cass, 1992.

Hooker, Edward N. "The Purpose of Dryden's *Annus Mirabilis.*" *Huntington Library Quarterly* 10 (1946): 49–67.

Hopkins, Robert H. "The Cant of Social Compromise: Some Observations on Mandeville's Satire." In *Mandeville Studies, 1670–1733,* ed. Irwin Primer, 168–92. The Hague: Martinus Nijhoff, 1975.

Hudson, Nicholas. "Dialogue and the Origins of Language: Linguistic and Social Evolution in Mandeville, Condillac, and Rousseau." In *Compendious Conversations: The Method of Dialogue in the Early Enlightenment.* New York: Peter Lang, 1992.

Hutton, Ronald. *The Restoration: A Political and Religious History of England and Wales, 1658–1667.* Oxford: Clarendon Press, 1985.

Irlam, Shaun. *Elations: The Poetics of Enthusiasm in Eighteenth-Century Britain.* Stanford, Calif.: Stanford University Press, 1999.

Jacob, Margaret. *The Newtonians and the English Revolution, 1689–1720.* Hassocks, U.K.: Harvester Press, 1976.

Johnston, David. *The Rhetoric of Leviathan.* Princeton: Princeton University Press, 1986.

Jones, J. R. *The First Whigs: The Politics of the Exclusion Crisis.* London: Oxford University Press, 1970.

———. *The Revolution of 1688 in England.* London: Weidenfeld and Nicholson, 1972.

Jones, John A. *Pope's Couplet Art.* Athens: Ohio University Press, 1969.

Keeble, N. H. *The Literary Culture of Nonconformity in Later-Seventeenth-Century England.* Athens: University of Georgia Press, 1987.

Kernan, Alvin. *The Canker'd Muse.* New Haven: Yale University Press, 1962.

Kinsley, James, and Helen Kinsley, eds. *Dryden: The Critical Heritage.* New York: Barnes and Noble, 1971.

Kinsley, William. "The *Dunciad* as Mock-Book." *Huntington Library Quarterly* 35 (1971): 29–47.

Kitchin, George. *A Survey of Burlesque and Parody in English.* London: Oliver and Boyd, 1931.

Klein, Lawrence, and Anthony J. LaVopa. *Enthusiasm and Enlightenment in Europe, 1650–1850.* Special issue of *Huntington Library Quarterly* 60 (1998).

Knoppers, Laura. *Constructing Cromwell: Ceremony, Portrait, and Print, 1645–1661.* Cambridge: Cambridge University Press, 2000.

———. *Historicizing Milton: Spectacle, Power, and Poetry in Restoration England.* Athens: University of Georgia Press, 1994.

———. "Milton's *The Readie and Easie Way* and the English Jeremiad." In *Politics, Poetics, and Hermeneutics in Milton's Prose,* ed. David Loewenstein and James Grantham Turner, 213–25. New York: Cambridge University Press, 1990.

Knox, R. A. *Enthusiasm: A Chapter in the History of Religion.* Oxford: Clarendon Press, 1950.

Kramnick, Jonathan Brody. "'Unwilling to be Short or Plain in Any Thing Concerning Gain': Bernard Mandeville and the Dialectic of Charity." *The Eighteenth Century* 33 (1992): 149–75.

Kroll, Richard. *The Material Word.* Baltimore: Johns Hopkins University Press, 1991.

Lake, Peter. *Anglicans and Puritans?: Presbyterian and English Conformist Thought from Whitgift to Hooker.* Boston: Unwin Hyman, 1988.

Leverenz, David. *The Language of Puritan Feeling: An Exploration in Literature, Psychology, and Social History.* New Brunswick, N.J.: Rutgers University Press, 1980.

Lewalski, Barbara. *Protestant Poetics and the Seventeenth-Century Religious Lyric.* Princeton: Princeton University Press, 1979.

Lewis, Jayne. *The English Fable: Aesop and Literary Culture, 1651–1740.* Cambridge Studies in Eighteenth-Century Literature and Thought, no. 28. Cambridge: Cambridge University Press, 1996.

Lyotard, Jean-François. *The Differend: Phrases in Dispute.* Trans. George Van Den Abeele. Minneapolis: University of Minnesota Press, 1988.

Macgillivray, Royce. *Restoration Historians and the English Civil Wars.* The Hague: Martinus Nijhoff, 1974.

Mack, Phyllis. *Visionary Women: Ecstatic Prophecy in Seventeenth-Century England.* Berkeley: University of California Press, 1992.

Mack, Maynard, ed. *Essential Articles for the Study of Alexander Pope.* Hamden, Conn.: Archon Books, 1968.

MacPherson, C. B. *The Political Theory of Possessive Individualism.* Oxford: Clarendon Press, 1962.

Mandell, Laura. "Bawds and Merchants: Engendering Capitalist Desires." *English Literary History* 59 (1992): 107–23.

McDowell, Paula. *The Women of Grub Street: Press, Politics, and Gender in the London Literary Marketplace, 1678–1730.* Oxford: Clarendon Press, 1998.

McFadden, George. *Dryden: The Public Writer, 1660–1685.* Princeton: Princeton University Press, 1978.

McKeon, Michael. *The Origins of the English Novel, 1600–1740.* Baltimore: Johns Hopkins University Press, 1987.

———. *Politics and Poetry in Restoration England.* Cambridge: Harvard University Press, 1975.

———. "The Politics of Discourse." In *Politics of Discourse: The Literature and History of Seventeenth-Century England,* ed. Kevin Sharpe and Steven Zwicker, 35–51. Berkeley: University of California Press, 1987.

McLynn, Frank. *Crime and Punishment in Eighteenth-Century England.* New York: Oxford University Press, 1991.

Miller, John. *Religion in the Popular Prints, 1600–1832.* The English Satirical Print, 1600–1832. Cambridge: Chadwick-Healey, 1986.

Miller, Perry. *The New England Mind: From Colony to Province.* Boston: Beacon Press, 1961.

Monod, Paul Kleber. *Jacobitism and the English People, 1688–1788.* New York: Cambridge University Press, 1989.

Morton, Timothy. "Trade Winds." *Essays and Studies* 49 (1996): 19–41.

Mumby, Frank Arthur. *Publishing and Bookselling.* New York: R. R. Bowker, 1949.

Nicholson, Colin. *Writing and the Rise of Finance: Capital Studies of the Early Eighteenth Century.* Cambridge Studies in Eighteenth-Century English Literature and Thought, no. 21. Cambridge: Cambridge University Press, 1994.

Norbrook, David. *Writing the English Republic: Poetry, Rhetoric, and Politics, 1627–1660.* Cambridge: Cambridge University Press, 1999.

Ogg, David. *England in the Reign of Charles II.* Oxford: Clarendon Press, 1934.

Okie, Laird. *Augustan Historical Writing.* New York: University Press of America, 1991.

Paulson, Ronald. *Breaking and Remaking: Aesthetic Practise in England, 1700–1820.* New Brunswick, N.J.: Rutgers University Press, 1989.

———. *Popular and Polite Art in the Age of Hogarth and Fielding.* Notre Dame, Ind.: University of Notre Dame Press, 1979.

———. "Satire, and Poetry, and Pope." In *Pope: Recent Essays by Several Hands,* ed. Maynard Mack and James A. Winn, 45–62. Hamden, Conn.: Archon Books, 1980.

Pears, Iain. *The Discovery of Painting.* New Haven: Yale University Press, 1988.

Peter, John. *Complaint and Satire in Early English Literature.* Oxford: Clarendon Press, 1956.

Plumb, J. H. *The Growth of Political Stability in England, 1675–1725.* New York: Macmillan, 1967.

Pocock, J. A. *The Ancient Constitution and the Feudal Law: A Study of English Historical Thought in the Seventeenth Century.* Cambridge: Cambridge University Press, 1957.

Potter, Lois. *Secret Rites and Secret Writing: Royalist Literature, 1640–1660.* New York: Cambridge University Press, 1989.

Price, Martin. "George Wither: The Poet as Prophet." *Studies in Philology* 59 (1962): 211–30.

———. *To the Palace of Wisdom: Studies in Order and Energy from Dryden to Blake.* Carbondale: Southern Illinois University Press, 1970.

Reichard, Hugo M. "Pope's Social Satire: Belles-Lettres and Business." *PMLA* 67 (1952): 420–34.

Reverend, Cedric. *Dryden's Final Poetic Mode: The Fables.* Philadelphia: University of Pennsylvania Press, 1988.

Roberts, Clayton. *The Growth of Responsible Government in Stuart England.* Cambridge: Cambridge University Press, 1966.

Rogers, Pat. *Literature and Popular Culture in Eighteenth-Century England.* Totowa, N.J.: Barnes and Noble Books, 1985.

Roper, Alan. *Dryden's Poetic Kingdoms.* London: Routledge and Kegan Paul, 1965.

Rupp, Gordon. *Religion in England, 1688–1791.* Oxford: Clarendon Press, 1986.

Schilling, Bernard N. *Dryden and the Conservative Myth.* New Haven: Yale University Press, 1961.

Schwartz, Hillel. *The French Prophets: The History of a Millenarian Group in Eighteenth-Century England.* Berkeley: University of California Press, 1980.

Scott, Jonathan. "England's Troubles: Exhuming the Popish Plot." In *The Politics of Religion in Restoration England,* ed. Tim Harris, Paul Seaward, and Mark Goldie, 107–32. Oxford: Basil Blackwell, 1990.

Seaward, Paul. "Gilbert Sheldon, the London Vestries, and the Defence of the Church." In *The Politics of Religion in Restoration England,* ed. Tim Harris, Paul Seaward, and Mark Goldie, 49–74. Oxford: Basil Blackwell, 1990.

Seidel, Michael. *Satiric Inheritence, Rabelais to Sterne.* Princeton: Princeton University Press, 1979.

Sena, John F. "Melancholic Madness and the Puritans." *Harvard Theological Review* 66 (1973): 293–311.

Sherburn, George. "The *Dunciad*, Book IV." *Texas Studies in Language and Literature* 24 (1944): 174–90.

Sitter, John. *The Poetry of Pope's Dunciad.* Minneapolis: University of Minnesota Press, 1971.

Skerpan, Elizabeth. *The Rhetoric of Politics in the English Revolution.* Columbia: University of Missouri Press, 1992.

Smith, Nigel. "Exporting Enthusiasm: John Perrot and the Quaker Epic." In *Literature and the English Civil War,* ed. Thomas Healy and Jonathan Sawday, 248–64. Cambridge: Cambridge University Press, 1990.

———. *Literature and Revolution in England, 1640–1660.* New Haven: Yale University Press, 1994.

———. *Perfection Proclaimed.* Oxford: Clarendon Press. 1989.

Sommerville, C. John. *Popular Religion in Restoration England.* University of Florida Social Sciences Monograph 59. Gainesville: University Presses of Florida, 1977.

Spurr, John. "'Virtue, Religion, and Government': The Anglican Uses of Providence." In *The Politics of Religion in Restoration England,* ed. Tim Harris, Paul Seaward, and Mark Goldie, 29–48. Oxford: Basil Blackwell, 1990.

Stachniewski, John. *The Persecutory Imagination: English Puritanism and the Literature of Religious Despair.* Oxford: Clarendon Press, 1991.

Stallybrass, Peter, and Allon White. *The Politics and Poetics of Transgression.* Ithaca, N.Y.: Cornell University Press, 1986.

Steadman, John. *Milton and the Renaissance Hero.* Oxford: Clarendon Press, 1967.

Stone, Lawrence. "The Results of the English Revolutions of the Seventeenth Century." In *Three British Revolutions: 1641, 1688, 1776,* ed. J. G. A. Pocock, 23–108. Princeton: Princeton University Press, 1980.

Tanner, Tony. "Reason and the Grotesque: Pope's *Dunciad.*" *Critical Quarterly* 7 (1965): 145–60.

Tawney, R. H. *Religion and the Rise of Capitalism.* New York: Harcourt, Brace, 1926.

Taylor, Rupert. *The Political Prophecy in England.* New York: Columbia University Press, 1911.

Thomas, Keith. *Religion and the Decline of Magic.* London: Weidenfeld and Nicolson, 1971.

Thomson, E. P. *Customs in Common.* New York: New Press, 1991.

Thorn-Drury, G. "Dryden's *Mac Flecknoe:* A Vindication." *Modern Language Review* 8 (1918): 276–81.

Todd, Dennis. *Imagining Monsters: Miscreations of the Self in Eighteenth-Century England.* Chicago: University of Chicago Press, 1995.

Tomashevsky, Boris. "Thematics." In *Russian Formalist Criticism: Four Essays,* ed. and trans. Lee T. Lemon and Marion J. Reis. Regents Critics Series. Lincoln: University of Nebraska Press, 1965.

Trickett, Rachel. *The Honest Muse.* Oxford: Clarendon Press, 1967.

Turner, James Grantham. *One Flesh: Paradisal Marriage and Sexual Relations in the Age of Milton.* Oxford: Clarendon Press, 1987.

Wall, Cynthia, *The Literary and Cultural Spaces of Restoration London.* Cambridge: Cambridge University Press, 1998.

Wallace, John. "'Examples Are Best Precepts': Readers and Meaning in Seventeenth-Century Poetry." *Critical Inquiry* 1 (1974): 273–90.

Walter, John, and Keith Wrightson. "Dearth and the Social Order in Early Modern England." *Past and Present* 71 (1976): 22–42.

Wasserman, George. "Carnival in *Hudibras.*" *English Literary History* 55 (1988): 79–87.

———. *Samuel "Hudibras" Butler.* Twayne's English Author Series, no. 193. Boston: Twayne, 1976.

Weber, Donald. *Rhetoric and History in Revolutionary New England.* Oxford: Oxford University Press, 1988.

Weber, Max. *Economy and Society: An Outline of Interpretive Sociology.* Ed. Guenther Roth and Claus Wittich. Berkeley: University of California Press, 1978.

Webster, C. M. "The Satiric Background of the Attack on Puritans in Swift's *Tale of a Tub.*" *PMLA* 50 (1935): 210–23.

———. "Swift and Some Earlier Satirists of Puritan Enthusiasm." *PMLA* 48 (1933): 1141–53.

———. "Swift's *Tale of a Tub* Compared with Earlier Satires of the Puritans." *PMLA* 47 (1932): 171–78.

Weinbrot, Howard. *Alexander Pope and the Traditions of Formal Verse Satire.* Princeton: Princeton University Press, 1982.

———. *Eighteenth-Century Satire.* New York: Cambridge University Press, 1988.

Wilding, Michael. *Dragons Teeth: Literature in the English Revolution.* Oxford: Clarendon Press, 1987.

Winn, James. *John Dryden and His World.* New Haven: Yale University Press, 1987.

Youngren, William H. "Generality, Science, and Poetic Language in the Restoration." *English Literary History* 35 (1968): 158–87.

Zwicker, Steven. *Dryden's Political Poetry.* Providence, R.I.: Brown University Press. 1972.

———. *Lines of Authority: Politics and English Literary Culture, 1649–1689.* Ithaca, N.Y.: Cornell University Press, 1993.

———. *Politics and Language in Dryden's Poetry.* Princeton: Princeton University Press, 1984.

# Index